Frank Rauch

Sounding Libretto Mastersingers

Richard Wagner's complete text of
Die Meistersinger von Nürnberg
with leitmotifs, note samples, and audio samples
on an included WebApp

MusiCosa Publishing
Munich, Germany

NOTICE TO THE READER

mastersinger motif   Leitmotifs are quoted on the outer margin at the place where they can be heard. The corresponding note samples are listed in the appendix in alphabetical order. Their numbering is corresponding to the order and the numbering of the samples on www.musicosa.com/ML17. We suggest you create a bookmark or add the link to the home screen of you mobile device.

Markers on the inner border on even pages refer to page and bar of the vocal score (e.g. page 201, bar 2055) of Schott (published 2012, ISBN 979-0-001-15250-1), which was the reference for the German text. On odd pages, reference is made to the English vocal score published by G. Schirmer (New York, 1904). Karl Klindworth translation in that score formed the basis for the English part of this libretto. In the second line, reference is made to the recording of the Staatskapelle Dresden under Herbert von Karajan in 1970 (Adam, Kollo, Donath, Schreier, Evans, Ridderbusch). CD number, track and time are indicated (e.g. CD 3, track 6, 5:35 minutes).

KA 201 ▶ 2055
CD 3/6 5:35

Passages jointly sung are marked with a bar on the inner margin of the book. Identical numbers indicate passages sung at the same time.

German names of a number of leitmotifs have become commonly accepted; for others, as for the English names, suitable names were chosen. As with the names of all leitmotifs, one should bear in mind that their name can never entirely describe their meaning.

© 2017 ZeroAltitude GmbH, Munich. Print: Amazon CreateSpace.
All rights reserved. Musicosa is a registered trademark of ZeroAltitude GmbH
www.musicosa.com
ISBN 978-3-9818225-7-1

Table of Content

Notice to the reader

Characters and place of action

Act 1

Prelude 9
Scene 1 – As our Saviour came to thee 13
Scene 2 – David! What is't? 33
Scene 3 – Be well assured 51

Act 2

Scene 1 – Midsummer day! Midsummer day! 111
Scene 2 – We'll see if Master Sachs is there 119
Scene 3 – Come here! – 'Tis well. 129
Scene 4 – Good evening, Master! 135
Scene 5 – There is he! 153
Scene 6 – Do't not! 165
Scene 7 – Oh, heaven! David! 205

Act 3

Scene 1 – Yes, Master! Here! 229
Scene 2 – Sir knight, I greet you! 243
Scene 3 – A trial song! By Sachs! 261
Scene 4 – Good day, my Ev'chen! 281
Scene 5 – Saint Crispin! Saint Crispin! 301

Appendix

Note Samples 340
Index of Motifs 352

Personen und Ort der Handlung
(nach dem Erstdruck der Partitur)

Hans Sachs, Schuster (Baß) ⎫
Veit Pogner, Goldschmied (Baß) ⎪
Kunz Vogelgesang, Kürschner (Tenor) ⎪
Konrad Nachtigal, Spengler (Baß) ⎪
Sixtus Beckmesser, Stadtschreiber (Baß) ⎪
Fritz Kothner, Bäcker (Baß) ⎪
Balthasar Zorn, Zinngießer (Tenor) ⎬ Meistersinger
Ulrich Eisslinger, Würzkrämer (Tenor) ⎪
Augustin Moser, Schneider (Tenor) ⎪
Hermann Ortel, Seifensieder (Baß) ⎪
Hans Schwarz, Strumpfwirker (Baß) ⎪
Hans Foltz, Kupferschmied (Baß) ⎭
Walther von Stolzing, ein junger Ritter aus Franken (Tenor)
David, Sachsens Lehrbube (Tenor)
Eva, Pogners Tochter (Sopran)
Magdalene, Evas Amme (Sopran)
Ein Nachtwächter (Baß)

Bürger und Frauen aller Zünfte.
Gesellen. Lehrbuben. Mädchen. Volk.

Nürnberg
Um die Mitte des 16. Jahrhunderts

Characters and place of action
(according to the first print of the score)

Mastersingers:
- Hans Sachs, Shoemaker (Bass)
- Veit Pogner, Goldsmith (Bass)
- Kunz Vogelgesang, Furrier (Tenor)
- Konrad Nachtigal, Tinsmith (Bass)
- Sixtus Beckmesser, Town Clerk (Bass)
- Fritz Kothner, Baker (Bass)
- Balthasar Zorn, Powterer (Tenor)
- Ulrich Eisslinger, Grocer (Tenor)
- Augustin Moser, Tailor (Tenor)
- Hermann Ortel, Soap-maker (Bass)
- Hans Schwarz, Stocking-weaver (Bass)
- Hans Foltz, Coppersmith (Bass)

Walther von Stolzing, a young knight from Franconia (Tenor)
David, Sachs's 'Prentice (Tenor)
Eva, Pogner's Daughter (Soprano)
Magdalene, Eva's Nurse (Soprano)
A Night-Watchman (Bass)

Men and women of all guilds.
Journeymen. Prentices. Girls. Folk.

Nuremberg
About the middle of the sixteenth century

1. Aufzug

Vorspiel

Richard Wagner beschrieb in einer *Programmatischen Erläuterung* anlässlich einer Aufführung den Inhalt des Meistersingervorspiels:

Meistersinger-M., Kunst-M.

Erregtheitstriller, Werbe-M.¹, (Eva-M.)

{ *König-David-M., Kreidestrich-M., Erregtheitstriller*

Erregtheitstriller, Kunst-M., Naturregel-M.

Erregtheitstriller, Kampf-M., Entzückung-M.

{ *Preislied (Liebesthema), Leidenschaft-M., Entzückung-M., (Eva-M.)*

Die Meistersinger ziehen im festlichen Gepränge vor dem Volke in Nürnberg auf; sie tragen in Prozession die „leges tabulaturae", diese sorglich bewahrten altertümlichen Gesetze einer poetischen Form, deren Inhalt längst verschwunden war.

KA 1 ▶ 1
CD 1/1 0:01

KA 2 ▶ 26
CD 1/1 0:57

Dem hochgetragenen Banner mit dem Bildnis des harfespielenden Königs David folgt die einzig wahrhaft volkstümliche Gestalt des Hans Sachs:

KA 3 ▶ 40
CD 1/1 1:40

seine eigenen Lieder schallen ihm aus dem Munde des Volkes als Begrüßung entgegen.

KA 3 ▶ 54
CD 1/1 2:14

Mitten aus dem Volk vernehmen wir aber den Seufzer der Liebe. Er gilt dem schönen Töchterlein eines Meisters, das, zum Preisgewinn eines Wettsingens bestellt, festlich geschmückt, aber bang und sehnsüchtig seine Blicke nach dem Geliebten aussendet, der wohl Dichter, aber nicht Meistersinger ist.

KA 5 ▶ 87
CD 1/1 3:30

Dieser bricht sich durch das Volk Bahn; seine Blicke, seine Stimme raunen der Ersehnten das alte Liebeslied der ewig neuen Jugend zu.

KA 5 ▶ 97
CD 1/1 4:02

---
¹ Musikalisch gibt es hier bereits einen ersten liebevollen Blickkontakt zwischen Eva und Walther, der in Wagners Erläuterung nicht extra erwähnt wird

Act 1
Prelude

Richard Wagner described in a *Programmatic Explanation* on the occasion of a performance the content of the Mastersingers' prelude:

VS 1 ▸ 1 CD 1/1 0:01	The mastersingers are appearing in front of the people of Nuremberg in festive chorus; They carry in procession the „leges tabulaturae", these carefully preserved ancient laws of a poetic form, the content of which had long disappeared.	*mastersinger motif, art motif*
VS 2 ▸ 7 CD 1/1 0:57		*courtship motif[1], (Eva motif)*
VS 3 ▸ 2 CD 1/1 1:40	The highly held up banner with the portrait of the harp-playing king David follows the only true folk figure, Hans Sachs:	*king David motif, chalk stroke motif, excitement trill*
VS 3 ▸ 16 CD 1/1 2:14	His own songs are echoed by the people as a welcome.	*excitement trill, art motif, nature motif*
VS 4 ▸ 26 CD 1/1 3:30	In the midst of the people we hear the sigh of love. It is the beautiful daughter of a master, who, in order to be won as the prize of a singing contest, festively decorated, but anxiously and longingly sends out her eyes to the beloved, who is probably a poet but not a mastersinger.	*excitement trill, competition motif., delight motif* *prize song (love theme), passion motif, delight motif, (Eva motif)*
VS 5 ▸ 9 CD 1/1 4:02	He breaks through the masses; His gaze, his voice, tell the old love-song of the eternally new youth.	

[1] *In the music, there is already a first loving eye contact between Eva and Walther, which is not mentioned in Wagner's explanation*

The Mastersingers of Nuremberg

{ Meistersinger-M. („me-
ckernd"), Erregtheits-
triller, Leidenschaft-M.,
Meistersinger-M.④,
Spott-M.,¹
Entzückung-M.

Eifrige Lehrbuben der Meister fahren mit kin- KA 7 ▸ 122
discher Gelehrttuerei dazwischen und stören CD 1/1 5:10
die Herzergießung, es entsteht Gedränge und
Gewirr.

{ Meistersinger-M.,
Preislied (Liebesthema),
Spott-M., Meistersin-
ger-M. („meckernd"),
Kunst-M.

Da springt Hans Sachs, der den Liebesgesang KA 10 ▸ 151
innig vernommen hat, dazwischen, erfaßt hilf- CD 1/1 6:22
reich den Sänger, und zwischen sich und der
Geliebten gibt er ihm einen Platz an der Spit-
ze des Festzuges der Meister.

{ König-David-M.,
Kunst-M.,
Meistersinger-M.,
Erregtheitstriller

Laut begrüßt sie das Volk – das Liebeslied tönt KA 12 ▸ 188
zu den Meisterweisen. CD 1/1 7:50

Pedanterie und Poesie sind versöhnt.

Meistersinger-M.,
König-David-M.

„Heil! Hans Sachs!" erschallt es mächtig. KA 14 ▸ 211
 CD 1/1 8:55

---

[1] Mit diesem Motiv kommentiert der Chor im 3. Aufzug in der 5. Szene den Auftritt Beckmessers („Scheint mir nicht der rechte")

Act 1, Prelude

VS 6 ▶ 15 CD 1/1 5:10	Eager apprentices of the masters interject with childish scholarship, and disturb the heart discharge, leading to hustle and confusion.	mastersinger motif („nagging"), excitement trill, passion motif, mastersinger motif ④, mockery motif,[1] delight motif
VS 9 ▶ 5 CD 1/1 6:22	Thereupon Hans Sachs, who has heard the love song intently, intersperses, grasps the singer, and between himself and the beloved he gives him a place at the head of the masters' parade.	mastersinger motif, prize song (love theme), mockery motif, mastersinger motif („nagging"), art motif
VS 12 ▶ 3 CD 1/1 7:50	They are greeted frenetically by the people – the love song is joined by the masters' tunes. Pedantry and poetry are reconciled.	king David motif, art motif, mastersinger motif, excitement trill
VS 13 ▶ 10 CD 1/1 8:55	„Hail! Hans Sachs!" it sounds powerfully.	mastersinger motif, king David motif

---

[1] With this motif, the choir in the third act, fifth scene comments on Beckmesser's performance („Surely she'll refuse him")

1. Szene – Da zu dir der Heiland kam

Die Bühne stellt das Innere der Katharinenkirche in schrägem Durchschnitt dar; von dem Hauptschiff, welches links ab, dem Hintergrunde zu, sich ausdehnend anzunehmen ist, sind nur noch die letzten Reihen der Kirchstühlbänke sichtbar: den Vordergrund nimmt der freie Raum vor dem Chor ein; dieser wird später durch einen schwarzen Vorhang gegen das Schiff zu gänzlich geschlossen. In der letzten Reihe der Kirchstühle sitzen Eva und Magdalene; Walther von Stolzing steht, in einer Entfernung, zur Seite an eine Säule gelehnt, die Blicke auf Eva heftend, die sich mit stummem Gebärdenspiel wiederholt zu ihm umkehrt.

Die Gemeinde

(überall verteilt, sehr voll)

Taufchoral

Da zu dir der Heiland kam,   KA 15 ▸ 222
CD 1/2 0:01

Werbe-M.

Walther drückt durch Gebärde eine schmachtende Frage an Eva aus.

willig deine Taufe nahm,

*Werbe-M.,
Eva-M.*

Evas Blick und Gebärde sucht zu antworten; doch beschämt schlägt sie das Auge wieder nieder.

weihte sich dem Opfertod,

Leidenschaft-M.

Walther zärtlich, dann dringender.

gab er uns des Heils Gebot:

Scene 1 – As our Saviour came to thee

The stage represents an oblique view of the church of St. Katherine; the last few rows of seats of the nave, which is on the left stretching towards the back, are visible; in front is the open space of the choir which is later shut off from the nave by a black curtain. In the last row of seats Eva and Magdalena sit. Walther von Stolzing stands at some distance at the side leaning against a column with his eyes fixed on Eva, who frequently turns round towards him with mute gestures.

The congregation

(distributed about, very full)

As our Saviour came to thee,   *choral of baptism*

> *Walther expresses by gestures a longing entreaty to Eva.*   *courtship motif*

by thy hand baptized to be,

> *Eva by look and gestures attempts to answer him, but casts her eyes down again ashamed.*   *courtship motif, Eva motif*

chose the Cross for man's release,

> *Walther tenderly, then more urgently.*   *passion motif*

teaching us his law of peace:

The Mastersingers of Nuremberg

Leidenschaft-M., *(Eva-M.)*	Eva: *Walthern schüchtern abweisend, aber schnell wieder seelenvoll zu ihm aufblickend.*	KA 17 ▸ 247 CD 1/2 1:14
Taufchoral, *Werbe-M.*	daß wir durch dein' Tauf' uns weihn,	
	Walther: *entzückt; höchste Beteuerungen; Hoffnung.*	
	Seines Opfers wert zu sein.	
Preislied (Liebesthema)	Eva: *selig lächelnd; – dann beschämt die Augen senkend.*	
Taufchoral	Edler Täufer!	
	(Walther: *dringend, – aber schnell sich unterbrechend*)	
	Christs Vorläufer!	
	Er nimmt die dringende Gebärde wieder auf, mildert sie aber sogleich wieder, um Eva sanft um eine Unterredung zu bitten.	
	Nimm uns gnädig an, dort am Fluß Jordan!	
Werbe-M., *Leidenschaft-M.,* *(Eva-M.)*	*Die Gemeinde erhebt sich. Alles wendet sich dem Ausgange zu und verläßt unter dem Nachspiele allmählich die Kirche. – Walther heftet in höchster Spannung seinen Blick auf Eva, welche ihren Sitz langsam verläßt und, von Magdalene gefolgt, langsam in seine Nähe kommt. – Da Walther Eva sich nähern sieht, drängt er sich gewaltsam, durch die Kirchgänger durch, zu ihr.*	
Leidenschaft-M.	**WALTHER** Verweilt! Ein Wort – Ein einzig' Wort!	KA 21 ▸ 290 CD 1/3 0:01

EVA

(*sich schnell zu Magdalene umwendend*)
Mein Brusttuch... schau!
                      wohl liegt's im Ort.

MAGDALENE

Vergeßlich' Kind! Nun heißt es: such!
Sie geht nach den Kirchstühlen zurück.

Act 1, Scene 1 – As our Saviour came to thee

VS 16▸7
CD 1/2 1:14

Eva shyly repels Walther, but quickly looks up at him with emotion.

    passion motif, (Eva motif)

let us share thy sacred rite,

  Walther: enraptured; love protestations; hope.

choral of baptism, courtship motif

and be sinless in his sight.

  Eva: smiling blissfully; – then sinking her eyes ashamed.

prize song (love theme)

Prophet, preacher!

  (Walther: pressingly, – but quickly stopping himself)

choral of baptism

Holy teacher!

  He resumes his urgent gestures, but immediately moderate them, as though to retreat tenderly for an interview.

Bless with thy hand,
there on Jordan's strand!

  The congregation rises. All turn to the door and gradually leave the church during the voluntary. Walther fixes his gaze in great anxiety on Eva, who leaves her place at the same time and, followed by Magdalena, comes slowly towards him. – Walther, seeing Eva coming, presses forcibly through the crowd to her.

courtship motif, passion motif, (Eva motif)

VS 20▸9
CD 1/3 0:01

WALTHER

    passion motif

Oh stay! A word – One single word!

EVA

(turning round quickly to Magdalena)
My kerchief... look!

                 'tis left behind.

MAGDALENE

Forgetful child! Now I must seek!

  She goes back to the seats.

WALTHER

(Eva-M.)
Fräulein! verzeiht der Sitte Bruch.
Eines zu wissen, eines zu fragen,
was müßt' ich nicht zu brechen wagen?
Ob Leben oder Tod? Ob Segen oder Fluch?

Werbe-M.
Mit einem Worte sei mir's vertraut: –
mein Fräulein, – sagt...

MAGDALENE

(wieder zurückkommend)

Hier ist das Tuch.

Eva-M.
EVA

O weh! die Spange?

MAGDALENE

Fiel sie wohl ab?
Sie geht abermals suchend nach hinten.

WALTHER

Ob Licht und Lust, oder Nacht und Tod?
Ob ich erfahr', wonach ich verlange,
ob ich vernehme, wovor mir graut: –
Mein Fräulein, – sagt...

MAGDALENE

(wieder zurückkommend)

Da ist auch die Spange.
Komm, Kind! Nun hast du Spang' und Tuch...
O weh! da vergaß ich selbst mein Buch!

(Eva-M.)
Sie geht nochmals eilig nach hinten.

WALTHER

Dies eine Wort, ihr sagt mir's nicht?
Die Silbe, die mein Urteil spricht?
Ja oder nein! – ein flücht'ger Laut:
(entschlossen und hastig)
mein Fräulein, sagt – seid ihr schon Braut?

Act 1, Scene 1 – As our Saviour came to thee

VS 21▸2
CD 1/3 0:13

WALTHER

Maiden! forgive my bold approach. *(Eva motif)*
Tell me but one thing, tell me I pray you.
To learn the truth what would I dare not?
If life be mine or death? If blessed I be or banned?
One single word will my fate decide: – *courtship motif*
fair maiden, – say...

MAGDALENE

(returning again)

                The kerchief's here.

EVA *Eva motif*

Alas! the buckle?

MAGDALENE

Lost is that, too?
She goes again to the back.

WALTHER

If light and life, or night and death?
Whether I learn the tidings I hope for,
whether I hear what sorely I dread: –
Fair maiden, – say...

MAGDALENE

(returning again)

           There hast thou the buckle.
Come, Child! Now hast though clasp and scarf...
Alack! now I have forgot my book!
She goes again hastily to the back. *(Eva motif)*

WALTHER

The word I crave, you speak it not?
The word that will forecast my lot?
Yes or no! – a fleeting sound:
   (resolutely and quickly)
are you as bride by promise bound?

MAGDALENE

die wieder zurückgekehrt ist und sich vor Walther verneigt:

Sieh da! Herr Ritter?
　　　　　Wie sind wir hochgeehrt:
mit Evchens Schutze
　　　　　habt ihr euch gar beschwert!
Darf den Besuch des Helden
ich Meister Pogner melden?

Entzückung-M.

WALTHER

(leidenschaftlich)

O, betrat ich doch nie sein Haus!

MAGDALENE

Ei! Junker, was sagt ihr da aus?
In Nürnberg eben nur angekommen,
wart ihr nicht freundlich aufgenommen?
Was Küch' und Keller, Schrein und Schrank
euch bot, verdient' es keinen Dank?

EVA

Werbe-M.

Gut' Lenchen, ach! das meint er ja nicht;
doch von mir wohl wünscht er Bericht, –
wie sag' ich's schnell?
　　　　　Versteh' ich's doch kaum!
Mir ist, als wär' ich gar wie im Traum!
Er frägt, ob ich schon Braut?

MAGDALENE

(heftig erschrocken)

Hilf Gott! Sprich nicht so laut!
jetzt laß uns nach Hause gehn,
wenn uns die Leut' hier sehn!

WALTHER

Nicht eh'r, bis ich alles weiß!

Act 1, Scene 1 – As our Saviour came to thee

MAGDALENE

who has again returned, courtseying to Walther:

Sir knight? I thank you!
                  Great honor, faith is ours:
for Eva's escort
                  receive our hearty thanks!
May I make known your coming
as guest to master Pogner?   *delight motif*

WALTHER

(passionate)

Would that ne'er I had seen his house!

MAGDALENE

Sir knight! Ah, what words do I hear?
In Nuremberg, tho' so new a comer,
have you not found all friendly welcome?
What kitchen, cellar, hearth and house
could give, doth that deserves no thanks?

EVA

Good Lene, ah! he means it not so;   *courtship motif*
but from me now fain would he know, –
'tis hard to say!
                  Bewildered I seem!
Methinks, around me all is a dream!
He asks, am I betrothed?

MAGDALENE

(in great alarm)

Oh God! Speak not so loud!
let us now betake us home,
if folk should see us here!

WALTHER

Not yet, till you tell me all!

EVA

(zu Magdalene)
's ist leer, die Leut' sind fort.

MAGDALENE

Drum eben wird mir heiß!
Herr Ritter, an andrem Ort!
> David tritt aus der Sakristei ein und macht sich darüber her, die schwarzen Vorhänge zu schließen.

WALTHER

(dringend)

Meistersinger-M. ⑤ Nein! Erst dies Wort!

EVA

(bittend zu Magdalene)
Dies Wort!
> Magdalene, die sich bereits umgewendet, erblickt David und hält an.

MAGDALENE

(zärtlich, für sich)

Meistersinger-M. ⑦ [1] David! Ei! David hier?

EVA

Was sag' ich? Sag' du's mir!

MAGDALENE

> wendet sich wieder zurück und zu Walther, zerstreut, öfter nach David sich umsehend:

Herr Ritter, was ihr die Jungfer fragt,
Meistersinger-M. ② das ist so leichtlich nicht gesagt.
Fürwahr ist Evchen Pogner Braut!

EVA

Erregtheitstriller *(lebhaft unterbrechend)*

---

[1] Der majestätische Beginn des Motivs repräsentiert die Ideale der Zunft, der weitere Verlauf das komplexe Klein-Klein des Regelwerks der Zunft. Die Zahl verweist auf die entsprechende Stelle des Notenbeispiels im Anhang.

Act 1, Scene 1 – As our Saviour came to thee

VS 26 ▶ 1
CD 1/3 2:30

EVA

(to Magdalena)
'tis safe, the folk are gone.

MAGDALENE

Just that 'tis, makes me fear!
Not now, Sir, some other time!
> *David enters from the sacristy and busies himself with closing the black curtains.*

WALTHER

(urgently)
No! First this word!   *mastersinger motif ⑤*

EVA

(appealingly to Magdalena)
This word!
> *Magdalene, who has turned round, sees David and pauses.*

MAGDALENE

(aside, tenderly)
David! Ei! David here?   *mastersinger motif ⑦* [1]

EVA

How tell him? Speak thou then!

MAGDALENE

> *she turns back again and towards Walther, at a loss, frequently looking round towards David:*

The answer you now would have, Sir knight,
no single word can give aright.   *mastersinger motif ②*
For though betrothed is Eva held!

EVA

(quickly interrupting)   *excitement trill*

---

[1] The majestic beginning of the motif represents the ideals of the guild, the further course the complex petty rule set of the guild. The number refers to the corresponding point in the note sample in the appendix.

Doch hat noch keiner den Bräut'gam erschaut!

KA 30 ▸ 394
CD 1/3 3:02

MAGDALENE

Meistersinger-M.

Den Bräut'gam wohl noch niemand kennt,
bis morgen ihn das Gericht ernennt,
das dem Meistersinger erteilt den Preis...

EVA

(enthusiastisch)

Und selbst die Braut ihm reicht das Reis.

WALTHER

(verwundert)

Dem Meistersinger?

EVA

(bang)

Seid ihr das nicht?

WALTHER

Ein Werbgesang?

MAGDALENE

Vor Wettgericht.

WALTHER

Den Preis gewinnt?

MAGDALENE

Wen die Meister meinen.

WALTHER

Die Braut dann wählt?...

EVA

(sich vergessend)

Euch, oder keinen!

Act 1, Scene 1 – As our Saviour came to thee

VS 27 ▶ 12
CD 1/3 3:02
Still hath no man yet the bridegroom
                              beheld!

MAGDALENE

None knows the bridegroom's name, } *mastersinger motif*
until tomorrow shall sound his fame,
when a mastersinger the prize hath won...

EVA

   (enthusiastically)
And him herself the bride will crown.

WALTHER

   (surprised)
The mastersinger?

EVA

   (anxiously)
                              Are you not that?

WALTHER
A trial song?

MAGDALENE
                              Before the guild.

WALTHER
The prize is won?

MAGDALENE
                              By the masters' favor.

WALTHER
The bride will choose?...

EVA

   (forgetting herself)
                              You and no other!

23

Walther wendet sich, in großer Aufregung auf- und abgehend, zur Seite. KA32▶417
CD 1/3 3:39

MAGDALENE

Unmut-M.
    (sehr erschrocken)
Was, Evchen! Evchen! Bist du von Sinnen?

EVA
Gut' Lene, laß mich den Ritter gewinnen!

MAGDALENE

Unmut-M. Sahst ihn doch gestern zum ersten Mal?

EVA
Das eben schuf mir so schnelle Qual,
daß ich schon längst ihn im Bilde sah!

David-M. Sag', trat er nicht ganz wie David nah?

MAGDALENE
    (höchst verwundert)
Bist du toll! Wie David?

EVA
                Wie David im Bild.

MAGDALENE

König-David-M. Ach! – Meinst du den König mit der Harfen
und langem Bart in der Meister Schild?

EVA
Nein! der, dess' Kiesel den Goliath warfen,
das Schwert im Gurt,
        die Schleuder zur Hand,

Erregtheitstriller   das Haupt von lichten Locken umstrahlt,
wie ihn uns Meister Dürer gemalt!

MAGDALENE
    (laut seufzend)

Unmut-M. Ach, David! David!

Act 1, Scene 1 – As our Saviour came to thee

VS 29 ▶ 8　*Walther turns away, walking up and down in*
CD 1/3 3:39　*great excitement.*

MAGDALENE

(very frightened)　　　　　　　　　　　　*resentment motif*

What, Eva! Eva! Lost are thy senses?

EVA

Good Lene, help but my lover to win me!

MAGDALENE

Yesterday didst thou hear his name?　　　　*resentment motif*

EVA

Even at once was my heart in flame,
long had I looked on his image fair!
Say, doth he not stay like David there?　　　*David motif*

MAGDALENE

(in great astonishment)

Art thou mad! Like David?

EVA

　　　　　　Like David the King.

MAGDALENE

Him mean'st thou with harp and crown and sceptre　*king David motif*
and flowing beard on the Masters' shield?

EVA

No! he who boldly Goliath vanquished,
with sword at side,
　　　and sling in hand,
　　　　　his head bedight with locks of gold,　*excitement trill*
as drawn of Master Dürer of old!

MAGDALENE

(sighing aloud)
Ah, David! David!　　　　　　　　　　　*resentment motif*

David

der hinausgegangen und jetzt wieder zurückkommt, ein Lineal im Gürtel und ein großes Stück weißer Kreide an einer Schnur schwenkend:

David-M.
                                Da bin ich: wer ruft?

Magdalene

Ach, David! Was ihr für Unglück schuft! –
(beiseite)
Der liebe Schelm! Wüßt' er's noch nicht? –
(laut)
Ei, seht, da hat er uns gar verschlossen?

David

(zärtlich)
Ins Herz euch allein!

Magdalene

(feurig)
                    Das treue Gesicht! –
Ei, sagt! Was treibt ihr hier für Possen?

David

Behüt' es! Possen? Gar ernste Ding':

Meistersinger-M.
für die Meister hier richt' ich den Ring.

Magdalene

Wie? Gäb' es ein Singen?

David

                      Nur Freiung heut:
der Lehrling wird da losgesprochen,
der nichts wider die Tabulatur verbrochen:

König-David-M.
Meister wird, wen die Prob' nicht reut.

Magdalene

Da wär' der Ritter ja am rechten Ort! –

Act 1, Scene 1 – As our Saviour came to thee

VS 32 ▶ 5
CD 1/4 0:01

DAVID

> *who has gone out and now returns, with a rule in his belt and a large piece of white chalk swinging by a string:*

                        Here am I: who calls?   *David motif*

MAGDALENE

Ah, David! Ill luck enough thou mak'st! –
   (aside)
The pretty rogue! Knows he not yet? –
   (aloud)
Ah, see, I trow we are locked in prison?

DAVID

   (tenderly)
But you in my heart!

MAGDALENE

   (ardently)
                  How true in his face! –
Now, say! What mumming here goes forward?

DAVID

Defend us! Mumming? Right weighty work:
for the Masters here making the ring.   *mastersinger motif*

MAGDALENE

What? Will there be singing?

DAVID

                    But trial today:
the pupil here will be made free, if
his voice fail not and never a rule be broken:
Master too, if the test goes well.   *king David motif*

MAGDALENE

So then the Knight has found his time and place! –

Jetzt, Evchen, komm! Wir müssen fort!

WALTHER

(schnell zu den Frauen sich wendend)

(Eva-M.) Zu Meister Pogner laßt mich euch geleiten.

MAGDALENE

Erwartet den hier, er ist bald da.
König-David-M. Wollt ihr Evchens Hand erstreiten,
rückt Zeit und Ort das Glück euch nah.

Zwei Lehrbuben kommen dazu und tragen Bänke herbei.

Jetzt eilig von hinnen!

WALTHER

Was soll ich beginnen?

MAGDALENE

Laßt David euch lehren,
die Freiung begehren. –
Davidchen! hör', mein lieber Gesell:
den Ritter hier bewahr' mir wohl zur Stell'!
David-M. Was Fein's aus der Küch'
bewahr' ich für dich,
und morgen begehr' du noch dreister,
König-David-M. wird hier der Junker heut Meister!
Erregtheitstriller *Sie drängt Eva zum Fortgehen.*

EVA

(zu Walther)

Kampf-M., Seh' ich euch wieder?
Entzückung-M.

WALTHER

(sehr feurig)

Heut abend gewiß!
Was ich will wagen,
wie könnt' ich's sagen?
Neu ist mein Herz, neu mein Sinn,
neu ist mir alles, was ich beginn'.

Act 1, Scene 1 – As our Saviour came to thee

VS 35 ▶ 4 Now, Eva, come! We must away!
CD 1/4 0:59

Walther

(turning quickly to the women)
To Master Pogner's door now let me lead you.   *(Eva motif)*

Magdalene

Nay, wait for him here, he soon will come.
If 'tis Eva's hand you sue for,   } king David motif
then take the time and place that serve.

> *Two prentices enter the scene, carrying benches.*

Now, hence let us hasten!

Walther

Say, what is to do, then?

Magdalene

Let David now teach you,
the rules of the trial. –
David! give ear, and heed what I tell:
this stranger here now help and counsel well!
Some sweet-meats fine   } David motif
as fee shall be thine,
tomorrow thy suit may run faster,
if here the Knight be made Master!   } king David motif

> *She urges Eva to go away.*   excitement trill

Eva

(to Walther)
When shall I see you?   } competition motif, excitement trill

Walther

(with much fervour)
This ev'ning, be sure!
Nought shall dismay me,
no power stay me?
New is my heart, my life is new,
new now are things I think and do.

29

(Eva-M.)

Preislied (Liebesthema) ②

Werbe-M.

Preislied (Liebesthema), Entzückung-M.

Eines nur weiß ich,
eines begreif' ich:
mit allen Sinnen
euch zu gewinnen! –
Ist's mit dem Schwert nicht,
              muß es gelingen,
gilt es als Meister euch zu ersingen.
Für euch Gut und Blut,
für euch Dichters heil'ger Mut!

KA 42 ▶ 534
CD 1/4 2:27

Eva

(mit großer Wärme)

Mein Herz, sel'ger Glut,
für euch liebesheil'ge Hut!

Magdalene

Schnell heim! sonst geht's nicht gut!

Magdalene zieht Eva eilig durch die Vorhänge nach sich fort.

David

der Walther verwunderungsvoll gemessen:

Gleich Meister? Oho! viel Mut!

Walther wirft sich, aufgeregt und brütend, in einen erhöhten, kathederartigen Lehnstuhl, welchen zuvor zwei Lehrbuben, von der Wand ab, mehr nach der Mitte zu, gerückt hatten.

Werbe-M.

Act 1, Scene 1 – As our Saviour came to thee

_{VS 38▶5} One bliss before me,   *(Eva motif)*
_{CD 1/4 2:27} only doth lure me:
one great endeavour   *prize song (love*
only and ever! –   *theme)* ②
If sword avail not,
                         in battle ringing,   *courtship motif*
then as a Master I win by singing.
① For thee goods and gold,   *prize song (love the-*
② all wealth of poet's heart for thee!   *me), delight motif*

EVA

(with great warmth)

① My heart's love untold,
② my holy rapture glows for thee!

MAGDALENE

② Now home! or evil I foresee!

Magdalena hurriedly pulls Eva away through the curtains.

DAVID

who has watched Walther with astonishment:

A master? Oho! so soon!

Walther throws himself excited and brooding, into a high ecclesiastical chair, which two of the prentices have previously moved from the wall towards the middle of the stage.   *courtship motif*

2. Szene – David! Was stehst?

Noch mehrere Lehrbuben sind eingetreten; sie tragen und stellen Bänke und richten alles zur Sitzung der Meistersinger her.

2. Lehrbube
David! Was stehst?

1. Lehrbube
      Greif an's Werck!

2. Lehrbube
Lebhaftigkeit-M. Hilf uns richten das Gemerk!

David
Zu eifrigst war ich vor euch allen;
schafft nun für euch, hab' ander Gefallen!

Lehrbuben
Was der sich dünkt!
     Der Lehrling' Muster!
Das macht,
   weil sein Meister ein Schuster!
Beim Leisten sitzt er mit der Feder!
Beim Dichten mit Draht und Pfriem!
Sein' Verse schreibt er auf rohes Leder.
 (mit entsprechender Gebärde)
Das, dächt' ich, gerbten wir ihm!

Sie machen sich lachend an die fernere Herrichtung.

Scene 2 – David! What is't?

More prentices have entered; they bring benches and place them in position, preparing everything for the sitting of the Mastersingers.

2ND PRENTICE
David! What is't?

1ST PRENTICE
Stirthy-self!

2ND PRENTICE
Come and help us with our work!   *liveliness motif*

DAVID
'Tis I have been ever the worker;
work now yourselves and leave me in quiet!

PRENTICES
Oho how pert!
How proud and haughty!
Because
he gets strapped when he's naughty!
He cobbles with a goose's feather!
Makes poems with awl and string!
He writes his verses on greasy leather.
(with appropriate gesture)
He knows, too, how it can sting!

They go on with the arrangements at back, laughing.

DAVID

KA 48 ▸ 588
CD 1/5 0:48

nachdem er den sinnenden Ritter eine Weile betrachtet:

Fanget an!

WALTHER

(verwundert)

              Was soll's?

DAVID

(noch stärker)

      Fanget an! So ruft der Merker: –
nun sollt ihr singen! Wißt ihr das nicht?

WALTHER

Wer ist der Merker?

DAVID

                  Wißt ihr das nicht?
Wart ihr noch nie bei 'nem Singgericht?

Erregtheitstriller

WALTHER

Noch nie, wo die Richter Handwerker.

DAVID

Seid ihr ein „Dichter"?

WALTHER

                Wär' ich's doch!

DAVID

Seid ihr „Singer"?

WALTHER

              Wüßt' ich's noch?

DAVID

Doch „Schulfreund" wart ihr
            und „Schüler" zuvor?

Act 1, Scene 2 – David! What is't?

DAVID
_{VS 44▸1}
_{CD 1/5 0:48}

after looking at the musing knight for awhile:

Now begin!

WALTHER

(surprised)
  What for?

DAVID

(louder)

Now begin! So cries the marker: –
straight must you sing then! Know you not that?

WALTHER
Who is the Marker?

DAVID
  Know you not that?
Were you ne'er yet at a singing trial?   } *excitement trill*

WALTHER
Ne'er yet, where the judges were craftsmen.

DAVID
Are you a „Poet"?

WALTHER
  Would I were!

DAVID
Are you a „Singer"?

WALTHER
  Would I knew?

DAVID
But „Schoolfriend" are you
  and „Scholar" at least?

WALTHER
Das klingt mir alles fremd vorm Ohr!

DAVID
Und so gradhin wollt ihr Meister werden?

WALTHER
Wie machte das so große Beschwerden?

DAVID
O Lene! Lene!

WALTHER
　　　　　　　　　　　　Wie ihr doch tut!

DAVID
O Magdalene!

WALTHER
　　　　　　　　　　　　Ratet mir gut!

DAVID

Erregtheitstriller　　*setzt sich in Positur:*
Mein Herr! Der Singer Meisterschlag
gewinnt sich nicht an einem Tag.
In Nüremberg der größte Meister,
mich lehrt die Kunst Hans Sachs;

Erregtheitstriller, schon voll ein Jahr mich unterweist er,
Schustermühe-M., daß ich als Schüler wachs'.
Kreidestrich-M. Schuhmacherei und Poeterei,
die lern' ich da alleinerlei;
hab' ich das Leder glatt geschlagen,

Erregtheitstriller lern' ich Vokal und Konsonanz sagen;
wichst' ich den Draht erst fest und steif,
was sich dann reimt, ich wohl begreif'.
Den Pfriemen schwingend
im Stich die Ahl',
was stumpf, was klingend,
was Maß, was Zahl, –
den Leisten im Schurz,

Act 1, Scene 2 – David! What is't?

WALTHER
The words my ears ne'er heard before!

DAVID
Yet now you would be at once a Master?

WALTHER
And why would that so hopeless a venture?

DAVID
O Lene! Lene!

WALTHER
What do you mean!

DAVID
O Magdalena!

WALTHER
Counsel me well!

DAVID
poses himself:
Sir Knight! The Mastersinger's seat
needs more than one short day to get.
for full a year our greatest Master,
has taught me art, ah me!
unless my steps go rather faster,
ne'er shall I scholar be.
Shoemaker's craft and poet's art,
both daily I learn by heart;
first all the leather smooth I hammer,
consonants then and vowels I stammer;
next must the thread be stiff with wax,
then I must learn, it rhymes with Sachs.
With awl and thread
I make stitches neat
and then I learn
about time and beat, –
with lapstone and last,

} *excitement trill*

} *excitement trill,*
} *cobbler's labor motif,*
} *chalk stroke motif*

} *excitement trill*

Erregtheitstriller	was lang, was kurz, was hart, was lind, hell oder blind, was Waisen, was Milben, was Klebsilben, was Pausen, was Körner, was Blumen, was Dörner, – das alles lernt' ich mit Sorg' und Acht: wie weit nun, meint ihr, daß ich's gebracht?	KA 53 ▶ 656 CD 1/6 1:00

WALTHER

Werbe-M.   Wohl zu 'nem Paar recht guter Schuh'? –

DAVID

Erregtheitstriller
Zunftgesetz-M.
    Ja, dahin hat's noch gute Ruh'!
Ein „Bar" hat manch' Gesätz' und Gebänd':
wer da gleich die rechte Regel fänd',
die richt'ge Naht
und den rechten Draht,
mit gut gefügten Stollen
den Bar recht zu versohlen.

Zunftgesetz-M.   Und dann erst kommt der „Abgesang",
daß der nicht kurz, und nicht zu lang,
und auch keinen Reim enthält,
der schon im Stollen gestellt.
Wer alles das merkt, weiß und kennt,
wird doch immer noch nicht Meister genennt.

WALTHER

Singkunst-M.   Hilf Gott! Will ich denn Schuster sein?
In die Singkunst lieber führ' mich ein!

DAVID

Ja – hätt' ich's nur selbst schon
                zum Singer gebracht!
Wer glaubt wohl, was das für Mühe macht!

Singkunst-M.   Der Meister Tön' und Weisen,   KA 57 ▶ 710
gar viel an Nam' und Zahl,   CD 1/7 0:01
die starken und die leisen,
wer die wüßte allzumal!
Der kurze, lang' und überlang' Ton;

Act 1, Scene 2 – David! What is't?

VS 49 ▶ 3
CD 1/6 1:00
the slow, the fast,
the hard, the light,
gloomy and bright,
the scissors and snippings,   *excitement trill*
and wordclippings,
the pauses and corns,
the flowers and thorns, –
I learn all such things with care and pains:
to what now think you all that attains?

Walther

Say, to a pair of right good shoon? –   *courtship motif*

David

Ah, think not that is reached so soon!   *excitement trill*
A „Bar" of many stanzas is made: *guild law motif*
and the rules alone would break your head,
and rightly stitched
and truly pitched
must words and music answer,
when bar is soled with stanza.
Then cometh first the „Aftersong",
and not to short nor yet too long,
and in it no rhyme may sound
that in the stanza is found.
Who all this has read, marked and learned,
hath e'en yet the name Master not earned.

Walther

Odd's life! Teach me not cobbler's trade?   *singing art motif*
Rather tell me how a singer's made!

David

Ah, would that a singer
                  already I were!
Who knoweth what time that needs and care!
VS 52 ▶ 9
CD 1/7 0:01
The Masters' tones and measures,   *singing art motif*
are many in name and kind,
the strong ones and the soft ones,
who at once the names can find!
The shortened, long, and overlong tones;

die Schreibpapier-, Schwarztintenweis';
der rote, blau' und grüne Ton;
die Hageblüh'-, Strohhalm-, Fengelweis';
der zarte, der süße, der Rosenton;
der kurzen Liebe, der vergeßne Ton;
die Rosmarin-, Gelbveigleinweis',
die Regenbogen-, die Nachtigallweis';
die englische Zinn-, die Zimtröhrenweis',
frisch Pomeranzen-, grün Lindenblüh'weis';
die Frösch-, die Kälber-, die Stieglitzweis',
die abgeschied'ne Vielfraßweis',
der Lerchen-, der Schnecken-, der Bellerton;
die Melissenblümlein-, die Mairanweis',
gelb Löwenhaut-,
> *(gefühlvoll)*

treu' Pelikanweis',
> *(prunkend)*

die buttglänzende[1] Drahtweis'!

WALTHER

Hilf Himmel! Welch endlos' Tönegeleis'!

DAVID

Erregtheitstriller

Das sind nur die Namen; nun lernt sie singen,
recht wie die Meister sie gestellt.
Jed' Wort und Ton muß klärlich klingen,
wo steigt die Stimm', und wo sie fällt;
fangt nicht zu hoch, zu tief nicht an,
als es die Stimm' erreichen kann.
Mit dem Atem spart, daß er nicht knappt,
und gar am End' ihr überschnappt;
vor dem Wort mit der Stimme
ja nicht summt,
nach dem Wort mit dem Mund
auch nicht brummt.
Nicht ändert an Blum' und Koloratur,
jed' Zierat fest nach des Meisters Spur.
Verwechseltet ihr, würdet gar irr,
verlört ihr euch und kämt ins Gewirr: –

---

[1] *Ein Druckfehler in einer Ausgabe der alten Meistersingermotive von Wagenseil, den Wagner entdeckte und als Verballhornung so übernahm (butt = Hintern). Es müsste eigentlich heißen: die gut(t)glänzende Drahtweis'*

Act 1, Scene 2 – David! What is't?

VS 53▸4
CD 1/7 0:48
the paper mode, black ink mode;
the scarlet, blue and verdant tones;
the hawthornbloom, strawhalm, fennel mode;
the tender, the dulcet, the rosy tone;
the passing passion, the forgotten tone;
the rosemary, wallflower mode,
the rainbow mode, and the nightingale mode;
the English tin, the cinnamon mode,
fresh pomegranates, green linden bloom mode;
the frog, the calf, the linnet mode,
the lonely gormandizer mode,
the skylark, the snail, the barking tone;
and the honeyflower, the marjoram mode,
the lion skin,

(with feeling)

                              true pelican mode,

(showily)

the bright glittering[1] thread mode!

WALTHER

Heav'n help me! What endless medleys of tones!

DAVID

Those are but the titles; now comes the singing,   *excitement trill*
e'en as the masters have decreed.
each word and tone right clearly ringing,
as voice doth rise and fall at need;
start not too high, too low in pitch,
but where the voice all notes can reach.
To the breath give heed and hold it well,
lest at the end your voice should fail;
Ere a word you pronounce

                        make not a groan,

when the word ends,

                the voice may not moan.

And alter not turns and colorature,
all gracenotes take from the Masters' store.
For if you go wrong, stumble or trip,
or lose yourself, or make but a slip: –

---

[1] *In the medieval book about the mastersingers' motifs by Wagenseil, Wagner found the mode described as „butt glittering" instead of „gutt glittering" (gutt = good). He quotes the misprint with a twinkle in the eye.*

Erregtheitstriller	wär sonst euch alles auch gelungen,	KA 64 ▸ 782
	da hättet ihr gar versungen!	CD 1/7 3:37
	Trotz großem Fleiß und Emsigkeit,	
	ich selbst noch bracht' es nicht so weit:	
Unmut-M.	So oft ich's versuch' und's nicht gelingt,	
	die Knieriemschlagweis'	
	der Meister mir singt.	
	(sanft)	
	Wenn dann Jungfer Lene nicht Hilfe weiß,	
	(greinend)	
Erregtheitstriller	sing' ich die eitel Brot- und Wasserweis'.	
	Nehmt euch ein Beispiel dran,	
	und laßt vom Meisterwahn!	
Zunftgesetz-M.	Denn Singer und Dichter müßt ihr sein,	
König-David-M.	eh' ihr zum Meister kehret ein.	

WALTHER

Wer ist nun „Dichter"?

LEHRBUBEN

(während der Arbeit)

Lebhaftigkeit-M.   David! David! Kommst her?

DAVID

(zu den Lehrbuben)

Wartet nur! Gleich! –

(schnell wieder zu Walther sich wendend)

	Wer „Dichter" wär'?
Erregtheitstriller	Habt ihr zum Singer euch aufgeschwungen
	und der Meister Töne richtig gesungen;
	fügtet ihr selbst nun Reim' und Wort',
Zunftgesetz-M.	daß sie genau an Stell' und Ort
	paßten zu eines Meisters Ton, –
König-David-M.,	dann trügt ihr den Dichterpreis davon.
Erregtheitstriller	

LEHRBUBEN

Lebhaftigkeit-M.   He! David! Soll man's dem Meister klagen?
                      Wirst' dich bald
                              deines Schwatzens entschlagen?

Act 1, Scene 2 – David! What is't?

VS 57▶8 CD 1/7 3:37 though you in all but that had thriven,	
that fault would not be forgiven!	*excitement thrill*
With all my faithful toil and care,	
I never yet have come so far:	
each hopeful attempt but failure brings,	*resentment motif*
the kneestrap stroke mode	
the Master me sings.	

   (tenderly)

When comfort from Lene I cannot gain,

   (weeping)

I sing alone the bread and water-strain.	*excitement thrill*
heed this lesson well,	
beware the Master spell!	
Till singer and poet he has been,	*guild law motif*
no one the Master's crown can win.	*king David motif*

Walther

Who is a „poet"?

Prentices

   (while they are working)

David! David! Come here?	*liveliness motif*

David

   (to the prentices)

Wait awhile! Wait! –

   (quickly turning again to Walther)

What „poet" means?	
When you as singer are chosen duly	*excitement trill*
and the Master tones have sung well and truly;	
if you yourself both rhyme and word,	
find and unite in true accord,	*guild law motif*
so that they fit some Master's tone, –	
then you've made the poet's prize your own.	*king David motif,* *excitement thrill*

Prentices

Hey! David! Must we then tell thy Master?	*liveliness motif*
Wilt thou never	
have done with thy chatter?	

DAVID

Oho! Ja wohl! denn helf' ich euch nicht,
ohne mich wird alles doch falsch gericht'!
Er will sich zu ihnen wenden.

WALTHER

(ihn zurückhaltend)
Nur dies noch: – wer wird „Meister" genannt?

DAVID

(schnell wieder umkehrend)
Damit, Herr Ritter, ist's so bewandt: –
(mit sehr tiefsinniger Miene)
Der Dichter, der aus eignem Fleiße,
zu Wort' und Reimen, die er erfand,
aus Tönen auch fügt eine neue Weise:
der wird als Meistersinger erkannt.

WALTHER

So bleibt mir einzig der Meisterlohn!
Muß ich singen,
kann's nur gelingen,
find' ich zum Vers auch den eignen Ton.

DAVID

der sich zu den Lehrbuben gewendet hat:
Was macht ihr denn da?
Ja, fehl' ich beim Werk,
verkehrt nur richtet ihr Stuhl und Gemerk!
Er wirft polternd und lärmend die Anordnungen der Lehrbuben, in Betreff des Gemerkes, um.
Ist denn heut Singschul'? Daß ihr's wißt!
Das kleine Gemerk! Nur Freiung ist.
Die Lehrbuben, welche in der Mitte der Bühne ein größeres Gerüste mit Vorhängen aufgeschlagen hatten, schaffen auf Davids Weisung dies schnell beiseite und stellen dafür ebenso

---

Singkunst-M. ②,
Werbe-M.,
König-David-M.,
Erregtheitstriller

Werbe-M.,
Entzückung-M.

Singkunst-M. ②

David-M.

Act 1, Scene 2 – David! What is't?

DAVID

_{VS 62▸2}
_{CD 1/7 5:45}

Oho! 'Tis so! if I help you not,
without me at hand all you do goes wrong!
> *He is about to go to them.*

WALTHER

> *(holding him back)*

But tell me: – who is „Master", in fine?

DAVID

> *(turning quickly back)*

Sir Knight, that title we thus assign: –
_{VS 63▸1}
_{CD 1/8 0:01}
> *(in a very solemn manner)*

The poet who by rules as stated,
to words and rhymes he himself has found,
can fit a new strain by himself created:
shall then as Mastersinger be crowned.

singing art motif ②,
courtship motif,
king David motif,
excitement trill

WALTHER

So doth then one only hope remain!
That by heaven
grace may be given
rightly to fashion a master strain.

courtship motif,
delight motif

singing art motif ②

DAVID

> *who has turned to the Prentices:*

What do you, then, there?
                 If I am not by,
then all your wits and your work go awry!
> *He fussily and noisily pulls down the prentices' arrangements for the marker's stage.*

Is today song-school? Know you not!
The small stage today! 'Tis trial day.
> *The Prentices, who had put up a large erection with curtains in the middle of the stage, put it aside under David's directions and substitute for it a smaller stage;*

David motif

eilig ein geringeres Brettergerüst auf; darauf stellen sie einen Stuhl, mit einem kleinen Pult davor, daneben eine große schwarze Tafel, daran die Kreide am Faden aufgehängt wird; um das Gerüst sind schwarze Vorhänge angebracht, welche zunächst hinten und an den beiden Seiten, dann auch vorn ganz zusammengezogen werden.

LEHRBUBEN

(während der Herrichtung)

David-M. Aller End' ist doch David der allergescheit'st;
nach hohen Ehren ganz sicher er geizt.
's ist Freiung heut: gewiß er freit;
als vornehmer Singer er schon sich spreizt!
Die Schlagreime fest er inne hat,
arm' Hungerweise singt er glatt!
Doch die harte Trittweis',
       die kennt er am best',

(mit der Gebärde zweier Fußtritte)

die trat ihm der Meister hart und fest.
 Sie lachen.

DAVID

Ja, lacht nur zu! Heut' bin ich's nicht.
Ein Andrer stellt sich zum Gericht;
Erregtheitstriller der war nicht Schüler, ist nicht Singer,
den Dichter – sagt' er – überspring' er;
denn er ist Junker,
und mit einem Sprung er
Erregtheitstriller denkt, ohne weit're Beschwerden
heut' hier Meister zu werden.
David-M. Drum richtet nur fein
das Gemerk dem ein!

(während die Lehrbuben vollends aufrichten)

Dorthin! Hierher! Die Tafel an die Wand, –
so daß sie recht dem Merker zur Hand! –

(zu Walther sich umwendend)

Beckmesser-M. Ja ja: dem Merker! – Wird euch wohl bang?

Act 1, Scene 2 – David! What is't?

VS 66▶1
CD 1/9 0:01

on this they place a chair with a small desk before it, near it a large black board, on which a piece of chalk is hung by a string; around the stage are hung black curtains which are pulled together first at the back and sides and then in front.

PRENTICES

(during their work)

Such a scholar as David yet never was seen;   } *David motif*
glory and honor he surely will win.
perhaps he may be freed today;
for finest of singers he long has been!
The strap-leather mode oft makes him smart,
the hunger tune he knows by heart!
And the hearty-kick-mode,
                             he carefully learns,

(with the action of two kicks)

his master employs them all by turns.

They laugh.

DAVID

Yes, laugh away! But not at me.
There comes another, you will see;
no scholar is he, singer neither,   } *excitement trill*
the poet's place he wants not either;
a noble knight, he,
in a single flight he
without let or disaster   *excitement trill*
here today be Master.
Then work ye right well   } *David motif*
at the marker's cell!

(while the prentices finish the erection)

Thither! Hither! The tablet on the wall, –
so the Marker's hand on it fall! –

(turning to Walther)

Aye, aye: the Marker! – Do you grow pale?   *Beckmesser motif*

The Mastersingers of Nuremberg

Beckmesser-M.
Erregtheitstriller,
Zunftgesetz-M.,
Kreidestrich-M.

Vor ihm schon mancher Werber versang.
Sieben Fehler gibt er euch vor,
die merkt er mit Kreide dort an:
wer über sieben Fehler verlor,
hat versungen und ganz vertan!
Nun nehmt euch in acht:
der Merker wacht!

KA 80 ▶ 935
CD 1/9 1:26

(derb in die Hände schlagend)

Lehrbuben-M.

Glück auf zum Meistersingen!
Mögt euch das Kränzlein erschwingen!

Kränzlein-M.

Das Blumenkränzlein aus Seiden fein,
wird das dem Herrn Ritter beschieden sein?

Die Lehrbuben, welche zu gleicher Zeit das Gemerk geschlossen haben, fassen sich an und tanzen einen verschlungenen Reigen um dasselbe.

LEHRBUBEN

Das Blumenkränzlein aus Seiden fein,
wird das dem Herrn Ritter beschieden sein?

Lebhaftigkeit-M.

Die Lehrbuben fahren sogleich erschrocken auseinander, als die Sakristei aufgeht und Pogner mit Beckmesser eintritt; sie ziehen sich nach hinten zurück.

Act 1, Scene 2 – David! What is't?

VS 70 ▶ 16
CD 1/9 1:26

Before him many candidates fail.
Seven faults the Marker lets by,
with chalk they are marked on his slate:
if more than seven faults he should spy,
then the singer has met his fate!
Good heed must you take:
his ear's awake!

Beckmesser motif
excitement trill,
guild law motif,
chalk stroke motif.

> *(clapping his hands loudly)*

God save you from this disaster!
May you today be a master!
The silken chaplet of flowers bright,
will that by good fortune be yours, sir knight?

prentices motif

chaplet motif

> *The Prentices who have first completed the marker's stage, take hands and dance in a ring around it.*

PRENTICES

The silken chaplet of flowers bright,
will that by good fortune be yours, Sir Knight?

> *The Prentices separate out in alarm as the sacristy opens and Pogner with Beckmesser enters.*

liveliness motif

3. SZENE – SEID MEINER TREUE WOHL VERSEHEN KA 85 ▸ 983
CD 1/10 0:01

Die Einrichtung ist nun folgendermaßen beendigt: – Zur Seite rechts sind gepolsterte Bänke in der Weise aufgestellt, daß sie einen schwachen Halbkreis nach der Mitte zu bilden. Am Ende der Bänke, in der Mitte der Bühne, befindet sich das „Gemerk" benannte Gerüste, welches zuvor hergerichtet worden. Zur linken Seite steht nur der erhöhte, kathederartige Stuhl („der Singstuhl") der Versammlung gegenüber. Im Hintergrunde, den großen Vorhang entlang, steht eine lange niedere Bank für die Lehrlinge. – Walther, verdrießlich über das Gespött der Knaben, hat sich auf die vordere Bank niedergelassen. Pogner und Beckmesser sind im Gespräch aus der Sakristei aufgetreten. Die Lehrbuben harren ehrerbietig vor der hinteren Bank stehend. Nur David stellt sich anfänglich am Eingang bei der Sakristei auf.

POGNER

(zu Beckmesser)

Zunftberatung-M.,
Zunftgesetz-M.

Seid meiner Treue wohl versehen,
was ich bestimmt, ist euch zu Nutz:
im Wettgesang müßt ihr bestehen,
wer böte euch als Meister Trutz?

BECKMESSER

Zunftberatung-M.,
Zunftideal-M.

Doch wollt ihr von dem Punkt nicht weichen,
der mich – ich sag's – bedenklich macht:
kann Evchens Wunsch den Werber streichen,
was nützt mir meine Meisterpracht?

Scene 3 – Be well assured

The arrangement of the stage is now thus completed: – On the right stuffed benches are placed in a curve facing the centre. At the end of the benches, in the middle of the stage is the „Gemerk" (the marker's stage) which has been erected. At the end stands a high ecclesiastical chair („the singing chair") opposite the benches. St the back in front of the great curtain stands a bench for the pupils. – Walther, vexed with the boys' mocking has sealed himself with the front bench. Pogner has come from the sacristy in conversation with Beckmesser. The prentices stand waiting respectfully before the back bench. Only David takes his place at first by the sacristy door.

Pogner

(to Beckmesser)

Be well assured of my good favour,   *guild council motif,*
what I have planned will serve you well: *guild law motif*
success will go with your endeavour,
who wields like you the master's spell?

Beckmesser

Yet will you not that point pass over,   *guild council motif,*
whereon, in truth, I'm doubtful still: *guild ideal motif*
if Eva's whim may choose her lover,
what booteth all my master skill?

Pogner
Ei sagt, ich mein', vor allen Dingen
sollt' euch an dem gelegen sein?
Könnt ihr der Tochter Wunsch nicht zwingen,
wie möget ihr wohl um sie frein?

Beckmesser

Zunftberatung-M.,
Zunftgesetz-M.

Ei ja! Gar wohl! Drum eben bitt' ich,
daß bei dem Kind ihr für mich sprecht,
wie ich geworben zart und sittig,
und wie Beckmesser grad euch recht.

Pogner

Zunftberatung-M.,
Zunftideal-M.

Das tu ich gern.

Beckmesser

(beiseite)

Zunftberatung-M.,
Zunftgesetz-M.,
Zunftideal-M.

                      Er läßt nicht nach.
Wie wehrt' ich da 'nem Ungemach?

Walther

der, als er Pogner gewahrt, aufgestanden und ihm entgegen gegangen ist, verneigt sich vor ihm:

Gestattet Meister!

Pogner

                 Wie, mein Junker?
Ihr sucht mich in der Singschul' hie?

Pogner und Walther wechseln Begrüßungen.

Beckmesser

(immer beiseite)

Verstünden's die Frau'n;
            doch schlechtes Geflunker
gilt ihnen mehr als all' Poesie.

Er geht verdrießlich im Hintergrunde auf und ab.

Act 1, Scene 3 – Be well assured

POGNER

But yet, meseems your first beginning
should be to find how ell you stand;
for if her heart you fail in winning,
how then can you desire her hand?

BECKMESSER

Ah yes! 'Tis true! I therefore pray you,   *guild council motif,*
that with the child you help my love,   *guild law motif*
that I am soft and tender, say you,
and that Beckmesser you approve.

POGNER

With right good will.   *guild council motif*
  guild ideal motif

BECKMESSER

(aside)

                     He won't give way.   *guild council motif*
How to avoid misfortune, say?   *guild law motif*
  guild ideal motif

WALTHER

who on seeing Pogner has risen and come to meet him, bow to him:

Your pardon Master!

POGNER

                   What, Sir Walther?
You seek me in the singing school?
Pogner and Walther exchange greetings.

BECKMESSER

(still aside)

If women had wits!
                     but high sounding folly
pleases them more than poesy's charms!
He walks up and down at back in vexation.

The Mastersingers of Nuremberg

WALTHER

Zunftberatung-M.,
Zunftideal-M.,
Zunftgesetz-M.,
Nürnberg-M.

Singkunst-M. ②

Singkunst-M. ①
(gekünstelt)

Hier eben bin ich am rechten Ort:
gesteh' ich's frei, vom Lande fort
was mich nach Nürnberg trieb,
war nur zur Kunst die Lieb'.
Vergaß ich's gestern euch zu sagen,
heut' muß ich's laut zu künden wagen:
ein Meistersinger möcht' ich sein!
   (sehr innig)
Schließt, Meister, in die Zunft mich ein!
   Kunz Vogelgesang und Konrad Nachtigal sind
   eingetreten.

POGNER

Zunftberatung-M.,
Zunftideal-M.,
Zunftgesetz-M.

   (freudig zu den Hinzutretenden sich wendend)
Kunz Vogelgesang! Freund Nachtigal!
Hört doch, welch ganz besondrer Fall:
der Ritter hier, mir wohlbekannt,
hat der Meisterkunst sich zugewandt.
   Vorstellungen und Begrüßungen; andre Mei-
   stersinger treten noch hinzu.

BECKMESSER

   (wieder in der Vordergrund tretend, für sich)
Noch such' ich's zu wenden;
         doch, sollt's nicht gelingen,
versuch' ich des Mädchens Herz zu ersingen:
in stiller Nacht, von ihr nur gehört,
erfahr' ich, ob auf mein Lied sie schwört.
   (Walther erblickend)
Wer ist der Mensch? –

POGNER

Meistersinger-M. ②
Singkunst-M. ②

   (sehr warm zu Walther fortfahrend)
         Glaubt, wie mich's freut!
Die alte Zeit dünkt mich erneut.

Act 1, Scene 3 – Be well assured

WALTHER

That here I find me is right and fit: *guild council motif,*
for truth to tell, what made me flit   *guild ideal motif,*
from home to Nürnberg town,   *guild law motif,*
was love of art alone.   *Nuremberg motif*
Though yesterday I failed to name it,   *singing art motif ②*
now, in this place I dare proclaim it
A Mastersinger would I be!   *singing art motif ①*

(cordially)   *(mannered)*

Pray, of your guild now make me free!

Enter Kunz Vogelgesang and Konrad Nachtigal.

POGNER

(turning joyfully to the new comers)   *guild council motif,*
    guild ideal motif,
Kunz Vogelgesang! Friend Nachtigal!   *guild law motif*
Hear now this passing strange event:
this noble knight, to me well known,
to our Master art his thought has bent.

Introductions and greetings; other Mastersingers come forward.

BECKMESSER

(coming again to the front, aside)

Again I will ask him;
                       and if I succeed not,
then straight will I try if my song she heed not:
I'll sing at night to her ears alone:
perchance by singing may she be won.

(seeing Walther)

What man is that? –

POGNER

(continuing very warmly to Walther)

                          Glad is my heart!   *mastersinger motif ②*
The ancient time is come again.   *singing art motif ②*

The Mastersingers of Nuremberg

Zunftberatung-M.,
Zunftgesetz-M.,
Zunftideal-M.

BECKMESSER
Er gefällt mir nicht!

POGNER
                    Was ihr begehrt,
soviel an mir, sei's euch gewährt.

BECKMESSER
Was will er hier? Wie der Blick ihm lacht!

POGNER
Half ich euch gern bei des Guts Verkauf,
in die Zunft nun nehm' ich euch
                    gleich gern auf.

BECKMESSER
Holla! Sixtus! Auf den hab acht!

WALTHER
    (zu Pogner)

Singkunst-M.
(gekünstelt)

Habt Dank der Güte
aus tiefstem Gemüte!
Und darf ich denn hoffen?
Steht heut mir noch offen,
zu werben um den Preis,
daß Meistersinger ich heiß'?

BECKMESSER
Oho! Fein sacht!
            Auf dem Kopf steht kein Kegel!

POGNER
Herr Ritter, dies geh' nun nach der Regel.
Doch heut ist Freiung, ich schlag' euch vor:

Zunftberatung-M.,
Zunftgesetz-M.,
Zunftideal-M.

mir leihen die Meister ein willig Ohr!

Die Meistersinger sind nun alle angelangt, zuletzt auch Hans Sachs.

Act 1, Scene 3 – Be well assured

BECKMESSER

I mislike the man!

guild council motif,
guild ideal motif,
guild law motif

POGNER

                     What you desire,
were't mine to grant, you might command.

BECKMESSER

What would be here? With his laughing looks!

POGNER

Freely I helped your land to sell,
in our guild I welcome you now as well.

BECKMESSER

Holla! Sixtus! Of him beware!

WALTHER

   (to Pogner)

My thanks now truly
from hearts depth I give you!
In this great endeavor,
then may I believe you?
The prize I too may gain,
if Master's rank I attain?

singing art motif
(mannered)

BECKMESSER

Ah, not too fast!
          Then the knight's on his mettle!

POGNER

Sir Walther, such things by rule we settle.
Today is trial, but have no fear:
I gain from the masters a willing ear!

   All the masters have now arrived, Hans Sachs
   last.

guild council motif,
guild ideal motif,
guild law motif

Zunftberatung-M.,
Zunftideal-M.,
Zunftgesetz-M.

SACHS
Gott grüß' euch, Meister!

VOGELGESANG
                    Sind wir beisammen?

BECKMESSER
Der Sachs ist ja da!

NACHTIGAL
                    So ruft die Namen!

KOTHNER
zieht eine Liste hervor, stellt sich zur Seite auf und ruft laut:
Zu einer Freiung und Zunftberatung
ging an die Meister ein' Einladung:
bei Nenn' und Nam',
ob jeder kam,
ruf' ich nun auf als letztentbot'ner,
der ich mich nenn' und bin Fritz Kothner. –
Seid ihr da, Veit Pogner?

POGNER
                    Hier zur Hand!
Er setzt sich.

KOTHNER
Kunz Vogelgesang?

VOGELGESANG
                    Ein sich fand.
Setzt sich.

KOTHNER
Hermann Ortel?

ORTEL
                    Immer am Ort.

Act 1, Scene 3 – Be well assured

SACHS

God greet you, Masters!

guild council motif,
guild ideal motif,
guild law motif

VOGELGESANG

                Are all together?

BECKMESSER

Yes, Sachs too, is here!

NACHTIGAL

                Let names be called, then!

KOTHNER

produces a list, takes his place apart, and calls aloud:

Now to a trial, as summoned hither,
Masters in counsil are come together:
if one and all,
the names I call,
and, as the last elected man, sirs,
Fritz Kothner names himself and answers. –
Are you there, Veit Pogner?

POGNER

                Here at hand!

Sits.

KOTHNER

Kunz Vogelgesang?

VOGELGESANG

                Here I stand.

Sits.

KOTHNER

Hermann Ortel?

ORTEL

                Aye on the spot.

Setzt sich.

Zunftberatung-M.,
Zunftgesetz-M.,
Zunftideal-M.

KOTHNER
Balthasar Zorn?

ZORN
Bleibt niemals fort.

Setzt sich.

KOTHNER
Konrad Nachtigal?

NACHTIGAL
Treu seinem Schlag.

Setzt sich.

KOTHNER
Augustin Moser?

MOSER
Nie fehlen mag.

Setzt sich.

KOTHNER
Niklaus Vogel? – Schweigt?

LEHRBUBE

(von der Bank aufstehend)

Ist krank!

KOTHNER
Gut Bess'rung dem Meister!

MEISTERSINGER
Walt's Gott!

LEHRBUBE
Schön Dank!

Er setzt sich wieder nieder.

Act 1, Scene 3 – Be well assured

VS 87 ▶ 1
CD 1/11 1:08 *Sits.*

KOTHNER
Balthasar Zorn?   *guild council motif,*
                                   guild law motif,
ZORN   *guild ideal motif*
                    Where is he not.
Sits.

KOTHNER
Konrad Nachtigal?

NACHTIGAL
                    True to his lay.
Sits.

KOTHNER
Augustin Moser?

MOSER
                    Ne'er stays away.
Sits.

KOTHNER
Niklaus Vogel? – Speaks not?

PRENTICE
    (rising from his seat)
                                Is ill!

KOTHNER
Good health to the Master!

MASTERSINGERS
                    Amen!

PRENTICE
                            His thanks!
He sits down again.

Singkunst-M.,
Zunftberatung-M.,
Zunftideal-M.,
Zunftgesetz-M.

KOTHNER

Hans Sachs?

DAVID

(vorlaut sich erhebend und auf Sachs zeigend)
        Da steht er!

SACHS

(drohend zu David)
                  Juckt dich das Fell?
Verzeiht, Meister! – Sachs ist zur Stell'!
Er setzt sich.

KOTHNER

Sixtus Beckmesser?

BECKMESSER

(während er sich setzt)
                Immer bei Sachs, –
daß den Reim ich lern'
           von „blüh' und wachs'".
Sachs lacht.

KOTHNER

Ulrich Eisslinger?

EISSLINGER

        Hier!
Setzt sich.

KOTHNER

            Hans Foltz?

FOLTZ

Bin da.
Setzt sich.

Act 1, Scene 3 – Be well assured

KOTHNER
Hans Sachs?

DAVID
(rising and pointing to Sachs)
There stands he!

SACHS
(threateningly to David)
Tingles thy face?
Forgive, Masters! – Sachs is in place!
Sits.

KOTHNER
Sixtus Beckmesser?

BECKMESSER
(as he takes his seat)
Ever by Sachs, –
so the rhyme I learn
of „bloom and wax".
Sachs laughs.

KOTHNER
Ulrich Eisslinger?

EISSLINGER
Here!
Sits.

KOTHNER
Hans Foltz?

FOLTZ
Here, too.
Sits.

singing art motif
guild council motif,
guild ideal motif
guild law motif

The Mastersingers of Nuremberg

Singkunst-M.

KOTHNER

Hans Schwartz?

KA 100 ▶ 1139
CD 1/11 1:58

SCHWARZ

Zuletzt: Gott wollt's!

Singkunst-M.,
Zunftgesetz-M.,
Zunftberatung-M.,
Zunftideal-M.

Setzt sich.

KOTHNER

Zur Sitzung gut und voll die Zahl.
Beliebt's, wir schreiten zur Merkerwahl?

VOGELGESANG

Wohl eh'r nach dem Fest?

BECKMESSER

(zu Kothner)

Pressiert's den Herrn?
Mein' Stell' und Amt laß' ich ihm gern.

POGNER

Nicht doch, ihr Meister; laßt das jetzt fort!
Für wicht'gen Antrag bitt' ich ums Wort.

Zunftberatung-M.

Die Meister stehen auf, nicken Kothner zu und setzen sich wieder.

KOTHNER

Singkunst-M. ②

Das habt ihr; Meister, sprecht!

POGNER

Entzückung-M.
Johannistag-M.

Nun hört, und versteht mich recht! –
Das schöne Fest, Johannistag,
ihr wißt, begehn wir morgen:
auf grüner Au, am Blumenhag,
bei Spiel und Tanz im Lustgelag,
an froher Brust geborgen,
vergessen seiner Sorgen,
ein jeder freut sich wie er mag.
Die Singschul' ernst im Kirchenchor
die Meister selbst vertauschen;

KA 102 ▶ 1167
CD 1/12 0:01

Act 1, Scene 3 – Be well assured

KOTHNER

    Hans Schwartz?   *singing art motif*

SCHWARZ

    At last: God speed!

Sits.   *singing art motif,*
guild council motif,
KOTHNER   *guild ideal motif*
The council, I declare, is met.   *guild law motif*
Shall we make choice of the marker now?

VOGELGESANG
The festival first?

BECKMESSER

(to Kothner)

    So pressing, sirs?
To you I gladly yield my place.

POGNER
Not so, my Masters; let me be heard!
For things of weight I ask for the word.   *guild council motif*
The masters rise, nod to Kothner, and reseat
themselves.

KOTHNER
You have it; Master, tell!   *singing art motif ②*

POGNER

delight motif
Then hear me, and heed me well! –   *Midsummer day motif*
The feast of John, Midsummer day,
ye know, we keep tomorrow:
In meadows green, by hedges gay,
with song and dance among the hay,
with heart filled full of gladness,
forgetting all his sadness,
let each rejoice as best he may.
To raise the solemn chant on high,
our singing school we borrow:

The Mastersingers of Nuremberg

Johannistag-M.   mit Kling und Klang hinaus zum Tor,
auf offne Wiese ziehn sie vor;
bei hellen Festes Rauschen
das Volk sie lassen lauschen
dem Freigesang mit Laienohr.
Zu einem Werb- und Wettgesang
gestellt sind Siegespreise,
und beide preist man weit und lang,
die Gabe, wie die Weise.
Nun schuf mich Gott zum reichen Mann;
und gibt ein jeder, wie er kann,
(Eva-M.)   so mußte ich wohl sinnen,
was ich gäb' zu gewinnen,
daß ich nicht käm' zu Schand':
so hört denn, was ich fand.
In deutschen Landen viel gereist,
hat oft es mich verdrossen,
daß man den Bürger wenig preist,
Johannistag-M.   ihn karg nennt und verschlossen.
(moll)   An Höfen, wie an niedrer Statt,
des bittren Tadels ward ich satt,
daß nur auf Schacher und Geld
sein Merk der Bürger stellt'.
Kunst-M.,   Daß wir im weiten deutschen Reich
Singkunst-M. ②   die Kunst einzig noch pflegen,
dran dünkt ihnen wenig gelegen.
Doch wie uns das zur Ehre gereich',
und daß mit hohem Mut
wir schätzen, was schön und gut,
was wert die Kunst, und was sie gilt,
das ward ich der Welt zu zeigen gewillt;
drum hört, Meister, die Gab',
die als Preis bestimmt ich hab'!
Johannistag-M.   Dem Singer, der im Kunstgesang
vor allem Volk den Preis errang,
am Sankt Johannistag,
sei er, wer er auch mag,
dem geb' ich, ein Kunstgewog'ner,
von Nürenberg Veit Pogner,
mit all meinem Gut, wie's geh' und steh',
Eva, mein einzig Kind, zur Eh'!

Act 1, Scene 3 – Be well assured

VS 93 ▶ 10
CD 1/12 0:59

through gate and door, with shout and cry,   *Midsummer day*
to open meadows all will hie;   *motif*
while there each one rejoices,
for ears unlearned our voices
a mastersong shall raise on high.
When gifts are won in strife of song
that blithely swells and rises,
the acclamations loud and long
will greet both songs and prizes.
As God has made me passing rich;
and wealth its duties lays on each,
I sought among my treasure,
a gift of goodly measure,
lest I to shame be brought:
and found then what I sought.
In German lands where'er I came,
my ears were oft offended,
hearing our burghers, to our shame,
as misers reprehended.   *Midsummer day*
In castle as in humble cot,   *motif (minor)*
this bitter slander ceases not
that only treasure and gold
the burgher's dreams can hold.
That in our empire's spacious bounds   *art motif,*
our art we alone have tended,   *singing art motif ②*
though 'tis little commended,
yet to our burghers' honour redounds.
And that in steadfast mood,
we treasure the fair and good,
the pow'r of art and all its worth
to that I would fain bear witness on earth;
this gift, then, I choose as prize:
may ye Masters deem it wise!
To him whose son among the rest   *Midsummer day*
in open strife ye judge the best,   *motif*
on John the Baptist's day,
be he, whoe'er he may,
then will I, as art's defender,
with all my goods surrender,
the dearest treasure of my life,
Eva, my only child, for wife!

67

The Mastersingers of Nuremberg

Die Meistersinger

Zunftberatung-M.,
Lebhaftigkeit-M.,
Johannistag-M.

(*sich erhebend und sehr lebhaft durcheinander*)

Das heißt ein Wort, ein Wort ein Mann!
Da sieht man, was ein Nürnberger kann!
Drob preist man euch, noch weit und breit,
den wackren Bürger, Pogner Veit!

Lehrbuben

(*lustig aufspringend*)
Alle Zeit!
Weit und breit!
Pogner Veit!

Vogelgesang

Wer möchte da nicht ledig sein!

Sachs

Sein Weib gäb' mancher gern wohl drein!

Kothner

Auf, ledig' Mann!
jetzt macht euch ran!

Die Meister setzen sich allmählich wieder nieder; die Lehrbuben ebenfalls.

Pogner

Meistersinger-M. ④

Nun hört noch, wie ich's ernstlich mein'!
Ein' leblos' Gabe geb' ich nicht;
ein Mägdlein sitzt mit zum Gericht:
den Preis erkennt die Meisterzunft;
doch gilt's der Eh', so will's Vernunft,
daß ob der Meister Rat
die Braut den Ausschlag hat.

Beckmesser

(*zu Kothner gewandt*)
Dünkt euch das klug?

Act 1, Scene 3 – Be well assured

Mastersingers

(rising and speaking to each other with great animation)

His words are brave, like word like man!
He speaks as none but Nürnbergers can!
Therefore our praises, far and wide,
shall sound aloud for Pogner!

guild council motif,
livelihood motif,
Midsummer day motif

Prentices

(springing up merrily)

All our days,
we will raise!
Pogner's praise!

Vogelgesang

Who would not now unwedded be!

Sachs

Some, being wed, would fain be free!

Kothner

Up, single man!
do what you can!

The masters gradually take their seats again; the Prentices also.

Pogner

Yet hear me, and my meaning see!
A lifeless gift I offer not;
the maid must help to cast the lot:
the prize shall go as wills the guild;
but maidens' hearts may not be willed,
whome'er the Masters choose,
the bride may still refuse.

mastersinger motif ④

Beckmesser

(turning to Kothner)

Doth that seem wise?

KOTHNER

                Versteh' ich gut,
ihr gebt uns in des Mägdleins Hut?

BECKMESSER
Gefährlich das!

KOTHNER

                Stimmt es nicht bei,
wie wäre dann der Meister Urteil frei?

BECKMESSER
Laßt's gleich wählen nach Herzens Ziel,
und laßt den Meistergesang aus dem Spiel!

POGNER

Meistersinger-M. ④   Nicht so! Wie doch? Versteht mich recht!
                Wem ihr Meister den Preis zusprecht,
(Eva-M.)   die Maid kann dem verwehren,
                doch nie einen andren begehren.
Meistersinger-M.   Ein Meistersinger muß er sein,
                nur wen ihr krönt, den soll sie frein.

SACHS

Erhebt sich.

Verzeiht,
vielleicht schon ginget ihr zu weit.
Ein Mädchenherz und Meisterkunst
erglühn nicht stets von gleicher Brunst:
(Eva-M.)   der Frauen Sinn, gar unbelehrt,
Naturregel-M.   dünkt mich dem Sinn des Volks gleich wert.
                Wollt ihr nun vor dem Volke zeigen,
                wie hoch die Kunst ihr ehrt,
                und laßt ihr dem Kind die Wahl zu eigen,
                wollt nicht, daß dem Spruch es wehrt, –
Meistersinger-M. ④ so laßt das Volk auch Richter sein:
                mit dem Kinde sicher stimmt's überein.

DIE MEISTERSINGER

Zunftideal-M.   Oho! Das Volk? Ja, das wäre schön!

Act 1, Scene 3 – Be well assured

VS 104▶6
CD 1/12 5:35

KOTHNER

I understand,
you place us in the maiden's hand?

BECKMESSER

That were not safe!

KOTHNER

Must we agree,
Who then could call the Masters' judgment free?

BECKMESSER

Whom she loves let her heart proclaim,
and leave the mastersong out of the game!

POGNER

Not so! How now? Hear me aright! *mastersinger motif* ④
If your judgment on one should light,
who fails to gain her favour, *(Eva motif)*
unwedded she lives then forever.
A Mastersinger must he be, } *mastersinger motif*
he whom ye crown, and none but he.

SACHS

rises.

KA 107▶1
CD 1/13 0:01

One word,
perchance already ye have erred.
A maiden's dreams and our desires
gain not their glow from selfsame fires:
and womans' mind, in art untaught, *(Eva motif)*
seems to the folk's alike in thought. *nature rule motif*
If you would show the people clearly
how high you hold our art,
and, granting the maid her choice sincerely,
would yet not the judgment thwart, –
then let the folk in judgment sit: *mastersinger motif* ④
with the maiden's their choice surely will fit.

MASTERSINGERS

Oho! The folk? That will be good! *guild ideal motif*

The Mastersingers of Nuremberg

        Ade dann Kunst und Meistertön'!   KA 121 ▶ 1333
                                                                    CD 1/13 0:53

Kothner

Nein, Sachs! Gewiß, das hat keinen Sinn!
Gebt ihr dem Volk die Regeln hin?

Sachs

Meistersinger-M. ④	Vernehmt mich recht! Wie ihr doch tut! Gesteht, ich kenn' die Regeln gut;
	und daß die Zunft die Regeln bewahr',
Naturregel-M.	bemüh' ich mich selbst schon manches Jahr.
	Doch einmal im Jahre fänd' ich's weise,
	daß man die Regeln selbst probier',
	ob in der Gewohnheit trägem Gleise
	ihr' Kraft und Leben nicht sich verlier'.
Naturregel-M.	Und ob ihr der Natur
	noch seid auf rechter Spur,
	das sagt euch nur,
	wer nichts weiß von der Tabulatur.
Lehrbuben-M.	*Die Lehrbuben springen auf und reiben sich die Hände.*

Beckmesser

Hei! Wie sich die Buben freuen!

Sachs

(eifrig fortfahrend)

	Drum mocht' es euch nie gereuen,
	daß jährlich am Sankt Johannisfest,
	statt daß das Volk man kommen läßt,
	herab aus hoher Meisterwolk'
	ihr selbst euch wendet zu dem Volk.
Zunftideal-M.	Dem Volke wollt ihr behagen;
Meistersinger-M. ② & ④	nun dächt' ich, läg' es nah, ihr ließt es selbst euch auch sagen,
	ob das ihm zur Lust geschah!
	Daß Volk und Kunst gleich blüh' und wachs'
Kunst-M.	bestellt ihr so, mein' ich, Hans Sachs!

Act 1, Scene 3 – Be well assured

VS 109▸2
CD 1/13 0:53

Farewell to art and masterhood!

KOTHNER

Nay, Sachs! indeed that plan has no sense!
Ruled by the folk, the art goes hence?

SACHS

Nay hear aright! Why chafe you so!
Confess, the rules right well I know;   *mastersinger motif ④*
and that the guild those rules well may guard,
for many a year I've laboured hard.   *nature rule motif*
'Twere well, when we meet each year together,
that we the rules themselves should try,
lest, soulless and tame in custom's tether,
their force and life should dwindle and die.
And if on nature's road   *nature rule motif*
your feet have firmly trod,
they know for sure,
who nought know of the Tabulature.

The prentices spring up and rub their hands.   *prentices motif*

BECKMESSER

Hey! see how the boys make merry!

SACHS

(eagerly continuing)

Believe me, you will not rue it,
if once on St. John's day each year
trusting the crowd ye should not fear,
to leave your realm of mist and cloud
and come yourselves towards the crowd.
If ye the people would flatter;   *guild ideal motif*
'twould surely help your aim,   *mastersinger motif*
to lay before them the matter,   *② & ④*
and ask what seems best to them!
That folk and art shall bloom and wax,
if this ye do, think I, Hans Sachs!   *art motif*

	VOGELGESANG	
Kunst-M.	Ihr meint's wohl recht!	
	KOTHNER	
	Doch steht's drum faul.	

VOGELGESANG
Ihr meint's wohl recht!

KOTHNER
                  Doch steht's drum faul.

NACHTIGAL
Wann spricht das Volk, halt' ich das Maul.

KOTHNER
Der Kunst droht allweil Fall und Schmach,
läuft sie der Gunst des Volkes nach.

Kreidestrich-M.

Lehrbuben-M., Kränzlein-M.

BECKMESSER
Drin bracht' er's weit, der hier so dreist:
Gassenhauer dichtet er meist.

POGNER
Freund Sachs! Was ich mein', ist schon neu;
zu viel auf einmal brächte Reu'.

Johannistag-M.

Er wendet sich zu den Meistern.

So frag' ich, ob den Meistern gefällt
Gab' und Regel, so wie ich's gestellt?

Zunftberatung-M., Zunftideal-M.

Die Meister erheben sich beistimmend.

SACHS
Mir genügt der Jungfer Ausschlagstimm'.

BECKMESSER
Der Schuster weckt doch stets mir Grimm!

Kreidestrich-M.

KOTHNER
Wer schreibt sich als Werber ein?
Ein Junggesell' muß es sein.

BECKMESSER
Vielleicht auch ein Witwer?
                    Fragt nur den Sachs!

Act 1, Scene 3 – Be well assured

VOGELGESANG
You mean right well! *— art motif*

KOTHNER
And yet 'tis wrong.

NACHTIGAL
If mobs may speak I hold my tongue

KOTHNER
But shame will fall upon our art,
if in our work the crowd have part.

BECKMESSER *— chalk stroke motif*
Shame has he brought, who talks so loud: *— prentices motif,*
doggrel rhymes he writes for the crowd. *chaplet motif*

POGNER
Friend Sachs! I offer what is new;
too much at one time we should rue.
He turns to the Masters. *— Midsummer day motif*
I ask then, if ye Masters allow
prize and promise as I state them now?
The Masters rise in assent. *— guild council motif,*
guild ideal motif

SACHS
With her final vote can I give in.

BECKMESSER *— chalk stroke motif*
The shoemaker awakes my spleen!

KOTHNER
Who cometh as suitor here?
Now batchelors, draw ye near.

BECKMESSER
A widower, maybe?
Ask but Hans Sachs!

Sachs
Nicht doch, Herr Merker!
                           Aus jüng'rem Wachs,
als ich und ihr, muß der Freier sein,
soll Evchen ihm den Preis verleih'n.

Beckmesser
Kreidestrich-M.

Als wie auch ich? – Grober Gesell'!

Kothner
Zunftberatung-M., Zunftideal-M.

Begehrt wer Freiung, der komm' zur Stell'!
Ist jemand gemeld't, der Freiung begehrt?

Pogner
Wohl, Meister, zur Tagesordnung kehrt,
und nehmt von mir Bericht,
wie ich auf Meisterpflicht
einen jungen Ritter empfehle,
der will, daß man ihn wähle

Zunftberatung-M.

und heut' als Meistersinger frei'!
Mein Junker Stolzing, – kommt herbei!

Stolzing-M.

Walther tritt vor und verneigt sich.

Beckmesser
(beiseite)

Dacht' ich mir's doch!
                         Geht's da hinaus, Veit? –
(laut)
Meister, ich mein', zu spät ist's der Zeit!

Die Meistersinger
Der Fall ist neu: Ein Ritter gar?
soll man sich freun? Wäre da Gefahr?
Immerhin hat's ein groß' Gewicht,
daß Meister Pogner für ihn spricht.

Kothner
Soll uns der Junker willkommen sein,
zuvor muß er wohl vernommen sein.

Act 1, Scene 3 – Be well assured

SACHS

Not so, Sir Marker!
                    Of younger wax,
than I and you must the wooer prove,
when Eva's heart bestows her love.

BECKMESSER

Than I, you say? – Ill-mannered boor! *chalk stroke motif*

KOTHNER

Who comes awooing? be not afraid! *guild counsel motif,*
Is anyone here who wishes to wed? *guild ideal motif*

POGNER

Now Masters, the order of the day!
And hear from me this news,
that on my Master's faith,
I this youthful knight now present you,
who wills that we admit him
today in our Masterguild! *guild counsel motif*
Sir knight of Stolzing, – hither come!

Walther comes forward and bows. *Stolzing motif*

BECKMESSER

(aside)

'Tis as I guessed!
                    Is that the plan, Veit? –

(aloud)

Masters methinks, the time is too late!

MASTERSINGERS

The case is new: A knight in sooth?
should we be glad? Is there danger here?
Ne'ertheless it must have great weight,
that Master Pogner for him speaks.

KOTHNER

Yet, if the knight is to join our guild,
he first must be tried and duly passed.

POGNER

Stolzing-M.
Vernehmt ihn wohl! Wünsch' ich ihm Glück,
nicht bleib' ich doch hinter der Regel zurück.
Tut, Meister, die Fragen!

KOTHNER

Kreidestrich-M.
So mög' uns der Junker sagen:
ist er frei und ehrlich geboren?

POGNER

Die Frage gebt verloren,
da ich euch selbst dess' Bürge steh',
daß er aus frei' und edler Eh':
Stolzing-M.
von Stolzing Walther aus Frankenland,
nach Brief und Urkund mir wohlbekannt.
Als seines Stammes letzter Spross
verließ er neulich Hof und Schloss
und zog nach Nürnberg her,
daß er hier Bürger wär'.

BECKMESSER

Neu–Junkerunkraut – tut nicht gut.

NACHTIGAL

Freund Pogners Wort Genüge tut.

SACHS

Wie längst von den Meistern beschlossen ist,
ob Herr, ob Bauer, hier nichts beschießt[1]:
Singkunst-M.
hier fragt sich's nach der Kunst allein,
wer will ein Meistersinger sein.

KOTHNER

Drum nun frag' ich zur Stell':
Singkunst-M.
welch Meisters seid ihr Gesell?

WALTHER

Vogelweid-M.
Am stillen Herd in Winterszeit,
wann Burg und Hof mir eingeschneit,
Eva-M.
wie einst der Lenz so lieblich lacht',

---
[1] *Laut Wörterbuch J. & W. Grimm Bd. 1 Sp. 1567 f.: es beschieszt = es hilft.*

Act 1, Scene 3 – Be well assured

POGNER

Mistake me not! Friend though he be, *) Stolzing motif*
yet I desire nought that the rules do not grant.
Put, Masters, the questions!

KOTHNER

So now let the knight first tell us: *chalk stroke motif*
are his birth and standing approved?

POGNER

That question I will answer,
for, as his surety here I stand,
that he is free and nobly born:
the knight of Stolzing in Frankenland, *) Stolzing motif*
by fame and letters to me well known.
Sole living scion of his race
of late he left his castle home,
and came to Nürnberg here,
to join our burghers' guild.

BECKMESSER

Raw, worthless coxcomb! Let him go!.

NACHTIGAL

Friend Pogner's word that is enough.

SACHS

The rule by the Masters made of old,
that lord and peasant alike we hold:
here nought is prized but art alone, *) singing art motif*
in those who seek the Master's crown.

KOTHNER

Then his answer I claim:
his Master now let him name? *) singing art motif*

WALTHER

In snowbound hall by fire side, *) Vogelweid motif*
when prisoned fast at wintertide,
how once the laughing spring did reign, *Eva motif*

The Mastersingers of Nuremberg

Vogelweid-M.,   und wie er bald wohl neu erwacht',
Eva-M.   ein altes Buch, vom Ahn vermacht,
               gab das mir oft zu lesen:
     Herr Walther von der Vogelweid',
               der ist mein Meister gewesen.

SACHS

Eva-M.   Ein guter Meister!

BECKMESSER

               Doch lang schon tot;
Vogelweid-M.   wie lehrt' ihn der wohl der Regeln Gebot?

KOTHNER

Doch in welcher Schul' das Singen
mocht' euch zu lernen gelingen?

WALTHER

Vogelweid-M.   Wann dann die Flur vom Frost befreit,
     und wiederkehrt' die Sommerszeit;
Eva-M.   was einst in langer Winternacht
     das alte Buch mir kund gemacht,
     das schallte laut in Waldes Pracht,
Entzückung-M.   das hört' ich hell erklingen:
     im Wald dort auf der Vogelweid'
               da lernt' ich auch das Singen.

BECKMESSER

Erregtheitstriller   Oho! Von Finken und Meisen
     lerntet ihr Meisterweisen?
     Das wird denn wohl auch danach sein!

VOGELGESANG

Entzückung-M.   Zwei art'ge Stollen faßt' er da ein.

BECKMESSER

Ihr lobt ihn, Meister Vogelgesang,
wohl weil vom Vogel er lernt' den Gesang?

KOTHNER

Was meint ihr, Meister, frag' ich noch fort?

Act 1, Scene 3 – Be well assured

VS 127▶4
CD 1/15 0:45
and, sleeping now, should wake again,
an ancient book, to heart and brain,
    the blessed tidings brought me:
Sir Walther of the Vogelweid',
    was then the Master who taught me.

Vogelweid motif,
Eva motif

SACHS

A goodly master!

Eva motif

BECKMESSER

    But long since dead;
from him I wonder what rules could be learned?

Vogelweid motif

KOTHNER

In what school of art well founded
in all our laws were you grounded?

WALTHER

And when the fields the frost defied,
and summer shown in radiant pride;
what during winter's dreary spell
that ancient book had taught so well,
that song I heard, o'er moor and fell
    through field and forest ringing:
from birds' son on the Vogelweid
    'twas there I learned my singing.

Vogelweid motif

Eva motif

delight motif

BECKMESSER

Oho! The finches and titmice
taught you our Mastersinging?
What manner of teaching was theirs!

excitement trill

VOGELGESANG

Two dainty stanzas, still, has he sung.

delight motif

BECKMESSER

You praise him, Master Vogelgesang,
because from birds he has learned all his song?

KOTHNER

What say ye, Masters, here shall we halt?

The Mastersingers of Nuremberg

Erregtheitstriller Mich dünkt, der Junker ist fehl am Ort.

Eva-M.
SACHS
Das wird sich bäldlich zeigen:
wenn rechte Kunst ihm eigen,
und gut er sie bewährt,
was gilt's, wer sie ihn gelehrt?

KOTHNER
(zu Walther)

Vogelweid-M. Seid ihr bereit, ob euch geriet
Erregtheitstriller, mit neuer Find' ein Meisterlied,
Eva-M. nach Dicht' und Weis' eu'r eigen,
zur Stunde jetzt zu zeigen?

WALTHER
Was Winternacht,
was Waldespracht,
was Buch und Hain mich wiesen,
was Dichtersanges Wundermacht
mir heimlich wollt' erschließen;
was Rosses Schritt
beim Waffenritt,
was Reihentanz
Vogelweid-M. bei heitrem Schanz,
mir sinnend gab zu lauschen:
Eva-M. gilt es des Lebens höchsten Preis
um Sang mir einzutauschen,
zu eignem Wort und eigner Weis'
will einig mir es fließen,
als Meistersang, ob den ich weiß,
Erregtheitstriller euch Meistern sich ergießen.

BECKMESSER
Entnahmt ihr was der Worte Schwall?

VOGELGESANG
Ei nun, er wagt's!

Act 1, Scene 3 – Be well assured

Methinks the knight is e'en now at fault.   *excitement trill*

SACHS   *Eva motif*

We must not judge too lightly
if art has led him rightly;
if well he sings by rule,
what matters master or school?

KOTHNER

(to Walther)

Are you prepared to show this throng   *Vogelweid-M.*
if you have found a Mastersong,   *excitement trill,*
with words and tune well mated,   *Eva motif*
and by yourself created?

WALTHER

The secret deep,
of winter's sleep,
of woods in summer's glory,
the hidden word of book and bird,
revealed in poet's story;
the warlike clash
when weapons flash,
and music meet
for dancing feet,   *Vogelweid motif*
with in my fancy ringing:
these now to gain life's highest need,   *Eva motif*
must I proclaim in singing.
Let word and tone in measure tread,
together sweetly mated,
a Mastersong, if fortune speed,
by me shall be created.   *excitement trill*

BECKMESSER

What sense is in the whirling words?

VOGELGESANG

In truth, 'tis bold!

NACHTIGAL
Merkwürd'ger Fall!

Meistersinger-M. ②

KOTHNER
Nun, Meister! Wenn's gefällt,
werd' das Gemerk bestellt.
(zu Walther)
Wählt der Herr einen heil'gen Stoff?

KA 151 ▸ 1592
CD 1/16 0:01

WALTHER
Erregtheitstriller
Was heilig mir, der Liebe Panier
schwing' und sing' ich, mir zu Hoff'.

Meistersinger-M. ②,
Erregtheitstriller

KOTHNER
Das gilt uns weltlich. Drum allein,
Meister Beckmesser, schließt euch ein!

BECKMESSER

Missgunst-M.[1]

erhebt sich und schreitet wie widerwillig dem Gemerk zu:

Ein saures Amt und heut zumal!
Wohl gibt's mit der Kreide manche Qual!

Stolzing-M.
("stolpernd")

Er verneigt sich gegen Walther.
Herr Ritter, wißt:

Erregtheitstriller-M.

Sixtus Beckmesser Merker ist;
hier im Gemerk

Missgunst-M.

verrichtet er still sein strenges Werk.
Sieben Fehler gibt er euch vor,
die merkt er mit Kreide dort an: –

Zunftgesetz-M.
Stolzing-M. (verfremdet, abgebrochen),
Missgunst-M.,
Beckmesser-M.

wenn er über sieben Fehler verlor,
dann versang der Herr Rittersmann.
Er setzt sich im Gemerk.
Gar fein er hört;
doch, daß er euch den Mut nicht stört,
säh't ihr ihm zu,
so gibt er euch Ruh',
und schließt sich gar hier ein, –
läßt Gott euch befohlen sein.

---

[1] *Das Missgunst-Motiv ist Beckmessers Karikatur des Stolzing-Motivs.*

Act 1, Scene 3 – Be well assured

NACHTIGAL
> Strange is the case!

KOTHNER — *mastersinger motif ②*
Now Masters! With your leave
the Marker takes his place.
> *(to Walther)*
Sings the knight on a holy theme?

WALTHER
My holy sign, the banner of love, — *excitement trill*
waiving over me, floats above.

KOTHNER — *mastersinger motif ②, excitement trill*
That soundeth worldly, therefore now,
Master Beckmesser, take your place!

BECKMESSER
> *rises and goes as if unwillingly to the „Gemerk":* — *envy motif[1]*

A bitter task today I trow!
The chalk will be busy, well I know!
> *He bows towards Walther.* — *Stolzing motif („stumbling")*

Sir Knight, give ear:
Sixtus Beckmesser marketh here; — *excitement trill*
here will he lurk
and silently do his cruel work. — *envy motif*
Seven faults he letteth pass by,
with chalk they are marked on the slate: –
but if more than seven faults he should spy, — *guild law motif*
then, Sir Knight, you have met your fate. — *Stolzing motif (distorted, disrupted), envy motif, Beckmesser motif*
> *He sits in the „Gemerk".*

His ears are keen;
but, lest your soul, if he were seen,
should be distressed,
he leaves you at rest,
and hides himself away, –
God grant you his grace today.

....
[1] *The envy motif is Beckmessers caricature of the Stolzing motif.*

Er streckt den Kopf, höhnisch freundlich nickend, heraus und verschwindet hinter dem zugezogenen Vorhange des Gemerkes gänzlich.

KOTHNER

winkt den Lehrbuben; zu Walther:

Erregtheitstriller, Meistersinger-M. ⑥ & ①, Stolzing-M. (gebrochen)

Was euch zum Liede Richt' und Schnur,
vernehmt nun aus der Tabulatur!

Die Lehrbuben haben die an der Wand aufgehängte Tafel der „Leges Tabulaturae" herabgenommen und halten sie Kothner vor; dieser liest daraus.

„Ein' jedes Meistergesanges Bar
stell' ordentlich ein Gemäße dar
aus unterschiedlichen Gesätzen,

Zunftgesetz-M. (mit Koloratur), Erregtheitstriller

die keiner soll verletzen.
Ein Gesätz besteht aus zweenen Stollen,
die gleiche Melodei haben sollen;
der Stoll' aus etlicher Vers' Gebänd',

Meistersinger-M. ④, Erregtheitstriller

der Vers hat seinen Reim am End.
Darauf so folgt der Abgesang,
der sei auch etlich' Verse lang,
und hab' sein' besondre Melodei,

Zunftgesetz-M. (mit Koloratur), Erregtheitstriller Meistersinger-M. ② Singkunst-M. ②

als nicht im Stollen zu finden sei.
Derlei Gemäßes mehre Baren
soll ein jed' Meisterlied bewahren;
und wer ein neues Lied gericht',
das über vier der Silben nicht
eingreift in andrer Meister Weis',

Zunftgesetz-M. (mit Koloratur), Erregtheitstriller

dess' Lied erwerb' sich Meisterpreis!"

Er gibt die Tafel den Lehrbuben zurück; diese hängen sie wieder auf.

Nun setzt euch in den Singestuhl!

WALTHER

Stolzing-M. (verfremdet), Kreidestrich-M.

(mit einem Schauer)
Hier – in den Stuhl?

Act 1, Scene 3 – Be well assured

He puts out his head with a mocking friendly nod, and then disappears behind the drawn curtains of the „Gemerk".

KOTHNER

beckons to the prentices; to Walther:

These rules to make your footsteps sure, now hear you from the tabulature!	*excitement trill, mastersinger motif ⑥ & ①, Stolzing motif (breaking)*
The prentices have taken down from the wall the board of the „Leges Tabulaturae" and hold it before Kothner who reads from it.	
„A song has „bars", as the Masters teach, which duly present a measure each: for this are sundry stanzas needed, with laws that must be heeded. In a stanza strophes two are mated, one tune for these must then be created:	*guild law motif (with colorature), excitement trill*
each must to several lines extend, each line or verse a rhyme must end. There follows then the aftersong, which is several verses long.	*mastersinger motif ④, excitement trill*
This also must have its melody, the which must not in the strophe be. The songs with „bars" of such a measure as Mastersongs we duly treasure. Of sequent notes as used before, our rules allow not more than four	*guild law motif (with colorature), excitement trill mastersinger motif ② singing art motif. ②*
who sings a song upon this wise, shall gain the Mastersinger's prize!"	*guild law motif (with colorature), excitement trill*
He gives the board back to the prentices; they hang it again to the wall.	
Now seat you in the singer's chair!	

WALTHER

(with a shudder)
Here – in this chair?

Stolzing motif (distorted), chalk stroke motif

The Mastersingers of Nuremberg

KOTHNER

Wie's Brauch der Schul'.

WALTHER

Missgunst-M.   *besteigt den Stuhl und setzt sich mit Widerstreben; beiseite:*

Für dich, Geliebte, sei's getan!

KOTHNER

(sehr laut)
Der Sänger sitzt.

BECKMESSER

(unsichtbar im Gemerk; sehr laut)
Fanget an!

WALTHER

„Fanget an!" –

Eva-M.,
Leidenschaft-M.[1]

So rief der Lenz in den Wald,
daß laut es ihn durchhallt:
und, wie in fern'ren Wellen
der Hall von dannen flieht,
von weit her naht ein Schwellen,
das mächtig näher zieht.

Lenzesgebot-M.
(rasch, in Walthers
Gesang)

Es schwillt und schallt,
es tönt der Wald,
von holder Stimmen Gemenge;
nun laut und hell,
schon nah zur Stell',
wie wächst der Schwall!
Wie Glockenhall
ertost des Jubels Gedränge!
Der Wald,
wie bald
antwortet er dem Ruf,
der neu ihm Leben schuf:

Kreidestrich-M.,
Beckmesser-M.

stimmte an das süße Lenzeslied.

Man hört aus dem Gemerk unmutige Seufzer
des Merkers und heftiges Anstreichen mit der

---
[1] *Das Leidenschaft-Motiv wird hier in rascher, beinahe gehetzter Folge immer wieder angespielt.*

Act 1, Scene 3 – Be well assured

KOTHNER

    'Tis custom here.

WALTHER

seats himself unwillingly; aside: *envy motif*

For thee, beloved, let it be!

KOTHNER

(very loud)
The singer sits.

BECKMESSER

(invisible in the „Gemerk"; very loud)
    Now begin!

WALTHER

    „Now begin!" –
So cried the spring through the land: *Eva motif,*
loud echoed her command,   *passion motif[1]*
and through the forest flying,
scarce reached its farthest bound,
when distant glens replying
gave back a mighty sound.
The woods ere long   *springtime's behest*
are filled with song   *motif (rapidly, in*
and sweetly clamourous voices;   *Walther's voice)*
now loud and clear
the sound draws near,
the tumult swells
like pealing bells,
and ev'ry creature rejoices!
All heard
spring's word,
and, answering her command,
that woke the sleeping land:
raised on high the tender song of spring.   *chalk stroke motif,*
     Beckmesser motif
    From the „Gemerk" are heard Marker's sighs
    of ill humor and vigourous scratching of the

---

[1] *The beginning of the passion motif is played in rapid, nearly hectic repetitions.*

| | Kreide. Auch Walther hat es bemerkt; nach | KA 163 ▸ 1742 |
| | kurzer Störung fährt er fort: | CD 2/1 1:31 |

Kreidestrich-M.,	In einer Dornenhecken
Beckmesser-M.	von Neid und Gram verzehrt,
	mußt' er sich da verstecken,
	der Winter, grimmbewehrt:
	von dürrem Laub umrauscht,
Kreidestrich-M.	er lauert da und lauscht,
	wie er das frohe Singen
	zu Schaden könnte bringen. –

Er steht vom Stuhle auf.

Passion motif	Doch: fanget an!
	So rief es mir in die Brust,
	als noch ich von Liebe nicht wußt'.
Flieder-M.	Da fühlt' ich's tief sich regen,
	als weckt' es mich aus dem Traum;
	mein Herz mit bebenden Schlägen
	erfüllte des Busens Raum:
Lenzesgebot-M.	das Blut, es wallt
	mit Allgewalt,
	geschwellt von neuem Gefühle;
	aus warmer Nacht,
	mit Übermacht,
	schwillt mir zum Meer
	der Seufzer Heer
Eva motif	in wildem Wonnegewühle.
	Die Brust, wie bald antwortet sie dem Ruf,
	der neu ihr Leben schuf;
	stimmt nun an das hehre Liebeslied.

BECKMESSER

Kreidestrich-M.	*(den Vorhang aufreißend)*
	Seid ihr nun fertig?	KA 168 ▸ 1795
		CD 2/2 0:01

WALTHER

Wie fraget ihr?

BECKMESSER

Mit der Tafel ward ich fertig schier.

Act 1, Scene 3 – Be well assured

VS 147▶1
CD 2/1 1:31

chalk; Walther hears it, too, and, after a few moments of discomposure, continues:

Deep hid in thorny cover — *chalk stroke motif,*
consumed by wrath and hate, — *Beckmesser motif*
when now his reign is over,
old Winter lies in wait:
in gloom of deepest woods,
he cowers there and broods, — *chalk stroke motif,*
how all this singing gladness
his spite may turn to sadness. –

He stands up.

But: now begin! — *passion motif*
    My heart, too, heard the behest,
ere love yet was born in my breast.
Methought I woke from dreaming; — *elder motif*
deep down my spirit was thrilled,
the blood in turbulence streaming,
my bosom with rapture filled:
my pulses beat — *springtime's behest*
with ardent heat, — *motif*
of unknown feelings thronging;
through sultry night,
with potent might,
tempests of sighs
in tumult rise
and tell my passion of longing. — *Eva motif*
I heard springs word and, answering her behest
that woke my sleeping breast,
raised on high the glorious song of love.

BECKMESSER

(tearing open the curtains) — *chalk stroke motif,*

VS 151▶1
CD 2/2 0:01

Say, have you finished?

WALTHER

                Why ask you that?

BECKMESSER

See, the slate here with your faults is full.

The Mastersingers of Nuremberg

Stolzing-M. (bricht ab und geht in absteigender Gelächterlinie unter)

Er hält die ganz mit Kreidestrichen bedeckte Tafel heraus. Die Meister brechen in ein Gelächter aus.

KA 169 ▶ 1800
CD 2/2 0:06

WALTHER

Hohn-M., Kreidestrich-M.

Hört doch, zu meiner Frauen Preis
gelang' ich jetzt erst mit der Weis'.

BECKMESSER

(das Gemerk verlassend)

Stolzing-M. (bricht ab und geht in absteigender Gelächterlinie unter)

Singt, wo ihr wollt! Hier habt ihr vertan! –
Ihr Meister, schaut die Tafel euch an:
so lang ich leb', ward's nicht erhört!
Ich glaubt's nicht, wenn ihr's all' auch schwört!

WALTHER

Stolzing-M. (bricht ab und geht in absteigender Gelächterlinie unter)

Erlaubt ihr's, Meister, daß er mich stört?
Blieb' ich von allen ungehört?

POGNER

Hohn-M.

Ein Wort, Herr Merker! Ihr seid gereizt!

BECKMESSER

Stolzing-M. (bricht ab, z.T. mit Gelächter)

Missgunst-M. (in Singstimme)

Sei Merker fortan, wer darnach geizt!
Doch daß der Junker hier versungen hat,
beleg' ich erst noch vor der Meister Rat.
Zwar wird's 'ne harte Arbeit sein:
wo beginnen, da wo nicht aus noch ein?
Von falscher Zahl und falschem Gebänd' –
schweig' ich schon ganz und gar:
zu kurz, zu lang – wer ein End' da fänd'?
Wer meint hier im Ernst einen Bar?

Kreidestrich-M.

Auf „blinde Meinung" klag' ich allein: –
Sagt, konnt' ein Sinn unsinniger sein?

MEHRERE MEISTERSINGER

Man ward nicht klug,
        ich muß gestehn,

Hohn-M., Kreidestrich-M.

ein Ende konnte keiner ersehn.

Act 1, Scene 3 – Be well assured

VS 151 ▶ 5 CD 2/2 0:06	*He holds out the slate quite covered with chalk marks; the Masters break out in laughter.*	*Stolzing motif (breaking off and going over to a descending line of laughter)*

WALTHER

But hear: my lady's praise to sound,
a fitting strain now have I found.

scorn motif,
chalk stroke motif

BECKMESSER

(leaving the „Gemerk")

Sing where you will! Here, fixed is your fate! –
Ye Masters, turn your eyes on the slate:
the like of this was never heard!
Nay never, though you pledge your word!

Stolzing motif (breaking off and going over to a descending line of laughter)

WALTHER

I ask you, Masters, is this not wrong?
May no-one hear me end my song?

Stolzing motif (breaking off and going over to a descending line of laughter)

POGNER

One word, Sir Marker! Not too much zeal!

scorn motif

BECKMESSER

Be Marker henceforth who ever will!
But, that the knight who sang is all unskilled,
that will I prove to all the master's guild.
'Faith, heavy toil the task will be!
Where begin it, when sense no man can see?
False beat and feet, without any law –
phrases too short, too long:
no form, no plan – ne'er an end I saw!
Who calls that in earnest a song?
His „hazy meaning" that is enough: –
Say now, what sense find ye in the stuff?

Stolzing motif (breaking off, some laughter)

envy motif (in voice)

chalk stroke motif

SEVERAL MASTERSINGERS

I found no sense,
        I must confess,
None there could find an end, I confess.

scorn motif,
chalk stroke motif

The Mastersingers of Nuremberg

Hohn-M.,
Kreidestrich-M.

BECKMESSER
Und dann die Weis', welch tolles Gekreis'
aus „Abenteuer-", „blau–Ritterspornweis',"
„hoch–Tannen"–, „stolz–Jüngling"–ton!

KOTHNER
Ja, ich verstand gar nichts davon.

BECKMESSER
Kein Absatz wo, kein' Koloratur;
von Melodei auch nicht eine Spur!

Die Meister sind im wachsenden Aufstand begriffen.

Passion motif

MEHRERE MEISTERSINGER
Wer nennt das Gesang?
Es ward einem bang!

VOGELGESANG
Eitel Ohrgeschinder!

ZORN
Auch gar nichts dahinter!

Hohn-M.

KOTHNER
Und gar vom Singstuhl ist er gesprungen!

BECKMESSER
Wird erst auf die Fehlerprobe gedrungen?
Oder gleich erklärt, daß er versungen?

SACHS

der vom Beginn an Walther mit wachsendem Ernst zugehört hat, schreitet vor:

Ablehnung-M. [1]
Freundschaft-M.

Halt, Meister! Nicht so geeilt!
Nicht jeder eure Meinung teilt. –
Des Ritters Lied und Weise,
sie fand ich neu, doch nicht verwirrt;
verließ er unsre Gleise,
schritt er doch fest und unbeirrt.

---

[1] *Das Motiv gewinnt seine Bedeutung im 2. Aufzug zu Sachs' Worten: "Mein Kind, für den ist alles verloren, und Meister wird der in keinem Land".*

Act 1, Scene 3 – Be well assured

BECKMESSER

And then the mode, what medley it showed *scorn motif,*
of „bold adventure", „blue rider-spur"-mode, *chalk stroke motif*
„high-firtree"–, „proud-stripling" tone!

KOTHNER

I understood nought, I must own.

BECKMESSER

no pause at all, no color or grace;
of melody not even a trace!

The Masters become more and more excited.

SEVERAL MASTERSINGERS

Who calls that a song? *passion motif*
We listen too long!

VOGELGESANG

Empty noise I find it!

ZORN

And nought is behind it!

KOTHNER

From seat up-springing while he was singing! *scorn motif*

BECKMESSER

The faults will ye weigh that I have detected,
or at once declare he is rejected?

SACHS

*who from the first has listened to Walther with
increasing earnestness, comes forward:*

Stay, Master! You go too far! *disapproval motif* [1]
All here your judgment do not share. –
The song that you are spurning, *friendship motof*
I found it new, but not confused;
Though from our courses turning,
with steady steps he firmly cruised.

---
[1] *The motif will gain its meaning in the 2nd act (page 145) to
Sachs's words: "My child, the man who meets such disaster, no
Master will be in any land".*

The Mastersingers of Nuremberg

Freundschaft-M.
Werbe-M.
(in Singstimme)

Wollt ihr nach Regeln messen,
was nicht nach eurer Regeln Lauf,
der eignen Spur vergessen,
sucht davon erst die Regeln auf!

KA 179 ▶ 1890
CD 2/3 0:33

BECKMESSER

Hohn-M.

Aha, schon recht! Nun hört ihr's doch:
den Stümpern öffnet Sachs ein Loch,
da aus und ein nach Belieben
ihr Wesen leicht sie trieben! –

Kreidestrich-M.

Singet dem Volk auf Markt und Gassen!
Hier wird nach den Regeln nur eingelassen.

SACHS

Kreidestrich-M.

Herr Merker, was doch solch ein Eifer?
Was doch so wenig Ruh'?
Eu'r Urteil, dünkt mich, wäre reifer,
hörtet ihr besser zu.
Darum so komm' ich jetzt zum Schluß,
daß den Junker man zu End' hören muß.

BECKMESSER

Kreidestrich-M.

Der Meister Zunft, die ganze Schul',
gegen den Sachs da sind wir Null!

SACHS

Kreidestrich-M.

Verhüt' es Gott, was ich begehr',
daß das nicht nach den Gesetzen wär'!

Meistersinger-M. ②,
Naturregel-M.

Doch da nun steht geschrieben:
„Der Merker werde so bestellt,
daß weder Hass noch Lieben

Freundschaft-M.
Johannistag-M.

das Urteil trübe, das er fällt."
Geht der nun gar auf Freiers Füßen,
wie sollt' er da die Lust nicht büßen,
den Nebenbuhler auf dem Stuhl
zu schmähen vor der ganzen Schul'?

Walther flammt auf.

NACHTIGAL

Ihr geht zu weit!

Act 1, Scene 3 – Be well assured

VS 160 ▶ 2   If ye by rules would measure,   *friendship motif*
CD 2/3 0:33   what doth not with your rules agree,   *courtship motif*
forgetting all your learning,   *(in voice)*
seek ye first what its rules may be!

Beckmesser

Aha, 'tis well! Now hear him pray: *scorn motif*
for bunglers Sachs reveals a way,
where they may roam at there pleasure
with none to take their measure! –
Though with their cries the streets are ringing,   *chalk stroke motif*
here singers are proved by the laws of singing.

Sachs

Sir Marker, why so hotly burning?   *chalk stroke motif*
What is it makes your spleen?
Your mind, methinks, were more discerning,
guided by ears more keen.
And so, now hear my final word,
that the singer to the end must be heard.

Beckmesser

The Masters' guild and all the schools,   *chalk stroke motif*
set against Sachs are nought but fools!

Sachs

God forbid that I should claim,   *chalk stroke motif*
to flout our laws or to thwart their aim!
But they speak in this fashion: *mastersinger motif*
„The Marker shall be chosen so,   *②, nature rule motif*
that free from hate and passion
he shall not swerve for friend or foe."   *friendship motif*
Now when our Marker goes awooing: *Midsummer day*
within his cell his aim pursuing,   *motif*
he brands his rival on the stool,
and shames him there before the school!

Walther flames up.

Nachtigal

You go too far!

KOTHNER

Johannistag-M.   Persönlichkeit!

POGNER

Freundschaft-M.   Vermeidet, Meister, Zwist und Streit!

Hohn-M.   BECKMESSER

Ei! Was kümmert doch Meister Sachsen,
auf was für Füßen ich geh'?
Kreidestrich-M   Ließ er doch lieber Sorge sich wachsen,
daß mir nichts drück' die Zeh'!
Doch seit mein Schuster ein großer Poet,
gar übel es um mein Schuhwerk steht:
da seht, wie's schlappt
und überall klappt!
All' seine Vers' und Reim'
ließ' ich ihm gern daheim,
Historien, Spiel' und Schwänke dazu,
Erregtheitstriller-M.,   brächt' er mir morgen die neuen Schuh'!
Unmut-M.

SACHS

Kreidestrich-M   *kratzt sich hinter den Ohren:*

Ihr mahnt mich da gar recht:
doch schickt sich's, Meister, sprecht,
daß – find' ich selbst dem Eseltreiber
ein Sprüchlein auf die Sohl',
dem hochgelahrten Herrn Stadtschreiber
ich nichts drauf schreiben soll?
Das Sprüchlein, das eu'r würdig sei,
mit all' meiner armen Poeterei,
fand ich noch nicht zur Stund'.
Stolzing-M.   Doch wird's wohl jetzt mir kund,

Walther steigt in großer Aufregung auf den Singstuhl und blickt stehend herab.

wenn ich des Ritters Lied gehört:
drum sing' er nun weiter ungestört!

BECKMESSER

Unmut-M.   Nicht weiter! Zum Schluß!

Act 1, Scene 3 – Be well assured

KOTHNER

    Of wrath beware!   *Midsummer day motif*

POGNER

I pray you, Masters, cease this jar!   *friendship motif*

BECKMESSER   *scorn motif*

Ei! What is it to Master Sachs, then,
how I may see fit to go?
Let him rather give heed to his cobbling,   *chalk stroke motif*
nought then will pinch my toe!
But since my cobbler a poet has been,
such shoes he makes as yet ne'er were seen:
unsound throughout
they flap all about!
All that he writes, I swear,
gladly to him I'd spare,
his lays and plays, in prose or in rhyme,
if he will bring me my shoes in time!   *excitement trill, resentment motif*

SACHS

    scratches behind his ear: *chalk stroke motif*

Your taunt comes not amiss:
but, Masters, tell me this:
I write on soles of donkey-drivers
some wisdom from my hoard;
were't fit our learned Sir Townwriter
should go without a word?
But words with worthy wisdom fraught,
among my poor verses long have I sought,
yet I found not the right.
But now they come in sight,   *Stolzing motif*

    Walther mounts on the singing seat in great excitement, and, standing there, looks down.

if I the singer apprehend:
then let him sing further to the end!

BECKMESSER

No further! Give o'er!   *resentment motif*

The Mastersingers of Nuremberg

DIE MEISTERSINGER

(außer Sachs und Pogner)

Unmut-M. Genug! Zum Schluß!

SACHS

(zu Walther)
Singt dem Herrn Merker zum Verdruß!

BECKMESSER

Beckmesser-M. Was sollte man da noch hören?
Wär's nicht, euch zu betören?
Er holt aus dem Gemerk die Tafel herbei und hält sie während des Folgenden, von einem zum andern sich wendend, den Meistern zur Prüfung vor.

WALTHER

Beckmesser-M., Kreidestrich-M.
Aus finst'rer Dornenhecken
die Eule rauscht hervor,
tät rings mit Kreischen wecken
der Raben heis'ren Chor:
in nächt'gem Heer zuhauf,
wie krächzen all' da auf,
mit ihren Stimmen, den hohlen,
die Elstern, Krähen und Dohlen!

BECKMESSER

Beckmesser-M., Kreidestrich-M.
Jeden Fehler, groß und klein,
seht genau auf der Tafel ein!
„Falsch' Gebänd" – „unredbare Worte" –
„Klebsilben", hier „Laster" gar!

DIE MEISTERSINGER

(ohne Sachs und Pogner)
Jawohl, so ist's; ich seh' es recht:
mit dem Herrn Ritter steht es schlecht!

WALTHER

Auf da steigt,

Act 1, Scene 3 – Be well assured

MASTERSINGERS

(except Sachs and Pogner)

No more! Give o'er! } *resentment motif*

SACHS

(to Walther)

Sing but to make the Marker sore!

BECKMESSER

What booteth then all our schooling? } *Beckmesser-M.*
Such singing is but fooling?

He fetches the slate from the „Gemerk" and, during the following, holds it out to one Master after another.

WALTHER

His gloomy cell foresaking, } *Beckmesser-M., chalk stroke motif*
the owl, to wreak his ire,
with hoots and cries awaking
the ravens' croaking choir,
now calls the dusty crowd
to rise and shriek aloud,
with voices hoarse and hollow,
the crows and jackdaws follow!

BECKMESSER

Ev'ry fault, both small and great! } *Beckmesser-M., chalk stroke motif*
Look you here, do but see the slate!
„Faulty verse" – „unsingable phrases" –
„Wordclippings", I reprehend!

MASTERSINGERS

(except Sachs and Pogner)

Ah yes, 'tis so; right well I see:
the knight will ne'er Master be!

WALTHER

Up then soars,

The Mastersingers of Nuremberg

	mit gold'nem Flügelpaar,
	ein Vogel wunderbar;
Flieder-M.	sein strahlend hell Gefieder
	licht in den Lüften blinkt;
Flieder-M.	schwebt selig hin und wieder,
Leidenschaft-M.	zu Flug und Flucht mir winkt.

BECKMESSER

„Aequivoca"!
                „Reim am falschen Orte".
„Verkehrt", „verstellt" der ganze Bar!

Flieder-M.   Ein „Flickgesang" hier zwischen den Stollen!

DIE MEISTER

(ohne Sachs und Pogner)

Mag Sachs von ihm halten, was er will,
hier in der Singschul' schweig' er still!
Bleibt einem jeden doch unbenommen,

Flieder-M.   wen er sich zum Genossen begehrt?

POGNER

(für sich)

Jawohl, ich seh's, was mir nicht recht:
mit meinem Junker steht es schlecht!

Flieder-M.   Weich' ich hier der Übermacht,

HANS SACHS

beobachtet Walther entzückt:

Ha! Welch ein Mut!
Begeist'rungsglut!
Ihr Meister, schweigt doch und hört!

Flieder-M.   Hört, wenn Sachs euch beschwört!

WALTHER

Lenzesgebot-M.,   Es schwillt das Herz
Leidenschaft-M.   vor süßem Schmerz;
der Not entwachsen Flügel:
es schwingt sich auf
zum kühnen Lauf,

Act 1, Scene 3 – Be well assured

on golden pinions borne,
a bird to greet the morn;
with wondrous plumage o'er me   *elder motif*
serene in Heaven high;
it gleams and floats before me,   *elder motif*
and lures me on to fly.   *passion motif*

Beckmesser

„Aequivoca"!
           „Rhymes in unfit places".
„Reversed", „misplaced" from end to end!
A „patchwork-song" here, filling the pauses!   *elder motif*

The Masters

(except Sachs and Pogner)

Let Sachs think of him as he may choose,
to make him Master we refuse!
Shall any Master, spite our denial,
as Master choose whomever he will?   *elder motif*

Pogner

(for himself)

Ah yes, in sooth, right well I see,
my knight will ne'er a master be!
If I should now be overborne,   *elder motif*

Hans Sachs

observes Walther with rapture:

Song of such fire
the heav'ns inspire!
Ye Masters, let him be heard!
Hear, if Sachs gives his word!

Walther

Now swells my heart   *springtime's behest*
with tender smart;   *motif, Passion motif*
as wings by need are given:
to mountain height
in dauntless flight,

The Mastersingers of Nuremberg

Lenzesgebot-M.,
Leidenschaft-M.

aus der Städte Gruft,
zum Flug durch die Luft,
dahin zum heim'schen Hügel,

BECKMESSER

„Blinde Meinung" allüberall!
„Unklare Wort'", „Differenz",
                      hie „Schrollen"!
Da „falscher Atem", hier „Überfall"!
Ganz unverständliche Melodei!
Aus allen Tönen ein Mischgebräu!

DIE MEISTER

(ohne Sachs und Pogner)

Wär uns der erste Best' willkommen,
was blieben die Meister dann wert?

POGNER

mir ahnet, daß mir's Sorge macht.
Wie gern säh' ich ihn angenommen!

HANS SACHS

Herr Merker dort, gönnt doch nur Ruh'!
Laßt andre hören, gebt das nur zu!
Umsonst! All' eitel Trachten!
Kaum vernimmt man sein eig'nes Wort;
des Junkers will keiner achten:
das nenn' ich Mut, singt der noch fort!

WALTHER

Vogelweid-M.
Lehrbuben-M.

dahin zur grünen Vogelweid',
Wo Meister Walther einst mich freit';
da sing' ich hell und hehr
der liebsten Frauen Ehr':

Kränzlein-M.

auf dann steigt,
ob Meisterkräh'n ihm ungeneigt,

Leidenschaft-M.

das stolze Liebeslied!
Ade, ihr Meister, hienied'!

Act 1, Scene 3 – Be well assured

from city's tomb, *springtime's behest*
towards its home, *motif, passion motif*
its wings are surely driven,

Beckmesser

"Hazy meaning" see, ev'rywhere!
"Unmeaning words", "braking off",
                    "lame clauses"!
There "faulty breathing", "surprises" here!
Incomprehensible melody!
A mixing up of all tones that be!

The Masters

(except Sachs and Pogner)

May all come in without a trial?
What good were the Masters?

Pogner

I fear the outcome I shall mourn.
Right fain were I to speed his suing!

Hans Sachs

Sir Marker there, let us have rest!
Let others hear him; grant that at least!
In vain! A vain endeavour!
Nought is heard, I may hold my tongue;
no use though he sing forever:
in sooth 'tis brave, striving so long!

Walther

to meadows where the song of birds, *Vogelweid motif*
The Master first revealed in words; *prentices motif*
where I my song will raise
in fairest women's praise:
there on high, *chaplet motif*
though ravenmasters croak and cry,
my song of love shall swell! *passion motif*
On earth, ye Masters, farewell!

Die Lehrbuben und David

Die Lehrbuben sind von der Bank aufgestanden und nähern sich dem Gemerk, um welches sie dann einen Ring schließen und sich zum Reigen ordnen.

Lehrbuben-M.

Kränzlein-M., Leidenschaft-M.

Glück auf zum Meistersingen!
Mögt' ihr euch das Kränzlein erschwingen;
das Blumenkränzlein aus Seiden fein,
wird das dem Herrn Ritter beschieden sein?

Sie fassen sich an und tanzen in Ringe immer lustiger um das Gemerk.

Beckmesser

Lehrbuben-M.

Kränzlein-M., Leidenschaft-M.

Scheutet ihr nicht das Ungemach,
Meister, zählt mir die Fehler nach!
Verloren hätt' er schon mit dem Acht',
doch so weit wie der
        hat's noch keiner gebracht:
wohl über fünfzig, schlecht gezählt!
Sagt, ob ihr euch den zum Meister wählt?
Nun, Meister, kündet's an!

Die Meister

(ohne Sachs und Pogner)

Lehrbuben-M.
Kränzlein-M., Leidenschaft-M.

Hei! Wie sich der Ritter da quält!
Der Sachs hat sich ihn erwählt!
Ha-ha! 's ist ärgerlich gar!
        Drum macht ein End'!
Auf, Meister! Stimmt und erhebt die Händ'!

Die Meister erheben die Hände.

Versungen und vertan!

Pogner

Lehrbuben-M.
Kränzlein-M.

Als Eidam wär' er mir gar wert:
nenn' ich den Sieger jetzt willkommen, –
wer weiß, ob ihn mein Kind erwählt?
Gesteh' ich's, daß mich's quält,
ob Eva den Meister wählt!

Act 1, Scene 3 – Be well assured

THE PRENTICES AND DAVID

The prentices have risen from the bench and form a ring around the „Gemerk", preparing to dance.

God save you from disaster!   *prentices motif*
And may you be a Master;
the silken chaplet of flowers bright,   *chaplet motif, passion*
may that by good fortune, be yours, sir knight?   *motif*

The take hands and dance in a circle round the „Gemerk" with increasing merriment.

BECKMESSER

If from this task ye shrink not now,   *prentices motif*
Masters, count but the faults I show!
Already at the eighth he was cast,   *chaplet motif, passion*
but so long as he   *motif*
           sure no man did e'er last:
well over fifty, that is clear!
Say, shall now the knight be Master here?
Now, Masters, judge aright!

THE MASTERS

(except Sachs and Pogner)

Hei! See how the knight is distraught!   *prentices motif*
Though Sachs for him well has fought!   *chaplet motif, passion*
Ha-ha! 'Tis not be borne!   *motif*
           Now make an end!
Each Master, speak, and uplift his hand!

The Masters raise their hands.

Rejected is the knight!

POGNER

Such kinsman would I not refuse: *prentices motif*
but when the winner comes awooing, –   *chaplet motif*
who knows if him my child will choose?
I fear that, when he woos,
the maid his suit will refuse!

HANS SACHS

Lehrbuben-M. Das Herz auf dem rechten Fleck:
ein wahrer Dichterreck'!
Kränzlein-M. Mach' ich Hans Sachs wohl Vers' und Schuh',
ist Ritter der und Poet dazu!

Walther verläßt mit einer stolz verächtlichen Gebärde den Stuhl und wendet sich rasch zum Fortgehen. –

Alles geht in großer Aufregung auseinander; lustiger Tumult der Lehrbuben, welche sich des Gemerkes, des Singstuhls und der Meisterbänke bemächtigen, wodurch Gedränge und Durcheinander der nach dem Ausgang sich wendenden Meister entsteht.

Lenzesgebot-M. *Sachs, der allein im Vordergrund geblieben, blickt noch gedankenvoll nach dem leeren Singstuhl;*

Kreidestrich-M., *als die Lehrbuben auch diesen erfassen, und*
Erregtheitstriller, *Sachs darob mit humoristisch unmutiger Ge-*
Kränzlein-M., *bärde sich abwendet, fällt der Vorhang.*
Meistersinger-M.,
Kreidestrich-M.

Act 1, Scene 3 – Be well assured

Hans Sachs

|2| With heart in its place aright: — *prentices motif*
a trueborn poet knight!
|3| Hans Sachs may make both verse and shoe, — *chaplet motif*
|4| but knight is he – knight and poet, too!

VS 188 ▶ 1
CD 2/3 6:34

Walther, with a proudly contemptuous gesture leaves the chair and quickly turns to go. –

General excitement, merry tumult of the prentices, who arm themselves with pieces of the „Gemerk", the seat and the benches, causing confusion among the masters who are making for the door.

Sachs, who has remained alone in front, still gazes thoughtfully at the empty singer's chair; — *springtime's behest motif*

As the boys remove this, and Sachs turns away with humourously indignant gesture, curtain falls. — *chalk stroke motif, excitement trill, chaplet motif, mastersinger motif, chalk stroke motif*

2. Aufzug
1. Szene – Johannistag! Johannistag!

Kreidestrich-M.,
Johannistag-M.
(verkürzt),
Erregtheitstriller

Die Bühne stellt im Vordergrunde eine Straße im Längendurchschnitte dar, welche in der Mitte von einer schmalen Gasse, nach dem Hintergrunde zu krumm abbiegend, durchschnitten wird, so daß sich im Front zwei Eckhäuser darbieten, von denen das eine, reichere, – rechts – das Haus Pogners, das andere, einfachere, – links das des Sachs ist. – Vor Pogners Haus eine Linde; vor dem Sachsens ein Fliederbaum. – Heitrer Sommerabend; im Verlaufe der ersten Auftritte allmählich einbrechende Nacht. – David ist darüber her, die Fensterläden nach der Gasse zu von außen zu schließen. Alle Lehrbuben tun das gleiche bei andren Häusern.

Lehrbuben

(während der Arbeit)

Johannistag! Johannistag!
Blumen und Bänder, so viel man mag!

David

(leise für sich)

Kränzlein-M.

„Das Blumenkränzlein aus Seiden fein"
möcht' es mir balde beschieden sein!

Act 2

Scene 1 – Midsummer day! Midsummer day!

The front of the stage represents a street in longitudinal section, intersected in the middle by a narrow, crooked alley winding towards the back; of the two corner houses thus presented in the front, the grander one on the right is Pogner's, the other, simpler one, is Sachs'. – Before Pogner's house is a lime tree, before Sachs's an elder. – A genial summer evening; in the course of the first scene night gradually falls. – David is engaged in closing from without the shutters of the windows towards the alley. All the prentices do the same for other houses.

> *chalk stroke motif,*
> *Midsummer day*
> *motiv (abbreviated),*
> *excitement trill*

Prentices

(during their work)

Midsummer day! Midsummer day!
Flowers and favours wear while you may!

David

(aside, softly)

„The silken chaplet of flowers fine"
would that tomorrow it might be mine!

> *chaplet motif*

The Mastersingers of Nuremberg

MAGDALENE

ist mit einem Korbe am Arm aus Pogners Haus gekommen und sucht, David unbemerkt sich zu nähern:

Bst! David!

DAVID

Kreidestrich-M.

(heftig nach der Gasse zu sich umwendend)
Ruft ihr schon wieder?
Singt allein eure dummen Lieder!
Er wendet sich unwillig zur Seite.

LEHRBUBEN

David, was soll's?
Wärst nicht so stolz,
schaut'st besser um,
wärst nicht so dumm! –

Kreidestrich-M.,
Johannistag-M.
(verkürzt),
Erregtheitstriller

„Johannistag! Johannistag!"
Wie der nur die Jungfer Lene
                   nicht kennen mag!

MAGDALENE

David-M.

David! Hör doch! Kehr dich zu mir!

DAVID

Ach, Jungfer Lene, ihr seid hier?

MAGDALENE

(auf ihren Korb deutend)

Meistersinger-M. ⑦

Bring' dir was Gut's, schau nur hinein:
das soll für mein lieb' Schätzel sein.
Erst aber schnell, wie ging's mit dem Ritter?
Du rietest ihm gut? Er gewann den Kranz?

Unmut-M.

DAVID

Versungen-M.

Ach, Jungfer Lene! Da steht's bitter:
der hat versungen und ganz vertan!

Act 2, Scene 1– Midsummer day! Midsummer day!

MAGDALENE

has come from Pogner's house with a basket on her arm, and tries to get near David unperceived:

Bst! David!

DAVID

(turning towards the alley)   *chalk stroke motif*
           Still are ye calling?
Sing alone there your silly ditties!
He turns angrily away.

PRENTICES

David, give ear?
proud be not here:
turn but thine eyes,
if thou art wise! –
„Midsummer day! Midsummer day!"   *chalk stroke motif,*
And he cannot see his Lene   *Midsummer day motif*
                   and turns away!   *(abbreviated),*
                                           excitement trill

MAGDALENE

David! Listen! Turn round to me!   *David motif*

DAVID

You, mistress Lene, do I see?

MAGDALENE

(pointing to her basket)

Look in and see what I have here: *mastersinger motif ⑦*
all this I've brought for thee, my dear.
But tell me first, what luck had Sir Walther?
Didst counsel him well? Did he win the crown?

DAVID   *resentment motif*

Ah, Mistress Lene, that went badly:
he was rejected, all hope is gone!   *rejection motif*

The Mastersingers of Nuremberg

MAGDALENE

(erschrocken)

David-M. Versungen? Vertan?

DAVID

Was geht's euch nur an?

MAGDALENE

Kreidestrich-M.
David-M.

(den Korb, nach welchem David die Hand ausstreckt, heftig zurückziehend)

Hand von der Taschen! Nichts zu naschen!

Unmut-M. Hilf Gott! Unser Junker vertan!

Versungen-M.

Sie geht mit Gebärden der Trostlosigkeit in das Haus zurück. David sieht ihr verblüfft nach.

DIE LEHRBUBEN

welche unvermerkt näher geschlichen waren und gelauscht hatten, präsentieren sich jetzt, wie glückwünschend, David.

Heil! Heil zur Eh' dem jungen Mann!
Wie glücklich hat er gefreit!
Wir hörten's all' und sahen's an,
der er sein Herz geweiht,
für die er läßt sein Leben,
die hat ihm den Korb – nicht gegeben!

DAVID

(auffahrend)

Was steht ihr hier faul?
Gleich haltet das Maul!

DIE LEHRBUBEN

schließen einen Ring um David und tanzen um ihn.

Kreidestrich-M.,
Johannistag-M.
(verkürzt)

„Johannistag! Johannistag!
Da freit ein jeder, wie er mag:
der Meister freit, der Bursche freit,
da gibt's Geschlamb' und Geschlumbfer!

Act 2, Scene 1– Midsummer day! Midsummer day!

VS 196 ▶ 4
CD 2/4 2:08

MAGDALENE

(alarmed)

Rejected? No hope? } *David motif*

DAVID

              What is that to thee?

MAGDALENE

(violently pulling back the basket towards   *chalk stroke motif*
which David has stretched out his hand)   *David motif*

Hands from the basket! Nought for supper!
Alas! Now mishap I foresee!   *resentment motif*

She goes back to the house with disconsolate   *rejection motif*
gestures. David looks after her in surprise.

THE PRENTICES

who unobserved have stolen nearer and listened, now presenting themselves as if congratulating David.

Hail! Hail oh man that fain would woo!
Bad luck 'tis if she be cold!
We heard it all and saw it too:
she who his heart doth hold,
to her most faithful lover
the basket she – not give over!

DAVID

(angrily)

What do you then there?
Now get you all gone!

THE PRENTICES

make a ring and dance round David

„Midsummer day! Midsummer day!   *chalk stroke motif,*
Each man must wed as best he may: *Midsummer day motif*
the master weds, the prentice weds,   *(abbreviated)*
fortune will follow the bold ones!

Kreidestrich-M., *Johannistag-M.* *(verkürzt)*	Der Alte freit die junge Maid, der Bursche die alte Jumbfer! Juchhei! Juchhei! Johannistag!"	KA 224 ▶ 91 CD 2/4 2:57

David ist im Begriff, wütend dreinzuschlagen, als Sachs, der aus der Gasse hervorgekommen, dazwischentritt. – Die Buben fahren auseinander.

SACHS

(zu David)

Unmut-M. — Was gibt's?

Treff' ich dich wieder am Schlag?

DAVID

Nicht ich:

Schandlieder singen die!

SACHS

Hör nicht drauf;

lern's besser wie sie!

Erregtheitstriller — Zur Ruh', ins Haus!

Schließ und mach Licht!

Die Lehrbuben zerstreuen sich.

DAVID

Hab' ich noch Singstund'?

SACHS

Nein, singst nicht

Schustermühe-M. — zur Straf' für dein heutig'

frech' Erdreisten![1]

Kreidestrich-M. — Die neuen Schuh' steck mir auf den Leisten![1]

Erregtheitstriller — *David und Sachs sind in die Werkstatt eingetreten und gehen durch innere Türen ab.*

---

[1] *Hier wird David melodisch aus dem ersten Aufzug zitiert. Dort sang er: „daß ich als Schüler wachs'" bzw. „hab' ich das Leder glatt geschlagen"*

Act 2, Scene 1– Midsummer day! Midsummer day!

VS 200 ▸ 1
CD 2/4 2:57
When grey-beards wed the youngest maids,   *chalk stroke motif,*
the prentices wed the old ones!   *Midsummer day motif*
Juchhei! Juchhei! Midsummer day!"   *(abreviated)*

> *David is on the point of fighting the boys when Sachs, who has come up the alley, comes between. – The prentices disperse.*

SACHS

(to David)

What now?
           Still do I find thee at strife?   *resentment motif*

DAVID

Not me:
           the all were mocking me!

SACHS

Heed them not;
           learn better than they!
Go in, lock up!
           Bring me a light!   *excitement trill*

The prentices disperse themselves.

DAVID

Have I to sing now?

SACHS

           No, not now,
because that today   *cobbler's labor motif*
           thou hast displeased me![1]
Now put the shoes on the lasts and leave me![1]   *chalk stroke motif*

David and Sachs have entered the workshop and go off through an inner door.   *excitement trill*

---

[1] *Here David is melodically quoted from the first act where he sang: „ne'er shall I scholar be" and „first all the leather smooth I hammer"*

2. Szene – Lass sehn, ob Meister Sachs zu Haus?

Erregtheitstriller

Pogner und Eva, – wie vom Spaziergang heimkehrend, – die Tochter leicht am Arm des Vaters eingehenkt, sind beide schweigsam die Gasse heraufgekommen.

POGNER

(durch eine Klinze im Fensterladen Sachsens spähend)

Laß sehn, ob Meister Sachs zu Haus?
Gern spräch' ich ihn; trät' ich wohl ein?

David kommt mit Licht aus der Kammer, setzt sich damit an den Werktisch am Fenster und macht sich an die Arbeit.

EVA

(spähend)

Unmut-M.,
Versungen-M.

Er scheint daheim: kommt Licht heraus.

POGNER

Tu' ich's? – Zu was doch? – Besser nein! –

Er wendet sich ab.

Will einer Selt'nes wagen,
was ließ er sich dann sagen? –

Er sinnt nach.

War er's nicht, der meint', ich ging zu weit? ...
Und, blieb' ich nicht im Geleise,
war's nicht auf seine Weise?

Scene 2 – We'll see if Master Sachs is there

Pogner and Eva, returning from a walk, have come in silence up the alley, the daughter lightly hanging on her father's arm

excitement trill

Pogner

(peeping through a chink in Sachs's shutter)

We'll see if Master Sachs is there.
I'd speak with him: shall I go in?

David comes from the inner room with a light, sits at the work-bench by the window and works.

Eva

(peeping)

He seems at home: his light shines out.

resentment motif
rejection motif

Pogner

Shall I? – Wherefor then? – Better not! –
He turns away.
On ways unwonted moving,
what man can brook reproving? –
He ponders.
And he 'twas who thought I went too far? ...
Yet, though old customs not heeding,
I followed so his leading?

Entzückung-M.

Doch war's vielleicht auch Eitelkeit? –
>*Er wendet sich zu Eva.*

Und du, mein Kind? Du sagst mir nichts?

EVA
Ein folgsam Kind, gefragt nur spricht's.

POGNER
Wie klug! Wie gut! Komm, setz dich hier
ein' Weil' noch auf die Bank zu mir.
>*Er setzt sich auf die Steinbank unter der Linde.*

EVA
Erregtheitstriller

Wird's nicht zu kühl?
's war heut gar schwül.
>*Sie setzt sich zögernd und beklommen Pogner zur Seite.*

POGNER
Nürnberg-M., Erregtheitstriller

Nicht doch, 's ist mild und labend,
gar lieblich lind der Abend: –
das deutet auf den schönsten Tag,
der morgen soll erscheinen.
O Kind! Sagt dir kein Herzensschlag,
welch Glück dich morgen treffen mag, –
wenn Nürenberg, die ganze Stadt,
mit Bürgern und Gemeinen,
mit Zünften, Volk und hohem Rat
vor dir sich soll vereinen,
daß du den Preis,

Werbe-M.

das edle Reis,
erteilest als Gemahl

Nürnberg-M.

dem Meister deiner Wahl?

EVA
Lieb Vater, muß es ein Meister sein?

POGNER
Hör wohl: ein Meister deiner Wahl.

Act 2, Scene 2 – We'll see if Master Sachs is there

VS 204 ▶ 17
CD 2/5 1:21
Yet still perchance some pride was there? –   } *delight motif*
> *He turns to Eva.*
And you, my child? Your thoughts are hid?

Eva
Good children only speak when bid.

Pogner
How wise! How good! Come, sit though here,
and taste with me the balmy air.
> *He sits on a stone bench under the lime tree.*

Eva
'Tis cool tonight?   *excitement trill*
Though day was bright.
> *She sits beside Pogner hesitating and anxious.*

Pogner
Ah no, the air is kindly,   *Nuremberg motif,*
and soft the night and friendly: –   *excitement trill*
'tis promise that the fairest day,
tomorrow will be bringing.
O child! Says not thy heart to thee,
what joy tomorrow thine may be, –
when Nüremberg, in all her state,
'mid acclamations ringing,
will come, with folk both small and great,
to see thee crown our singing,
and thou as bride,
 shalt stand beside   *courtship motif*
the man who gains her voice,
a Master of thy choice?   *Nuremberg motif*

Eva
Dear father, Master, the, must he be?

Pogner
But hear: a Master thou shalt choose.

David-M.

Magdalene erscheint an der Türe und winkt Eva.

EVA

(zerstreut)

Ja, – meiner Wahl. – Doch tritt nun ein –

(laut, zu Magdalene gewandt)

(gleich, Lene, gleich!) – zum Abendmahl.

Sie steht auf.

POGNER

Unmut-M.

(ärgerlich aufstehend)

's gibt doch keinen Gast?

EVA

Meistersinger-M. ④

(wie zuvor)

      Wohl den Junker?

POGNER

(verwundert)

              Wieso?

EVA

Sahst ihn heut nicht?

POGNER

(halb für sich; nachdenklich zerstreut)

        Ward sein' nicht froh. –

(sich zusammennehmend)

Nicht doch... Was denn? –

(sich vor die Stirn klopfend)

           Ei! Werd' ich dumm?

EVA

Lieb' Väterchen, komm!

           Geh, kleid dich um.

Act 2, Scene 2 – We'll see if Master Sachs is there

Magdalene appears at the door and beckons to Eva. — *David motif*

EVA

(absently)
Yes, – I may choose. – But go within –
(aloud turning to Magdalene)
(Lene, I come!) – our evening meal.
She rises.

POGNER

(irritably rising) — *resentment motif*
But we have no guest?

EVA

(as before) — *mastersinger motif ④*
        Not Sir Walther?

POGNER

(surprised)
                        How so?

EVA
Saw'st thou him not?

POGNER

(half aside; meditatively and absently)
                He pleased me not. –
(collecting himself)
Yet no... What now? –
(tapping his forehead)
                    Ah! Am I blind?

EVA
Dear father, now come!
               Go change thy dress.

POGNER

(während er ins Haus vorangeht)
Hm! Was geht mir im Kopf doch 'rum?

MAGDALENE

(heimlich zu Eva)
Hast' was heraus?

EVA

       Blieb still und stumm.

MAGDALENE

Sprach David, meint', er habe vertan.

EVA

(erschrocken)
Der Ritter? Hilf Gott! Was fing' ich an?
Ach, Lene, die Angst! Wo was erfahren?

MAGDALENE

Hoffnung-M.   Vielleicht vom Sachs?

EVA

(heiter)
      Ach! Der hat mich lieb:
gewiß, ich geh' hin.

MAGDALENE

     Laß drin nichts gewahren;
Versungen-M.   der Vater merkt' es, wenn man jetzt blieb'.
Nach dem Mahl!
   Dann hab' ich dir noch was zu sagen,
  (im Abgehen auf der Treppe)
was jemand geheim mir aufgetragen.

EVA

(sich umwendend)
Wer denn? Der Junker?

Act 2, Scene 2 – We'll see if Master Sachs is there

POGNER

(as he goes before her into the house)
Hm! What thought in my head goes round?

MAGDALENE

(secretly to Eva)
What hast thou heard?

EVA

No word he spoke.

MAGDALENE

My David says, the knight is undone.

EVA

(alarmed)
Sir Walther? Ah me! What shall I do?
Ah, Lene, the fear! How to discover?

MAGDALENE

Perchance from Sachs?   *hope motif*

EVA

(cheerfully)
Ah! He loves me well:
to him will I go.

MAGDALENE

Give heed to thy father;
lest he should miss thee, if thou art late.   *rejection motif*
In the night;
then I shall have something to tell thee;
(on the steps as she goes off)
a secret that someone told me lately.

EVA

(turning round)
Who then? Sir Walther?

MAGDALENE
> Nichts da! Nein!

Unmut-M. Beckmesser.

EVA
> Das mag was Rechtes sein!
> *Sie geht in das Haus; Magdalene folgt ihr.*

Act 2, Scene 2 – We'll see if Master Sachs is there

VS 210 ▶ 11
CD 2/5 5:17

MAGDALENE

                Not he! No!
Beckmesser.   *resentment motif*

EVA

            A pretty secret, that!

She goes into the house; Magdalene follows her.

3. Szene – Zeig her! – 's ist gut.

KA 237 ▶ 244
CD 2/6 0:01

Sachs ist, in leichter Hauskleidung, von innen in die Werkstatt zurückgekommen. Er wendet sich zu David, der an seinem Werktische verblieben ist.

Sachs

Erregtheitstriller,
Zunftideal-M.
Unmut-M.

Zeig her! – 's ist gut. – Dort an die Tür
rück mir Tisch und Schemel herfür.
Leg dich zu Bett, steh auf bei Zeit:
verschlaf die Dummheit,
                sei morgen gescheit!

David

Schafft ihr noch Arbeit?

Sachs

                Kümmert dich das?

David

während er den Tisch und Schemel richtet, für sich:

Was war nur der Lene? – Gott weiß, was! –
Warum wohl der Meister heute wacht?

Sachs

Was stehst noch?

David

            Schlaft wohl, Meister!

Scene 3 – Come here! – 'Tis well.

Sachs in a light indoor dress has returned from the inner room to the shop. He turns to David who is still at his bench.

Sachs

Come here! – 'tis well. – There at the door *excitement trill,*
put my stool and table outside. *guild ideal motif*
Then go to bed, and early rise: *resentment motif*
sleep off thy folly,
                tomorrow be wise!

David

More work this evening?

Sachs

                What's that to thee?

David

as he arranges bench and stool, aside:

What was it with Lene? – God knows what! –
But why doth the Master work tonight?

Sachs

Not yet gone?

David

         Sleep well, Master!

The Mastersingers of Nuremberg

SACHS

Unmut-M.

Gut' Nacht!

David geht in die der Gasse zu gelegene Kammer ab. – Sachs legt sich die Arbeit zurecht,
Lenzesgebot-M. *setzt sich an der Tür auf den Schemel, läßt aber die Arbeit wieder liegen und lehnt, mit dem Arm auf den geschlossenen Unterteil des*
Flieder-M. *Türladens gestützt, sich zurück.*

(sehr zart)

Was duftet doch der Flieder
so mild, so stark und voll!
Mir löst es weich die Glieder,
Lenzesgebot-M. will, daß ich was sagen soll.
Was gilt's, was ich dir sagen kann?
Bin gar ein arm einfältig' Mann!
Soll mir die Arbeit nicht schmecken,
gäbst, Freund, lieber mich frei:
tät' besser, das Leder zu strecken,
Unmut-M., und ließ' alle Poeterei!
Schaffenslust-M.

Er nimmt heftig und geräuschvoll die Schusterarbeit vor. Er läßt wieder ab, lehnt sich von
Lenzesgebot-M. *neuem zurück und sinnt nach.*
übergehend in
Leidenschaft-M. Und doch, 's will halt nicht gehn: –
Ich fühl's und kann's nicht verstehn; –
kann's nicht behalten, –
               doch auch nicht vergessen:
und fass' ich es ganz,
Entzückung-M.   kann ich's nicht messen! –
Doch wie wollt' ich auch messen,
(Tristanmotive)   was unermeßlich mir schien.
Kein' Regel wollte da passen, –
Lenzesgebot-M.   und war doch kein Fehler drin.
übergehend in Es klang so alt, – und war doch so neu, –
Leidenschaft-M. wie Vogelsang im süßen Mai!
Wer ihn hört
und wahnbetört
sänge dem Vogel nach,
dem brächt' es Spott und Schmach: –
Lenzesgebot-M. Lenzes Gebot,
die süße Not,

Act 2, Scene 3 – Come here! – 'Tis well.

SACHS

        Good night!   *resentment motif*

David goes into the room on the alley side. –
Sachs arranges his work, sits on the stool at
the door, then lays down his work again and
leans back, his arm resting on the closed lower
half of the door.

(very tenderly)
The elder's scent floats round me,
so mild, so rich it falls!
Its sweetness weighs upon me;
words from out my heart it calls. *springtime's behest*
What boot such words as I can find *motif*
within my poor unlettered mind?
When with my work I'm weary,
then, friend, let me go free:
'twere better with leather to plague me,
and let all this poetry be! *resentment motif,*
He begins to work abruptly and noisily. He *work lust motif*
leaves off again and leans back in thought.

 springtime's behest
 motif, merging into
And still, that strain I hear: – *passion motif*
I fell, yet nothing is clear; –
cannot forget it, –
      nor can I enfold it:
I measure it not,
    e'en when I hold it! – *delight motif*
Yet what could gauge its greatness?
    A measure no mortal hath seen. *(Tristan motifs)*
I found no rule that would fit it, – *springtime's behest*
    and yet was no fault therein. *motif, merging into*
It sounded old, – and yet was newborn, – *passion motif*
like song of birds on blithe May morn!
If one heard
and madly dared
that song again to sing;
but scorn and shame 'twould bring: –
Springtime's behest, *springtime's behest*
within hist breast, *motif*

Vogelweid-M.   die legt' es ihm in die Brust: –
nun sang er, wie er mußt';
und wie er mußt', so konnt er's, –
das merkt' ich ganz besonders.
Dem Vogel, der heut sang,
dem war der Schnabel hold gewachsen;
macht' er den Meistern bang,
gar wohl gefiel er doch Hans Sachsen!

> *Er nimmt mit heitrer Gelassenheit seine Arbeit vor.*

Act 2, Scene 3 – Come here! – 'Tis well.

VS 216 ▶ 13
CD 2/7 4:10

on heart and voice there was laid: –
then sang he as Nature bade;   } *Vogelweid motif*
and to his need the power
was granted from her dower.
The bird who sang this morn,
from Nature's self had learned his singing;
Masters that song may scorn,
for aye Hans Sachs will hear it ringing!

He resumes his work with cheerful composure.

4. Szene – Gut'n Abend, Meister!

Eva-M.

Eva ist auf die Straße getreten, hat sich schüchtern der Werkstatt genähert und steht jetzt unvermerkt an der Türe bei Sachs.

Eva
Gut'n Abend, Meister! Noch so fleißig?

Sachs

fährt, angenehm überrascht, auf.

Anmut-M.
Ei, Kind! Lieb' Evchen? Noch so spät? –
Und doch, warum so spät noch, weiß ich:
die neuen Schuh'?

Eva
Wie fehl er rät!
Die Schuh' hab' ich noch gar nicht probiert;

Entzückung-M.
sie sind so schön und reich geziert,
daß ich sie noch nicht an die Füß' mir getraut.

Hoffnung-M.
Sie setzt sich dicht neben Sachs auf den Steinsitz.

Sachs
Doch sollst sie morgen tragen als Braut?

Eva
Wer wäre denn Bräutigam?

Sachs

Eva-M.,
Hoffnung-M.
Weiß ich das?

Scene 4 – Good evening, Master!

Eva has come into the street and shyly approached Sachs's shop, and now stands unnoticed by Sachs's door.   *Eva motif*

Eva

Good evening, Master! Still aworking?

Sachs

starts in agreeable surprise.

Ah child! Sweet Evchen? Still awake? –   *grace motif*
Yet, why so late awake, well know I:
the new made shoes?

Eva

                How you mistake!
The shoes scarcely have greeted my sight.
They look so fine, so richly dight,   *delight motif*
that they on my feet have not even been tried.

She seats herself near Sachs on the stone seat.   *hope motif*

Sachs

Tomorrow thou must wear them as bride?

Eva

Say, who will be bridegroom, then?

Sachs

                Who can tell?   *Eva motif, hope motif*

The Mastersingers of Nuremberg

Eva-M.,
Hoffnung-M.

EVA
Wie wißt ihr denn, daß ich Braut?

SACHS
                          Ei, was!
Das weiß die Stadt.

EVA
              Ja! Weiß es die Stadt,
Freund Sachs gute Gewähr dann hat!
Ich dacht' – er wüßt' mehr.

SACHS
                    Was sollt' ich wissen?

EVA
Ei, seht doch! Werd' ich's ihm sagen müssen?
Ich bin wohl recht dumm?

SACHS
                      Das sag' ich nicht.

EVA
Werbe-M.
Dann wärt ihr wohl klug?

SACHS
                    Das weiß ich nicht.

EVA
Ihr wißt nichts? Ihr sagt nichts? –
                    Ei, Freund Sachs,
Werbe-M.
jetzt merk' ich wahrlich, Pech ist kein Wachs.
Ich hätt' euch für feiner gehalten.

SACHS
                              Kind,
Anmut-M., Eva-M.,
Entzückung-M.
beid', Wachs und Pech bekannt mir sind:
mit Wachs strich ich die seid'nen Fäden
damit ich dir die zieren Schuh' gefaßt:
heut' fass' ich die Schuh'

Act 2, Scene 4 – Good evening, Master!

VS 219 ▸ 14
CD 2/8 1:01

EVA

How know you I shall be bride?   *Eva motif, hope motif*

SACHS

                     Ah well!
All the folk know.

EVA

                Yes! All folk know!,
Friend Sachs good warrant, no doubt, can show!
I thought – he knew more.

SACHS

           What should I know then?

EVA

Look now! Must I my secret show, then?
Am I, then, so dull?

SACHS

              I say not that.

EVA

'Tis you, then, are crafty?   *courtship motif*

SACHS

            I know not that.

EVA

You know naught? You say naught? –
         Ah, friend Sachs,
now I see truly, pitch is not wax.   *courtship motif*
Methought that your cunning was finer.

SACHS

                 Oh!
both wax and pitch right well I know:
'tis wax strengthens the silken stitching,   *grace motif, Eva motif,*
wherewith for thee those dainty shoes I sewed: *delight motif*
shoes now are in hand

The Mastersingers of Nuremberg

Erregtheitstriller   mit dicht'ren Drähten,
da gilt's mit Pech für den derb'ren Gast.

EVA
Wer ist denn der? Wohl was recht's?

SACHS

Anmut-M.   Das mein' ich!
Ein Meister, stolz auf Freiers Fuß;
denkt morgen zu siegen ganz alleinig:
Herrn Beckmessers Schuh' ich richten muß.

EVA
So nehmt nur tüchtig Pech dazu:

Erregtheitstriller   da kleb' er drin, und lass' mir Ruh'!

SACHS
Er hofft, dich sicher zu ersingen.

EVA
Wieso denn der?

SACHS
              Ein Junggesell', –
's gibt deren wenig dort zur Stell'.

EVA

Hoffnung-M.,   Könnt's einem Witwer nicht gelingen?
Eva-M.

SACHS
Mein Kind, der wär' zu alt für dich.

EVA

Werbe-M.   Ei, was! Zu alt? Hier gilt's der Kunst;
wer sie versteht, der werb' um mich.

SACHS
Lieb' Evchen, machst mir blauen Dunst?

EVA
Nicht ich, ihr seid's, ihr macht mir Flausen!

Act 2, Scene 4 – Good evening, Master!

that call for a pitching, *excitement trill*
to fit a churl on his stony road.

EVA
Who, the, is he? Someone great?

SACHS
Aye truly! *grace motif*
A Master proud who boldly woos,
and hopes, too, to win, if honoured duly:
for Beckmesser's feet I make these shoes.

EVA
Then pitch in plenty let there be:
may he stick there and leave me free! *excitement trill*

SACHS
His song he hopes will speed his suing.

EVA
A man like that?

SACHS
A scanty band
of batchelors is here at hand.

EVA
Might not a widower go wooing? *hope motif*
Eva motif

SACHS
My child, too old were he for thee.

EVA
Ah, what! too old? What wins is art; *courtship motif*
and all who sing, to woo are free.

SACHS
Sweet Evchen, wouldst thou snare my heart?

EVA
Not I, 'tis you are an impostor!

Eva-M., Hoffnung-M., Werbe-M.	Gesteht nur, daß ihr wandelbar. Gott weiß, wer euch jetzt im Herzen mag hausen! Glaubt' ich mich doch drin so manches Jahr.	KA 255 ▶ 458 CD 2/8 3:30

Sachs

Werbe-M., Eva-M.	Wohl, da ich dich gern auf den Armen trug?

Eva

Ich seh', 's war nur, weil ihr kinderlos.

Sachs

Hatt' einst ein Weib und Kinder genug.

Eva

Doch, starb Eure Frau, so wuchs ich groß?

Sachs

Eva-M., Anmut-M., Werbe-M.	Gar groß und schön!

Eva

                  Da dacht' ich aus,
Ihr nähmt mich für Weib und Kind ins Haus?

Sachs

Da hätt' ich ein Kind, und auch ein Weib!
's wär gar ein lieber Zeitvertreib!
Ja, ja! Das hast du dir schön erdacht.

Eva

	Ich glaub',
Leidenschaft-M., Eva-M.	der Meister mich gar verlacht? Am End' auch ließ' er sich gar gefallen, daß unter der Nas' ihm weg vor allen der Beckmesser morgen mich ersäng'?

Sachs

Hohn-M. Beckmesser-M., Kreidestrich-M.	Wer sollt's ihm wehren, wenn's ihm geläng'? Dem wüßt' allein dein Vater Rat.

Act 2, Scene 4 – Good evening, Master!

VS 225 ▸ 2
CD 2/8 3:30
Admit now, your affections veer;
Heav'n knows whom now
     your heart may foster!
I'd thought it my own this many a year.

Eva motif
hope motif.,
courtship motif

Sachs

Because in my arms thou hast often lain?

courtship motif, Eva motif

Eva

I see why 'twas; you were childless then.

Sachs

Yet once were wife and children my own.

Eva

But gone is your wife, and I am grown?

Sachs

Aye, tall and fair!

Eva motif, grace motif, courtship motif

Eva

    The thought would come,
that I might be wife and child at home.

Sachs

The I should have wife and child indeed!
how gainly then the time would speed!
Aye, aye, that thought in thy brain was born.

Eva

Methinks,
  the Master doth nought but scorn?
At last, in sooth, he will feel no sorrow,
if under his nose from all tomorrow,
old Beckmesser's singing wins me too!

passion motif, Eva motif

Sachs

Who can gainsay him? What could we do?
Thy father 'tis, who grants the prize.

scorn motif
Beckmesser motif, chalk stroke motif

The Mastersingers of Nuremberg

Unmut-M.

EVA
Wo so ein Meister den Kopf nur hat!
Käm' ich zu euch wohl, fänd' ich's zu Haus?

KA 260 ▶ 497
CD 2/8 4:55

SACHS
(trocken)
Ach, ja! Hast recht: 's ist im Kopf mir kraus.
Hab' heut manch Sorg' und Wirr' erlebt:
da mag's dann sein, daß was drin klebt.

EVA
(wieder näher rückend)

Ablehnung-M.
Wohl in der Singschul'? 's war heut' Gebot?

SACHS
Ja, Kind! Eine Freiung machte mir Not.

EVA
Ja, Sachs! Das hättet ihr gleich soll'n sagen,
quält' euch dann nicht
                mit unnützen Fragen. –
Nun sagt, wer war's, der Freiung begehrt?

Ablehnung-M., Stolzing-M.

SACHS
Ein Junker, Kind, gar unbelehrt.

EVA
Ein Ritter? Mein', sagt! Und ward er gefreit?

Stolzing-M. (bricht ab, Gelächter) Hohn-M.

SACHS
Nichts da, mein Kind! 's gab gar viel Streit.

Kreidestrich-M.

EVA
So sagt, – erzählt, – wie ging es zu?
Macht's euch Sorg', wie ließ' mir es Ruh'?

Hoffnung-M.
So bestand er übel und hat vertan?

Stolzing-M., Unmut-M., Hohn-M.

SACHS
Ohne Gnad' versang der Herr Rittersmann.

Act 2, Scene 4 – Good evening, Master!

EVA
Where doth a Master now keep his eyes?
If in his head, then must it be crazed? *resentment motif*

SACHS
(drily)
Ah yes, art right; 'tis my head is dazed.
Today my brain was sore perplexed,
and 'tis not strange if I am vexed.

EVA
(again coming nearer)
'Twas in the school, then? Will you not tell?

SACHS
Yes child, at a trial all went not well.

EVA
Ah, Sachs! That should you at once have told me,
lest all my talk should.
              tempt you to scold me. –
Now tell what man your favour besought?

SACHS
A knight, my child, and all untaught. *disapproval motif, Stolzing motif*

EVA
A knight 'twas? Ah me! Then say, did he pass?

SACHS
Not so, my child! much strife there was. *Stolzing motif (breaks off, laughter)*
   scorn motif

EVA
Then tell, – relate; – how did it go? *chalk stroke motif*
Can I be calm if it plagues you so?
So ill-luck befel him? was he undone? *hope motif*

SACHS
For the knight all hope for the prize has gone. *Stolzing motif, resentment motif, scorn motif*

The Mastersingers of Nuremberg

MAGDALENE

kommt zum Hause heraus und ruft leise:

Ablehnung-M. — Bst, Evchen! Bst!

EVA

(eifrig zu Sachs gewandt)

                Ohne Gnade? Wie?
Kein Mittel gäb's, das ihm gedieh'?
Sang er so schlecht, so fehlervoll,

Entzückung-M. — daß nichts mehr zum Meister ihm helfen soll?

SACHS

Ablehnung-M. — Mein Kind, für den ist alles verloren,
und Meister wird der in keinem Land,
denn wer als Meister geboren,
der hat unter Meistern

Kreidestrich-M. —   den schlimmsten Stand.

MAGDALENE

(vernehmlicher rufend)

Der Vater verlangt.

EVA

(immer dringender zu Sachs)

Hoffnung-M. —   So sagt mir noch an,
ob keinen der Meister
                zum Freund er gewann?

SACHS

Ablehnung-M. — Das wär' nicht übel, Freund ihm noch sein!
Ihm, vor dem sich alle fühlten so klein?

Kreidestrich-M.,
Hohn-M. — Den Junker Hochmut, laßt ihn laufen!
Mag er durch die Welt sich raufen;
was wir erlernt mit Not und Müh',
dabei laßt uns in Ruh' verschnaufen:
hier renn' er uns nichts übern Haufen;
sein Glück ihm anderswo erblüh'!

Act 2, Scene 4 – Good evening, Master!

VS 231▶7
CD 2/8 6:18

MAGDALENE

Comes out of the house and calls softly:
Bst, Evchen! Bst! — *disapproval motif*

EVA

(eagerly turning to Sachs)
       Is it hopeless? Say:
to give him aid, was there no way?
Was, then, his song of fault so full
that none might defend him in all your school?

SACHS

My child, the man who meets such disaster, — *disapproval motif*
no Master will be in any land.
Whoe'er is born as a master,
finds ever with Masters
       the lowest stand. — *chalk stroke motif*

MAGDALENE

(calling more audibly)
Thy father has called.

EVA

(still more urgently to Sachs)
       But say, in the end, — *hope motif*
if none of the Masters?
       he won as a friend?

SACHS

Ah, how could that be? Friend who might call — *disapproval motif*
him, before whose greatness all felt so small?
His knightly highness! devil take him! — *chalk stroke motif, scorn motif*
Let the bustling world awake him.
Shall he then rob and leave us bare
of what by labour we have won us:
Here never shall he overrun us:
let fortune greet him otherwhere!

	EVA	KA 269 ▶ 576 CD 2/8 7:43
Unmut-M.	*erhebt sich zornig:*	
Kreidestrich-M., *Hohn-M.,* *Leidenschaft-M.*	Ja! Anderswo soll's ihm erblühn, als bei euch garst'gen, neid'schen Mannsen, – wo warm die Herzen noch erglühen, trotz allen tück'schen Meister Hannsen! –	
	(zu Magdalene)	
Kreidestrich-M., *Hohn-M., Unmut-M.,* *Erregtheitstriller*	Gleich, Lene, gleich! Ich komme schon! Was trüg' ich hier für Trost davon? Da riech's nach Pech, daß' Gott erbarm': – brennt' er's lieber, da würd' er doch warm!	
	Sie geht sehr aufgeregt mit Magdalene über *die Straße hinüber und verweilt in großer Un-* *ruhe unter der Türe des Hauses.*	
	SACHS	
	sieht ihr mit bedeutungsvollem Kopfnicken *nach:*	
Ablehnung-M., *Hohn-M., Eva-M.*	Das dacht' ich wohl. Nun heißt's: schaff Rat!	
	Er ist während des Folgenden damit beschäf- *tigt, auch die obere Ladentür so weit zu schlie-* *ßen, daß sie nur ein wenig Licht noch durch-* *läßt: er selbst verschwindet so fast gänzlich.*	
	MAGDALENE	
Hohn-M., *Ablehnung-M.*	Hilf Gott! Wo bliebst du nur so spat? Der Vater rief.	KA 272 ▶ 603 CD 2/9 0:01
	EVA	
Hohn-M., *Entzückung-M.*	Geh zu ihm ein: ich sei zu Bett, im Kämmerlein.	
	MAGDALENE	
Beckmessers *Leidenschaft-M.*	Nicht doch, – hör mich! – Komm' ich dazu? Beckmesser fand mich; er läßt nicht Ruh': zur Nacht sollst du dich ans Fenster neigen, er will dir was Schönes singen und geigen, mit dem er dich hofft zu gewinnen, das Lied,	

Act 2, Scene 4 – Good evening, Master!

EVA

VS 234 ▶ 11
CD 2/8 7:43

    rises angrily: *resentment motif*

Aye, otherwhere shall fortune greet!   *chalk stroke motif,*
whatever an envious,   *scorn motif,*
                 churlish man says, –   *passion motif*
where hearts with loving ardour beat
in spite of cross-grained Master Hanses! –

    (to Magdalene)

Yes, Lene, yes! At once I'll come,   *chalk stroke motif,*
and better comfort seek at home.   *scorn motif,*
Lest smell of pitch should do you harm,   *resentment motif,*
burn it rather, and make yourself warm!   *excitement trill*

    In great excitement she crosses the street with
    Magdalene, and stops awhile, much agitated at
    the house door.

SACHS

    looks after her, nodding his head meaningly:

I thought as much, now help must come!   *disapproval motif,*
    During the following he closes the upper half   *scorn moti, Eva motif*
    of the door so far that only a little light pass-
    es out: he himself disappears almost entirely.

MAGDALENE

VS 237 ▶ 2
CD 2/9 0:01

So late! Why art thou not at home?   *scorn motif,*
Thy father called.   *disapproval motif*

EVA

                 Go thou instead: *scorn motif,*
say I had gone at once to bed   *delight motif*

MAGDALENE

Nay, may, – listen! – How shall I tell?   *Beckmesser's passion*
Beckmesser found me and told his tale: *motif*
to hear his ditty he means to bring thee
tonight to thy window, when he will sing thee
the song that shall capture both thee and thy love,

The Mastersingers of Nuremberg

ob das dir nach Gefallen geriet.

EVA

Ablehnung-M., Das fehlte auch noch! – Käme nur er!
Beckmessers
Leidenschaft-M. **MAGDALENE**
Hast' David gesehn?

EVA

       Was soll mir der?

Sie späht aus.

MAGDALENE

(für sich)
Ablehnung-M. Ich war zu streng; er wird sich grämen.

EVA
Siehst du noch nichts?

MAGDALENE

Tut, als spähe sie.
Hoffnung-M.   's ist, als ob Leut' dort kämen.

EVA
Wär' er's!

MAGDALENE

    Mach und komm jetzt hinan!

EVA
Nicht eh'r, bis ich sah den teuersten Mann!

MAGDALENE

Beckmessers Ich täuschte mich dort; er war es nicht.
Leidenschaft-M. Jetzt komm, sonst merkt der Vater
       die Geschicht'.

EVA

Ablehnung-M. Ach, meine Angst!

Act 2, Scene 4 – Good evening, Master!

VS 238 ▶ 5
CD 2/9 0:25

to find if thou his lay dost approve.

EVA
Must that be borne, too! – Would he but come!   *disapproval motif, Beckmesser's passion motif*

MAGDALENE
Has David been here?

EVA
What's he to me?

She looks out.

MAGDALENE
(aside)
I was too hard; now he'll be pining.   *disapproval motif*

EVA
See'st thou naught yet?

MAGDALENE
Appears to look out.   *hope motif*
It sounds like people coming.

EVA
He, 'tis!

MAGDALENE
Come, 'tis time to go in!

EVA
Not yet, until I my lover have seen!

MAGDALENE
My ear was deceived, it was not he.   *Beckmesser's passion motif*
Now come, for thy father aught
should guess.

EVA
Ah, how I fear!   *disapproval motif*

MAGDALENE

Unmut-M.,
Beckmessers
Leidenschaft-M.

Auch laß uns beraten,
wie wir des Beckmessers uns entladen!

EVA
Zum Fenster gehst du für mich.

MAGDALENE
Wie? Ich? –
(für sich)
Das machte wohl David eiferlich?
Er schläft nach der Gassen: hihi! 's wär fein! –

EVA

Unmut-M.

Da hör' ich Schritte.

MAGDALENE
(zu Eva)
Jetzt komm, es muß sein.

EVA
Jetzt näher!

MAGDALENE
Du irrst; 's ist nichts, ich wett'.
Ei, komm! Du mußt, bis der Vater zu Bett.

POGNER
(von innen)
He! Lene! Eva!

MAGDALENE
's ist höchste Zeit.
Sie zieht die sich sträubende Eva am Arm die Stufen zur Tür hinauf.
Hörst du's? Komm! Dein Ritter ist weit.

Act 2, Scene 4 – Good evening, Master!

MAGDALENE

                The let us take counsel,
how we from Beckmesser now may rid us!

resentment motif, Beckmesser's passion motif

EVA

To the window go thou for me.

MAGDALENE

                        What? I? –

(aside)

How jealous then David's heart would be?
He sleeps t'ward the alley: hihi! 'twere fine! –

EVA

I hear a footstep.

resentment motif

MAGDALENE

(to Eva)

                Now come, it must be.

EVA

Now nearer!

MAGDALENE

           Thou err'st, 'tis nought, I swear.
Ah, come! Thou must, till thy father's in bed.

POGNER

(from inside)

He! Lene! Eva!

MAGDALENE

                'Tis time, indeed.

She pulls the resisting Eva up the steps to the house.

Hear'st thou? Come! Your knight is not there.

5. Szene – Da ist er!

Stolzing-M.

Walther ist die Gasse heraufgekommen; jetzt biegt er um die Ecke herum; Eva erblickt ihn.

Eva

Da ist er!

Sie reißt sich von Magdalene los und stürzt Walther auf die Straße entgegen.

Magdalene

Da haben wir's! Nun heißt's: gescheit!
Sie geht eilig in das Haus.

Eva

(außer sich)

Hoffnung-M.

Ja! Ihr seid es; nein! Du bist es!
Alles sag' ich, denn ihr wißt es;
alles klag' ich, denn ich weiß es:
ihr seid beides, Held des Preises
und mein einz'ger Freund!

Walther

Ablehnung-M.

Ach! Du irrst: bin nur dein Freund,
doch des Preises noch nicht würdig,
nicht den Meistern ebenbürtig:
mein Begeistern fand Verachten,
und ich weiß es, darf nicht trachten
nach der Freundin Hand.

Scene 5 – There is he!

Walther has come up the alley; he now turns the corner; Eva sees him.   } *Stolzing motif*

Eva

There is he!

She tears herself away from Magdalene, and rushes towards Walther.

Magdalene

Now wit alone can help us out!

She goes hastily into the house.

Eva

(beyond herself)

Yes, 'tis you, love; no, 'tis thou, love!   } *hope motif*
All I tell thee, for thou knowest;
all is ruthless, and I know it:
you are truly hero, poet,
and my only friend!

Walther

Ah! thou err'st: thy friend alone;
but as poet Masters blame me,
and as Master will not name me: } *disapproval motif*
all my passion found but scorning,
and I know it; vain my yearning
for my lady's hand.

The Mastersingers of Nuremberg

EVA

Hoffnung-M.,
Werbe-M.

Wie du irrst! Der Freundin Hand,
erteilt nur sie den Preis,
wie deinen Mut ihr Herz erfand,
reicht sie nur dir das Reis.

WALTHER

Leidenschaft-M.

Ach, nein! Du irrst: der Freundin Hand,
wär' keinem sie erkoren,
wie sie des Vaters Wille band,
mir wär' sie doch verloren!

Meistersinger-M.

„Ein Meistersinger muß es sein;
nur wen ihr krönt, den darf sie frein!"
So sprach er festlich zu den Herrn;
kann nicht zurück, möcht' er auch gern! –
Das eben gab mir Mut:
wie ungewohnt mir alles schien,
ich sang voll Lieb' und Glut,

Lenzesgebot-M.,
Erregtheitstriller,
Kreidestrich-M.

daß ich den Meisterschlag verdien'. –
Doch, diese Meister!

   (wütend)

                Ha! Diese Meister! –
Dieser Reimgesetze
                Leimen und Kleister! –
Mir schwillt die Galle,
das Herz mir stockt,
denk' ich der Falle,
darein ich gelockt.

Vogelweid-M.,
Entzückung-M.

Fort, in die Freiheit! Dahin gehör' ich, –
dort, wo ich Meister im Haus!
Soll ich dich frein heut,
                dich nun beschwör' ich,
komm und folg mir hinaus!
Nichts steht zu hoffen;

Beckmessers
Leidenschaft-M.

keine Wahl ist offen! –
Überall Meister,
wie böse Geister,
seh' ich sich rotten,
mich zu verspotten:

Lebhaftigkeit-M.

mit den Gewerken,

Act 2, Scene 5 – There is he!

EVA

How thou err'st! her hand shall give
the victor's prize alone,
within thy heart my heart doth live,
thine then shall be the crown.

hope motif,
courtship motif

WALTHER

Ah, no! Thou err'st: my lady's hand,
e'en though none else should gain it
if fast thy father's word doth stand,
never may I attain it!
„A Mastersinger must he be!
he whom ye choose, and none but he!"
The word that he so firmly spake;
though he should wish, he may not break! –
That thought my courage fired:
how strange all seemed around me then,
I sang, by love inspired,
that I the Master's crown might gain. –
But all these Masters!

passion motif

mastersinger motif

springtime's behest motif
excitement trill,
chalk stroke motif

(furiously)

Ha! all these Masters! –
all this stanza-rhyming pack
of poetasters! –
With shame I think on
what I endured,
cursing the pitfall
whereto I was lured.
Hence let me fly now! Freedom doth call me
where I am Master by right!
Wilt thou be mine now,
whate'er befall me,
fly with me, then, tonight!
Hope is bereft us;
not a choice is left us! –
Nought but disasters,
Ev'rywhere Masters!
There they are flocking
round me and mocking:
ev'rywhere judges,

Vogelweid motif,
delight motif

Beckmesser's passion motif

liveliness motif

The Mastersingers of Nuremberg

Lebhaftigkeit-M., aus den Gemerken,   KA 288 ▶ 751
Beckmessers aus allen Ecken,   CD 2/10 3:24
Leidenschaft-M. auf allen Flecken,
seh' ich zu Haufen
Meister nur laufen,
mit höhnendem Nicken
frech auf dich blicken,
in Kreisen und Ringeln
Lebhaftigkeit-M. dich umzingeln,
näselnd und kreischend
zur Braut dich heischend,
als Meisterbuhle
auf dem Singestuhle,
zitternd und bebend,
hoch dich erhebend!
Und ich ertrüg' es, sollt' es nicht wagen,
gradaus tüchtig drein zu schlagen?

(Tritonus)   *Man hört den starken Ruf eines Nachtwächter-*
horns.

Ha!

Walther hat mit empathischer Gebärde die
Hand an das Schwert gelegt und starrt wild
vor sich hin.

Eva

Sommernacht-   *(faßt ihn besänftigend bei der Hand)*
zauber-M.,   Geliebter, spare den Zorn;   KA 291 ▶ 775
Eva-M.   's war nur des Nachtwächters Horn. –   CD 2/11 0:01
Unter der Linde
birg dich geschwinde;
hier kommt der Wächter vorbei.

Magdalene

(ruft leise unter der Türe)
Ev'chen! 's ist Zeit: mach dich frei!

Walther

Preislied (Liebes-   Du fliehst?
thema)

Act 2, Scene 5 – There is he!

<small>VS 251 ▶ 2
CD 2/10 3:24</small> markers with grudges;
out from all alleys
making their sallies,
crowds of them hustling,
Masters are bustling;
in jeering grimaces
twisting their faces;
in circles about thee,
so to flout thee;
snuffling and screeching,
thy hand beseeching;
as Master's plaything
on the throne they place thee,
trembling and quaking,
there to disgrace thee!
And I must bear it, tamely attend them,
dare not fall on them and rend them?

*liveliness motif,
Beckmesser's passion motif*

liveliness motif

> *The loud horn of the night-watchman is heard.*

(tritone)

Ha!

> *Walther has laid his hand with emphatic gesture on his sword and stares wildly before him.*

EVA

(takes his hand soothingly)

<small>VS 253 ▶ 3
CD 2/11 0:01</small>   Beloved, curb now thy scorn;
'twas but the night-warder's horn. –
Under the linden
hide thyself swiftly;
for here the warder will pass.

*summer night's magic motif,
Eva motif*

MAGDALENE

(calls softly from the door)

Evchen! 'tis time: come away!

WALTHER

Thou flee'st?

prize song (love theme)

Preislied (Liebesthema)

EVA

(lächelnd)

Muß ich denn nicht?

WALTHER

Entweichst?

EVA

(mit zarter Bestimmtheit)

Dem Meistergericht.

Sie verschwindet mit Magdalene im Hause. Der Nachtwächter ist währenddem in der Gasse erschienen, kommt singend nach vorn, biegt um die Ecke von Pogners Haus und geht nach links zu weiter ab.

NACHTWÄCHTER

Hört, ihr Leut', und laßt euch sagen,
die Glock' hat zehn geschlagen;
bewahrt das Feuer und auch das Licht,
daß niemand kein Schad' geschicht.
Lobet Gott den Herrn! –

SACHS

welcher hinter der Ladentüre dem Gespräche gelauscht, öffnet jetzt, bei eingezogenem Lampenlicht, ein wenig mehr.

Unmut-M., Sommernachtzauber-M.

Üble Dinge, die ich da merk':
eine Entführung gar im Werk?
Aufgepaßt! Das darf nicht sein. –

WALTHER

(hinter der Linde)

Käm' sie nicht wieder? O, der Pein! –

Eva kommt in Magdalenes Kleidung aus dem Hause.

Doch ja, sie kommt dort? –

(die Gestalt gewahrend)

Act 2, Scene 5 – There is he!

EVA

(smiling)

> Must I not flee?

prize song (love theme)

WALTHER

Escap'st?

EVA

(with gentle decision)

> The Masters' decree.

She disappears with Magdalene into the house. The night-watchman has appeared in the meantime in the alley and comes to the front, singing; he turns the corner of Pogner's house and goes off to the left.

NIGHT-WATCHMAN

Hear, all folk, the warder's ditty!
'tis ten o' clock in our city;
heed well your fire and eke your light,
that none may be harmed this night.
Praise ye God the Lord! –

SACHS

who has listened to the conversation from behind the door, now withdraws the lamp and opens the door a little further.

Evil doings now are in hand:
flitting of lovers being planned?
Now, to watch! That may not be. –

resentment motif, summer night's magic motif

WALTHER

(behind the lime tree)

Cometh she not, then? Woe is me! –

Eva comes in Magdalene's dress out of the house.

Ah, yes, she comes there? –

(catching sight of her figure)

The Mastersingers of Nuremberg

Sommernachtzau-
ber-M., Preislied
(Liebesthema)

              Weh mir! – nein! –
Die Alte ist's. –
    Eva erblickt Walther und eilt auf ihn zu.
            Doch – aber – ja!

KA 294 ▶ 819
CD 2/12 0:22

EVA

Preislied (Liebes-
thema)

Das tör'ge Kind, da hast du's, da!
    Sie wirft sich ihm heiter an die Brust.

WALTHER

    (hingerissen)
O Himmel! Ja, nun wohl ich weiß,
daß ich gewann den Meisterpreis.

EVA

Doch nun kein Besinnen!
Von hinnen! Von hinnen!
O, wären wir schon fort!

WALTHER

Hier durch die Gasse, dort
finden wir vor dem Tor
Knecht und Rosse vor.

Unmut-M.

    Nachtwächterhorn entfernt. Als sich beide
    wenden, um in die Gasse einzubiegen, läßt
    Sachs, nachdem er die Lampe hinter eine
    Glaskugel gestellt, durch die ganz wieder ge-
    öffnete Ladentüre einen grellen Lichtschein
    quer über die Straße fallen, so daß Eva und
    Walther sich plötzlich hell erleuchtet sehen.

EVA

    (Walther hastig zurückziehend)
O weh! Der Schuster! Wenn er uns säh! –
Birg dich – komm ihm nicht in die Näh'!

WALTHER

Sommernacht-
zauber-M.

Welch andrer Weg führt uns hinaus?

Act 2, Scene 5 – There is he!

Woe's me! – no! – *summer night's magic*
the old one 'tis. – *motif, prize song (love*
  Eva sees Walther and hastens towards him. *theme)*
Yet – surely – ah!

EVA

The foolish child, thou hast her, there! *prize song (love*
  She throws herself joyfully on his breast. *theme)*

WALTHER

  (carried away)
I know now, gazing in thine eyes,
that I have won the Master-prize.

EVA

But no more delaying!
Away now! Away now!
Oh, would that we were gone!

WALTHER

Here through the alley.
Ready, without the gate,
squire and horses wait.

  Night-watchman's horn from the distance. As *resentment motif*
  they both turn to go into the alley, Sachs, after
  placing his lamp behind a glass globe, lets a
  bright beam of light fall across the alley
  through the opened shutter so that Eva and
  Walther suddenly find themselves clearly illu-
  minated.

EVA

  (hastily drawing Walther back)
Alas! The cobbler! If he should see! –
Hide there – do not come in his way!

WALTHER

What other way leads to the gate? *summer night's magic*
  motif

*Sommernachtzau-
ber-M.*

EVA
Dort durch die Straße: doch der ist kraus,
ich kenn' ihn nicht gut; auch stießen wir dort
auf den Wächter.

WALTHER
                Nun denn, durch die Gasse.

EVA
Der Schuster muß erst vom Fenster fort.

WALTHER

Eva-M.   Ich zwing' ihn, daß er's verlasse.

EVA
Zeig dich ihm nicht: er kennt dich.

WALTHER
                    Der Schuster?

EVA
's ist Sachs.

WALTHER
              Hans Sachs? Mein Freund!

EVA
                    Glaub's nicht!

Unmut-M.   Von dir Übles zu sagen nur wußt' er.

WALTHER
Wie? Sachs? Auch er? –
                Ich lösch' ihm das Licht. –

KA 296 ▶ 842
CD 2/12 1:08

Act 2, Scene 5 – There is he!

EVA — *summer night's magic motif*

Round through the street, there: 'tis hard to find,
I scarce know it well; and there we should come
on the warder.

WALTHER

So then, through the alley.

EVA

But wait we must till the cobbler goes.

WALTHER

I'll make him turn from his window.

Eva motif

EVA

Show thyself not: he knows thee.

WALTHER

The cobbler?

EVA

'tis Sachs.

WALTHER

Hans Sachs? My friend!

EVA

Not so!
For he speaks of thee only to flout thee.

resentment motif

WALTHER

What? Sachs? He too? –
I'll put out his light. –

6. Szene – Tu's nicht!

Beckmesser ist dem Nachtwächter nachschleichend, die Gasse heraufgekommen, hat nach den Fenstern von Pogners Haus gespäht, und, an Sachsens Haus angelehnt, stimmt er jetzt seine mitgebrachte Laute.

Eva

(Walther zurückhaltend)

Laute-M.

Tu's nicht! – Doch horch! –

Walther

Einer Laute Klang.

Eva

Ach! meine Not!

Als Sachs den ersten Ton der Laute vernommen, hat er, von einem plötzlichen Einfall erfaßt, das Licht wieder etwas eingezogen und öffnet leise den unteren Teil des Ladens.

Walther

Wie wird dir bang?
Der Schuster, sieh! zog ein das Licht:
so sei's gewagt!

Eva

Weh! Siehst du denn nicht?
Ein andrer kam und nahm dort Stand.

Scene 6 – Do't not!

Beckmesser has come up the alley, slinking behind the night watchman, and has scanned the windows of Pogner's house; he now tunes a lute he has brought, as he leans against Sachs's house.

Eva

(holding back Walther)

Do't not! – But hark! –   *lute motif*

Walther

'Tis a lute that sounds.

Eva

Ah! My distress!

As Sachs hears the first sounds of the lute he withdraws his light a little, as if struck by a sudden thought, and opens the lower part of the door.

Walther

What, art afraid?
The cobbler, see! puts out his light:
now the, to fly!

Eva

Ah! Seest thou not there?
Another came and took his stand.

WALTHER
Ich hör's und seh's: ein Musikant.
Was will der hier so spät des Nachts?

> Sachs hat unvermerkt seinen Werktisch ganz unter die Tür gestellt; jetzt erlauscht er Evas Ausruf.

EVA
's ist Beckmesser schon!

SACHS
                    Aha! – ich dacht's.
> Er setzt sich leise zur Arbeit zurecht.

WALTHER
Der Merker? Er? In meiner Gewalt?
Drauf zu! Den Lung'rer mach' ich kalt.

EVA
Um Gott! So hör!
               Willst du den Vater wecken?

Unmut-M., Laute-M.

Er singt ein Lied, – dann zieht er ab. –
Laß dort uns im Gebüsch verstecken! –
Was mit den Männern ich Müh' doch hab'!

> Sie zieht Walther hinter das Gebüsch auf die Bank unter der Linde. Beckmesser, eifrig nach dem Fenster lugend, klimpert voll Ungeduld heftig auf der Laute. Als er sich endlich auch zum Singen rüstet, schlägt Sachs sehr stark mit dem Hammer auf den Leisten, nachdem er soeben das Licht wieder hell auf die Straße hat fallen lassen.

SACHS
(sehr stark)

Unmut-M., Schaffenslust-M.

Jerum! Jerum! Hallahallohe!
O ho! Tralalei! Tralalei! O ho!

Act 2, Scene 6 – Do't not!

WALTHER

I hear and see: a singer 'tis.
What wants he here so late at night?

> *Sachs unperceived has placed his work bench in the doorway; he now overhears Eva's cry.*

EVA

'Tis Beckmesser, ah!

SACHS

Aha! – I guessed.

> *He noiselessly prepares the work.*

WALTHER

The Marker? He? And here in my power?
Then on! The drone shall feel my sting.

EVA

Now God forbid!
    Wouldst thou, then, wake my father?
He'll sing a song, – and leave us then. –   } *resentment motif,*
Let's hide behind the foliage rather! –   } *lute motif*
What trouble ever I have with men!

> *She draws Walther on to the seat behind the foliage under the lime tree. Beckmesser, eagerly gazing at the window, strums loudly on the lute, in impatience. When he at length prepares to sing, Sachs strikes a heavy blow with his hammer on the last, after turning the light of his lamp full on the street again.*

SACHS

(very loud)

Jerum! Jerum! Hallahallohe!   } *resentment motif,*
O ho! Tralalei! Tralalei! O ho!   } *work lust motif*

The Mastersingers of Nuremberg

BECKMESSER

springt ärgerlich von dem Steinsitz auf und gewahrt Sachs bei der Arbeit.

Schaffenslust-M., Unmut-M.

Was soll das sein? –
                Verdammtes Schrei'n!

SACHS

Schusterlied

Als Eva aus dem Paradies
von Gott dem Herrn verstoßen,
gar schuf ihr Schmerz der harte Kies

Schustermühe-M.

an ihrem Fuß, dem bloßen.

BECKMESSER

Was fällt dem groben Schuster ein?

SACHS

Das jammerte den Herrn;

WALTHER

(flüsternd zu Eva)

Was heißt das Lied?
            Wie nennt er dich?

SACHS

Ihr Füsschen hatt er gern,
und seinem Engel rief er zu:

EVA

(flüsternd zu Walther)

Ich hört' es schon;
        's geht nicht auf mich:
doch eine Bosheit steckt darin.

SACHS

da, mach der armen Sünd'rin Schuh';
und da der Adam, wie ich seh,
an Steinen dort sich stößt die Zeh',

Act 2, Scene 6 – Do't not!

BECKMESSER

springs up angrily from the seat and perceives Sachs at work.

What can that be? –   *work lust motif,*
          Accursed noise!   *resentment motif*

SACHS

When Eve from Paradise was cast,   *cobbler's song*
her sin she soon repented,
for, toiling o'er the stony waste,
her feet were sore tormented.   *cobbler's labor motif*

BECKMESSER

What plan is in the cobbler's head?

SACHS

Thereat the Lord was moved;

WALTHER

(whispering to Eva)

What means the song?
          Thy name I hear?

SACHS

her tender feet he loved,
some comfort he might not refuse:

EVA

(whispering to Walther)

I heard it well;
          but 'tis not I:
yet malice hidden lieth there.

SACHS

so bade an angel make her shoes.
then, seeing Adam limping tread
with feet all torn with stones, he said;

The Mastersingers of Nuremberg

WALTHER

Schusterlied,   Welch Zögernis!
Schaffenslust-M.   Die Zeit geht hin.

SACHS

Daß recht fortan er wandeln kann,
so miß dem auch Stiefeln an!

BECKMESSER

tritt zu Sachs heran:

Kreidestrich-M., Un-   Wie? Meister! Auf? Noch so spät zur Nacht?
mut-M., Beckmessers
Leidenschaft-M.   **SACHS**

Herr Stadtschreiber! Was? Ihr wacht? –
Beckmessers   Die Schuh' machen euch große Sorgen?
Leidenschaft-M.   Ihr seht, ich bin dran: ihr habt sie morgen. –

(arbeitet)

BECKMESSER

Unmut-M.   *(zornig)*

Hol' der Teufel die Schuh'!
Hier will ich Ruh'!

SACHS

Unmut-M.,   Jerum! Hallahallohe!
Schaffenslust-M.   O ho! Tralalei! Tralalei! O he!
Schusterlied   O Eva! Eva! Schlimmes Weib,
das hast du am Gewissen,
daß ob der Füß' am Menschenleib
Schustermühe-M.   jetzt Engel schustern müssen!

WALTHER

(wie vorher)

Uns oder dem Merker,
           wem spielt er den Streich?

EVA

(wie vorher)

Act 2, Scene 6 – Do't not!

WALTHER

Why stay we now! *cobbler's song,*
         The time goes by. *work lust motif*

SACHS

tough, truth to tell, in sin he fell,
measure him for boots as well!

BECKMESSER

comes up to Sachs:
What? Master! Up? and so late at night? *chalk stroke motif,*
   resentment motif,
SACHS *Beckmesser's passion*
   motif
You, Beckmesser! What awake? –
Your shoes bring you still nought but sorrow? *Beckmesser's passion*
You see I'm at work against tomorrow. – *motif*
   (works)

BECKMESSER

(angry)   *resentment motif*
Let the fiend take the shoes!
Here I want peace!

SACHS

         Jerum! Hallahallohe! *resentment motif,*
O ho! Tralalei! Tralalei! O he! *work lust motif*
O Eve on thee this guilt has lain, *cobbler's song*
and caused thee bitter ruing,
that now the feet of mortal men
the angels must be shoeing! *cobbler's labor motif*

WALTHER

(as before)
Is't we or the Marker?
         At whom does he jeer?

EVA

(as before)

Schusterlied — Ich fürcht', uns dreien gilt er gleich.

SACHS
Bliebst du im Paradies,
da gab es keinen Kies:
um deiner jungen Missetat
hantier' ich jetzt mit Ahl' und Draht,
und ob Herrn Adams übler Schwäch'
versohl' ich Schuh' und streiche Pech!

EVA
O weh, der Pein! Mir ahnt nichts Gutes.

WALTHER
Mein süßer Engel, sei guten Mutes!

EVA
Mich betrübt das Lied.

WALTHER
                         Ich hör' es kaum;
du bist bei mir: welch holder Traum!
Er zieht Eva zärtlich an sich.

SACHS
Wär' ich nicht fein
          ein Engel rein,
Schaffenslust-M. — der Teufel möchte Schuster sein!
Je – – –

BECKMESSER
(drohend auf Sachs zufahrend)
Gleich höret auf! Spielt ihr mir Streich'?
Unmut-M. — Bleibt ihr tags und nachts euch gleich?

SACHS
Wenn ich hier sing', was kümmert's euch?
Die Schuhe sollen doch fertig werden?

His song reproves all three, I fear. — *cobbler's song*

SACHS

Stones were not ever found,
on Eden's holy ground:
for that offence that wrought thy fall,
I sit at work with thread and awl,
and eke to pay for Adam's crime,
in soling shoes I spend my time!

EVA

Ah, woe is me! I fear some evil.

WALTHER

My sweetest angel, comfort thy spirit!

EVA

'Tis the song that wounds.

WALTHER

                            I hear it not;
thou art by me: What blissful dream!

He draws Eva tenderly to him.

SACHS

Were I not, too,
          an angel true,
devils might make shoes for you! — *work lust motif*
Je – – –

BECKMESSER

(coming threatening towards Sachs)

Come to an end! What is the trick?
Night and day are you the same? — *resentment motif*

SACHS

If I here sing, What's that to you?
And look you! shoes will you need tomorrow!

BECKMESSER

Unmut-M.   So schließt euch ein, und schweigt dazu still!

SACHS

Des Nachts arbeiten macht Beschwerden;
wenn ich da munter bleiben will,
so brauch' ich Luft und frischen Gesang:
drum hört, wie der dritte Vers gelang!

Unmut-M.,
Schaffenslust-M.
Jerum! Jerum! Hallahallohe!
O ho! Tralalei! Tralalei! O he!

BECKMESSER

Er macht mich rasend! –
                Das grobe Geschrei!
Am End' denkt sie gar, daß ich das sei!

Er hält sich die Ohren zu und geht, verzweiflungsvoll sich mit sich beratend, die Gasse vor dem Fenster auf und ab.

SACHS

Wahn-M.[1],
Schusterlied

Schustermühe-M.

Schaffenslust-M.,
Erregtheitstriller

O Eva! Hör mein' Klageruf,
mein' Not und schwer Verdrüßen!
Die Kunstwerk', die ein Schuster schuf,
sie tritt die Welt mit Füßen!
Gäb' nicht ein Engel Trost,
der gleiches Werk erlost,
und rief' mich oft ins Paradies,
wie ich da Schuh' und Stiefel ließ'!
Doch wenn mich der im Himmel hält,
dann liegt zu Füßen mir die Welt,
und bin in Ruh
        Hans Sachs, ein Schuhmacher und Poet dazu!

BECKMESSER

Unmut-M.   Das Fenster geht auf!

Er späht nach dem Fenster, welches jetzt leise geöffnet wird, und an welchem vorsichtig Magdalene in Evas Kleidung sich zeigt.

---

[1] *Als Kontrapunkt in den Holzbläsern.*

Act 2, Scene 6 – Do't not!

BECKMESSER

The hold your peace, and get you within! } *resentment motif*

SACHS

But night shoe-making bringeth sorrow;
to cheer my heart and cure my spleen,
fresh air I need and song must be heard:
now hark as I sing you verse the third!
Jerum! Jerum! Hallahallohe! } *resentment motif,*
O ho! Tralalei! Tralalei! O he! } *work lust motif*

BECKMESSER

He drives me frantic! –
                      This infamous noise!
At last, she will think 'tis I who sing!

He stops his ears and walks in despair up and down the alley before the window, ruminating.

SACHS

O Eve, my woes must wring thy heart, } *delusion motif[1],*
and make us morn together! } *cobbler's song*
The world contemns the cobbler's art
and treads upon his leather! } *cobbler's labor*
Were not an angel there, } *motif*
to charm away my care,
to Paradise oft calling me,
I soon would let my cobbling be!
But when enthroned in Heaven's seat,
the world doth lie beneath my feet:
then born anew,
        I am a shoe-
maker and a poet too! } *work lust motif,*
                                           excitement trill

BECKMESSER

The window's unclosed! } *resentment motif*

He looks at the window which is gently opened, and at which Magdalena, in Eva's dress, cautiously shows herself.

---
[1] *As counterpoint in the woodwinds.*

EVA

(mit großer Aufgeregtheit)

Wahn-M., Schusterlied

Mich schmerzt das Lied,
           ich weiß nicht wie!
O fort! Laß uns fliehen!

WALTHER

(auffahrend)
           Nun denn: mit dem Schwert!

EVA

Nicht doch! Ach, halt!

BECKMESSER

           Herr Gott! 's ist sie. –

WALTHER

(die Hand vom Schwert nehmend)
Kaum wär' er's wert.

EVA

Ja, besser Geduld!

BECKMESSER

Jetzt bin ich verloren, singt der noch fort!

Er tritt zu Sachs an den Laden heran und klimpert, während des Folgenden, mit dem Rücken der Gasse zugewendet, seitwärts auf der Laute, um Magdalene am Fenster festzuhalten.

EVA

Schustermühe-M.
           O, bester Mann!
Daß ich so Not dir machen kann!

BECKMESSER

Laute-M.
Freund Sachs!
           So hört doch nur ein Wort! –

Act 2, Scene 6 – Do't not!

EVA

(in great agitation)
His song doth pain me,
            I now not why!
Away let us hasten!! — *delusion motif, cobbler's song*

WALTHER

(impetuously)
            Aye now; with my sword!

EVA

Ah no! Not that!

BECKMESSER

            Good god!'Tis she! –

WALTHER

(taking his hand from the sword)
'Tis scarce worthwhile.

EVA

Yes, patience is best!

BECKMESSER

Now if he sings longer I am undone!

He comes up to Sachs at the shop, and during the following, stands with his back to the alley, but playing his lute sideways as to Magdalene at the window, to hold her attention.

EVA

            O best of men! — *cobbler's labor motif*
that I should bring distress to thee!

BECKMESSER

Friend Sachs!
            Let me but speak a word! – — *lute motif*

WALTHER

(leise zu Eva)
Wer ist am Fenster?

BECKMESSER
Wie seid ihr auf die Schuh' versessen!

EVA

(leise)
's ist Magdalene.

BECKMESSER
Ich hatt' sie wahrlich schon vergessen.

WALTHER
Das heiß' ich vergelten!

BECKMESSER
Als Schuster seid ihr mir wohl wert,

WALTHER
Fast muß ich lachen.

BECKMESSER
als Kunstfreund doch weit mehr verehrt.

EVA
Wie ich ein End' und Flucht mir ersehne!

WALTHER
Ich wünscht',
er möchte den Anfang machen.

Walther und Eva, auf der Bank sanft aneinandergelehnt, verfolgen des Weiteren den Vorgang zwischen Sachs und Beckmesser mit wachsender Teilnahme.

Unmut-M.,
Erregtheitstriller,
Laute-M.,

BECKMESSER
Eu'r Urteil, glaubt, das halt' ich wert[1];

---
[1] *So laut Schott. Meist wird hier allerdings "hoch" gesungen, um den Reim auf "doch" zu bilden.*

Act 2, Scene 6 – Do't not!

WALTHER
(low Eva)
Who's at thy window?

BECKMESSER
Why let the shoes so much distress you.

EVA
(softly)
'Tis Magdalene.

BECKMESSER
I give my word I'd clean forgot them.

WALTHER
I call that requital!

BECKMESSER
As cobbler well I know your worth,

WALTHER
It moves my laughter.

BECKMESSER
in art your place is first on earth.

EVA
Would we might fly and end all this trouble!

WALTHER
If only, he would begin his story.

Walther and Eva, leaning tenderly together on the seat, follow the scene between Sachs and Beckmesser with growing interest.

resentment motif,
excitement trill,
lute motif,

BECKMESSER
Your judgment, too, is seldom wrong;

The Mastersingers of Nuremberg

Unmut-M.,	drum bitt' ich, hört das Liedlein doch,	KA 321 ▶ 1035
Erregtheitstriller,	mit dem ich morgen möcht' gewinnen,	CD 2/15 0:55
Laute-M., Beckmessers Ständchen	ob das auch recht nach euren Sinnen.	

Er klimpert wiederholt seitwärts, ängstlich nach dem Fenster gewandt.

SACHS

Kreidestrich-M., O ha! Wollt mich beim Wahne fassen?
Erregtheitstriller Mag mich nicht wieder schelten lassen.
Seit sich der Schuster dünkt Poet,[1]
gar übel es um eu'r Schuhwerk steht:
Kreidestrich-M. ich seh', wie's schlappt,
und überall klappt;
drum lass' ich Vers und Reim'
gar billig nun daheim,
Verstand und Witz, und Kenntnis dazu,
Erregtheitstriller mach' euch für morgen die neuen Schuh'!

BECKMESSER

(kreischend)

Unmut-M., Laute-M. Laßt das doch sein! Das war ja nur Scherz.

(wie vorher)

Vernehmt besser, wie's mir ums Herz. –
Kreidestrich-M., Vom Volk seid ihr geehrt,
Erregtheitstr., Zunftge- auch der Pognerin seid ihr wert:
setz-M., Nürnberg-M. will ich vor aller Welt
nun morgen um die werben,
sagt! – könnt's mich nicht verderben,
Laute-M. wenn mein Lied ihr nicht gefällt?
Naturregel-M.[2] Drum hört mich ruhig an,
und sang ich, sagt mir dann,
was euch gefällt, was nicht, –
Laute-M., daß ich mich danach richt'!
Kreidestrich-M.

SACHS

Ei! Laßt mich doch in Ruh',
wie käme solche Ehr' mir zu?
Kränzlein-M., Nur Gassenhauer dicht' ich zum meisten:
Hohn-M., Unmut-M. Drum sing' ich zur Gassen

---
[1] Auch musikalisch ein Zitat aus der 3. Szene des 1. Aufzugs.
[2] Ein weiteres musikalisches Zitat: Hans Sachs sang im 1. Aufzug: „und ob ihr der Natur noch seid auf rechter Spur".

Act 2, Scene 6 – Do't not!

VS 279 ▶3
CD 2/15 0:55
so, pray you, hear this little song;
for, help from you I fain would borrow,
that I might win the prize tomorrow.

> *He strums repeatedly on his lute, half turning towards the window.*

resentment motif,
excitement trill,
lute motif,
Beckmesser's song

SACHS

Aha! Then by my craze you'd catch me?
Not again will I let you teach me
how since the cobbler poet has been,[1]
such shoes he makes as ne'er yet were seen:
unsound throughout,
they flap all about!
Writing of songs, I swear;
for you I would forbear
my laws and plays, in prose or rhyme
that I may send your shoes in time!

chalk stroke motif,
excitement trill

chalk stroke motif

excitement trill

BECKMESSER

(shrieking)

Nay, let that be! 'Twas nought but a jest.

(as before)

No malice, truly, lives in my breast. –
The folk all feel your spell,
and the maiden, too, loves you well:
if I tomorrow came,
to win the people's favour,
were't not a vain endeavour,
if my song Hans Sachs should blame?
Now listen to my song,
and tell me what is wrong;
then, to attain my end, –
your words my work shall mend!

resentment motif,
lute motif

chalk stroke motif,
excitement trill,
guild law motif,
Nuremberg motif

lute motif

nature rule motif[2]

lute motif,
chalk stroke motif

SACHS

Ah, cease and let me be,
how could such honour come to me?
If nought but doggrel rhymes I can stammer,
then doggrel I sing

chaplet motif,
scorn motif,
resentment motif

---

[1] *Also melodically a quote from the 3rd scene of the 1st act.*
[2] *Another melodic quote: Hans Sachs sang in the 1st act: „and if on nature's road your feet have firmly trod".*

The Mastersingers of Nuremberg

Unmut-M.,
Schaffenslust-M.

               und hau' auf den Leisten! –
Jerum! Jerum! Hallahallohe!
O ho! Tralalei! Tralalei! O he!

BECKMESSER

Verfluchter Kerl! Den Verstand verlier' ich,
mit seinem Lied voll Pech und Schmierich!
Schweigt doch! Weckt ihr die Nachbarn auf?

SACHS

Die sind's gewöhnt. 's hört keiner drauf!

Schusterlied   O Eva! Eva!

BECKMESSER

(in höchste Wut ausbrechend)

Kreidestrich-M.   Oh, ihr boshafter Geselle!
Ihr spielt mir heut den letzten Streich:
Schweigt ihr jetzt nicht auf der Stelle,
so denkt ihr dran, das schwör' ich euch!

Laute-M.   *Er klimpert wütend.*

Neidisch seid ihr, nichts weiter:
dünkt ihr euch auch gleich gescheiter;
daß andre auch was sind,

Hohn-M.   ärgert euch schändlich:
glaubt, ich kenne euch aus-
                        und inwendlich!
Daß man euch noch nicht

Hohn-M.   zum Merker gewählt,
Unmut-M.,
Erregtheitstriller   das ist's, was den gallichten Schuster quält.
               Nun gut! So lang' als Beckmesser lebt,
Zunftideal-M.   und ihm noch ein Reim
                      an den Lippen klebt;
               so lang' ich noch bei den Meistern was gelt',
Meistersinger-M. ② ob Nürnberg blüh' und wachs',
& ④   das schwör' ich Herrn Hans Sachs,
               nie wird er je zum Merker bestellt.

Laute-M.   *Er klimpert in höchster Wut.*

Act 2, Scene 6 – Do't not!

as my leather I hammer! –
Jerum! Jerum! Hallahallohe! *resentment motif,*
O ho! Tralalei! Tralalei! O he! *work lust motif*

BECKMESSER

Accursed rogue! All my senses leave me,
amid his song that reeks of blacking!
Silence! Folk now to bed are gone?

SACHS

They know me well; they will sleep on!
O Eve! O Eve, how *cobbler's song*

BECKMESSER

(In a transport of rage)

Oh, you base, black hearted rascal! *chalk stroke motif*
More tricks like this you'll play not here!
Now at once, silence that howling,
or you'll repent your trick, I swear!

He strums furiously. *lute motif*

Envy-cursed were you ever:
though you deem yourself so clever:
that others, too, have wits
             ever enraged you: *scorn motif*
through and through, believe me,
             I have gauged you!
That the most of Marker
             you cannot win *scorn motif*
'tis that wakes the rancourous cobbler's spleen. *resentment motif,*
Ah well, so long as Beckmesser sings; *excitement trill*
while a single rhyme
             to his lips be brings; *guild ideal motif*
so long as I among the Masters am famed,
though Nüremberg bloom and wax, *mastersinger motif ②*
I swear to you Hans Sachs, *& ④*
never shall you as Marker be named.

He plays in intense fury. *lute motif*

SACHS

Sommernachtzauber-M. (Beginn)

der ihm ruhig und aufmerksam zugehört hat:
War das eu'r Lied?

BECKMESSER

Der Teufel hol's!

SACHS

Hohn-M.

Zwar wenig Regel, doch klang's recht stolz.

BECKMESSER

Unmut-M.

Wollt ihr mich hören?

SACHS

Kreidestrich-M.

In Gottes Namen,
singt zu: ich schlag' auf die Sohl' die Rahmen.

BECKMESSER

Unmut-M.

Doch schweigt ihr still?

SACHS

Ei, singet ihr,
die Arbeit, schaut, fördert's auch mir.
Er klopft auf seinen Leisten.

BECKMESSER

Unmut-M.
Hohn-M.

Das verfluchte Klopfen wollt ihr doch lassen?

SACHS

Wie sollt' ich die Sohl' euch richtig fassen?

BECKMESSER

Erregtheitstriller

Was? Ihr wollt klopfen, und ich soll singen?

SACHS

Euch muß das Lied, mir der Schuh gelingen.

BECKMESSER

Unmut-M.

Ich mag keine Schuh'!

Act 2, Scene 6 – Do't not!

SACHS

who has listened to him quietly and attentively: *summer night's magic*
Was that your song?   *motif (beginning)*

BECKMESSER

               Ill-mannered hound!

SACHS

The rules were lacking, but brave the sound.   *scorn motif*

BECKMESSER

Will you not hear me?   *resentment motif*

SACHS

            For heaven's sake then,
sing you; while shoes for your feet I make, then.   *chalk stroke motif*

BECKMESSER

But, you'll keep still?   *resentment motif*

SACHS

              Oh, sing you on,
my cobbling, too, is not yet done.
   He knocks on his last.

BECKMESSER   *resentment motif*
That accursed knocking passes all bearing!   *scorn motif*

SACHS
But must your shoes be fit for wearing?

BECKMESSER
What! must I sing, then, while you beat leather?   *excitement trill*

SACHS
Both song and shoe must advance together.

BECKMESSER
I want not the shoes!   *resentment motif*

SACHS

Erregtheitstriller

Das sagt ihr jetzt:
in der Singschul'
Ihr mir's dann wieder versetzt. –
Kreidestrich-M. Doch hört! Vielleicht sich's richten läßt;
zweieinig geht der Mensch am best'.
Naturregel-M Darf ich die Arbeit nicht entfernen,
die Kunst des Merkers möcht' ich erlernen;
darin kommt euch nun keiner gleich:
Meistersinger-M. ④ ich lern' sie nie, wenn nicht von euch.
Drum, singt ihr nun, ich acht' und merk',
und fördr' auch wohl dabei mein Werk.

BECKMESSER

Merkt immer zu; und was nicht gewann,
Meistersinger-M. ④ nehmt Eure Kreide und streicht mir's an.

SACHS

Nein, Herr! Da fleckten die Schuh' mir nicht:
mit dem Hammer auf den Leisten
halt' ich Gericht.

BECKMESSER

Verdammte Bosheit! – Gott, und 's wird spät!
Am End' mir die Jungfer vom Fenster geht!
Laute-M. *Er klimpert eifrig.*

SACHS

Fanget an, 's pressiert:
sonst sing' ich für mich. –

BECKMESSER

Haltet ein! Nur das nicht!
(Teufel! Wie ärgerlich!) –
Naturregel-M,
Unmut-M. Wollt ihr euch denn als Merker erdreisten,
nun gut, so merkt mit
Meistersinger-M. ④ dem Hammer auf den Leisten:
Naturregel-M,
Unmut-M. nur mit dem Beding,
nach den Regeln scharf,
Meistersinger-M. ④ aber nichts, was nach den Regeln ich darf.

Act 2, Scene 6 – Do't not!

SACHS

                You say so now:
but tomorrow morn   *excitement trill*
          you will blame me, I trow. –
Yet hear! Perchance it may be done;   *chalk stroke motif*
two comrades better speed than one.
Although my work brooks no denial,   *nature rule motif*
in Marker's craft now give me a trial.
In that you have no peer, 'tis true:
how learn the art if not from you?   *mastersinger motif* ④
Then sing you on, I'll heed and mark,
and yet go forward with my work.

BECKMESSER

Mark for me, then, and if I go wrong,
score with your chalk as I sing my song.   *mastersinger motif* ④

SACHS

Ah no! Not so will your shoes be soled:
by my hammer on the last
                let judgment be told.

BECKMESSER

Accursed malice! God, and 'tis late!
and long at the window she will not wait!
   He strums eagerly.   *lute motif*

SACHS

Now begin, time flies:
                or I too shall sing. –

BECKMESSER

Nay, not that! Be silent!
            (Devil now take the thing) –
Would you as Marker make a beginning?   *nature rule motif,*
'Tis well; but strike only   *resentment motif*
                if you catch me sinning: *mastersinger motif* ④
yet, be it agreed,   *nature rule motif,*
                by the rules alone;   *resentment motif*
do not blame me what by the rules may be done.   *mastersinger motif* ④

Hohn-M.,
Kreidestrich-M.,
Unmut-M.

SACHS
Nach den Regeln,
    wie sie der Schuster kennt,
dem die Arbeit unter den Händen brennt.

BECKMESSER
Auf Meisterehr'?

SACHS
    Und Schustermut!

BECKMESSER

Prügel-M.
Erregtheitstriller

    Nicht einen Fehler: glatt und gut.

SACHS
Dann ging't ihr morgen unbeschuht!
Nachtwächterhorn sehr entfernt.

WALTHER

Sommernacht-
zauber-M.

(leise zu Eva)
Welch toller Spuk! Mich dünkt's ein Traum:
den Singstuhl, scheint's, verließ ich kaum.

EVA
(sanft an Walthers Brust gelehnt)
Die Schläf umwebt mir's wie ein Wahn:

Eva-M.

ob's Heil, ob Unheil, was ich ahn'?

SACHS
Sachs deutet auf den Steinsitz vor der Ladentüre.
Setzt euch denn hier!

BECKMESSER
(zieht sich nach der Ecke des Hauses zurück)
    Laßt mich hier stehen.

Act 2, Scene 6 – Do't not!

SACHS
On the rules,
                the cobbler takes his stand,
though his work is burning beneath his hand.

scorn motif,
chalk stroke motif,
resentment motif

BECKMESSER
By Masters' rule?

SACHS
              With cobbler's tool!

BECKMESSER
              Never a fault, then, fair and good.

beating motif
excitement trill

SACHS
Then you tomorrow go unshod!
    Night-watchman far off, on his horn.

WALTHER
    (Low to Eva)
'Tis like the tricks of crazy dreams;
still am I in the school meseems.

summer night's magic motif

EVA
    (leaning softly on Walther's breast)
My brain is dazed as by a spell:
if good or ill-fate, who can tell?

Eva motif

SACHS
    Sachs pointing to a stone seat at the shop door.

Seat you, then, here!

BECKMESSER
    (draws back to the corner of the house)
              I'll stand her, rather.

The Mastersingers of Nuremberg

Sommernacht-zauber-M.

SACHS
Warum so weit?

BECKMESSER
Euch nicht zu sehen,
wie's Brauch der Schul' vor dem Gemerk'.

SACHS
Da hör' ich euch schlecht.

BECKMESSER
Der Stimme Stärk'
ich so gar lieblich dämpfen kann.
Er stellt sich ganz um die Ecke dem Fenster gegenüber auf.

SACHS
(Wie fein!) –
Nun, gut denn! Fanget an!

BECKMESSER
Er stimmt die in der Wut unversehens zuvor hinaufgeschraubte D-Saite wieder herunter.

Laute-M., Beckmessers Ständchen, Kreidestrich-M.

„Den Tag seh' ich erscheinen,
Sachs holt mit dem Hammer aus.
der mir wohl gefalln tut;
Sachs schlägt auf. Beckmesser schüttelt sich.
da faßt mein Herz sich einen
Sachs schlägt auf. Beckmesser setzt heftig ab, singt aber weiter.
guten und frischen" –
Sachs hat aufgeschlagen. Beckmesser wendet sich wütend um die Ecke herum.
Treibt ihr hier Scherz?
Was wär' nicht gelungen?

SACHS
Besser gesungen:

Act 2, Scene 6 – Do't not!

SACHS
But why so far?

summer night's magic motif

BECKMESSER
Because the marker must not be seen; so says the rule.

SACHS
Then I shall not hear.

BECKMESSER
My voice is full; more sweetly so your ear 'twill win.

He takes his place quite round the corner, opposite the window.

SACHS
(How fine!) –
'Tis well, then! Now begin!

BECKMESSER

He tunes down the D string which he has unconsciously screwed up in his rage.

lute motif, Beckmesser's song, chalk stroke motif

„I see now dawning daylight,

Sachs raising his hammer.

that gives me delight true;

Sachs strikes. Beckmesser shakes himself.

and wakes in me a gay, light

Sachs strikes. Beckmesser breaks off suddenly but resumes.

heart and a courage" –

Sachs has struck. Beckmesser turns round in a rage.

Is that a jest?
What fault do you find there?

SACHS
Better have sung there:

The Mastersingers of Nuremberg

Beckmessers
Ständchen,
Kreidestrich-M.

„Da faßt mein Herz
sich einen guten, frischen"?

BECKMESSER

Wie soll sich das reimen
auf „seh' ich erscheinen"?

SACHS

Kreidestrich-M.

Ist euch an der Weise nichts gelegen?
Mich dünkt, sollt' passen Ton und Wort?

BECKMESSER

Mit euch zu streiten?
                        Laßt von den Schlägen,
sonst denkt ihr mir dran!

SACHS

                        Jetzt fahret fort!

BECKMESSER

– Bin ganz verwirrt! –

SACHS

                    So fangt noch mal an:
drei Schläg' ich jetzt pausieren kann.

BECKMESSER

(beiseite)

Laute-M., Beckmes-
sers Ständchen,
Kreidestrich-M.

Am besten, wenn ich ihn gar nicht beacht':
Wenn's nur die Jungfer nicht irre macht!
„Den Tag seh' ich erscheinen,
der mir wohl gefall'n tut;
da faßt mein Herz sich einen
guten und frischen Mut:
da denk' ich nicht an Sterben,

Sachs schlägt.

Beckmessers
Werbe-M.

lieber an Werben
um jung Mägdeleins Hand.

Sachs schlägt.

KA 341 ▶ 1227
CD 2/16 0:55

Act 2, Scene 6 – Do't not!

_{VS 297 ▶ 6} „and makes in me a gay, light *Beckmesser's song,*
_{CD 2/16 0:55} heart and courage"? *chalk stroke motif*

BECKMESSER

Pray how would it rhyme, then,
with „now dawning day-light"?

SACHS

Is accent to you so small a matter? *chalk stroke motif*
Methinks, the phrase should fit the rhyme?

BECKMESSER

I will not wrangle!
     Silence that clatter,
or you will repent!

SACHS

    You lose your time!

BECKMESSER

– I'm all distraught! –

SACHS

    Begin, then, once more:
three faults I pass as marked before.

BECKMESSER

 (aside)

'Twere best to heed not a word he may say: *lute motif,*
If only she, too, no heed will pay! *Beckmesser's song,*
„I see now dawning day-light, *chalk stroke motif*
that gives me delight true;
and wakes in me a gay,
light heart and a courage new:
I think not now of dying;
 Sachs strikes.
rather of trying *Beckmesser's*
to win a young maid's hand. *courtship motif*
 Sachs strikes.

The Mastersingers of Nuremberg

Laute-M., Beckmessers Ständchen, Kreidestrich-M.	Warum wohl aller Tage	KA 345 ▸ 1251 CD 2/16 2:18

        (Schlag)

schönster mag dieser sein?

        (Beckmesser ärgerlich)

Allen hier ich es sage:
weil ein schönes Fräulein

        (zwei Schläge)

Beckmessers Werbe-M.   von ihrem lieb'n Herrn Vater,

        Sachs nickt ironisch beifällig.

wie gelobt hat er,

        (viele kleine Schläge)

ist bestimmt zum Eh'stand.

Erregtheitstriller   *(Schläge, Beckmesser sehr ärgerlich)*
Ärger-M.   Wer sich getrau',

        (Schlag)

                der komm' und schau'

        (Schlag)

Beckmessers Werbe-M.   da stehn die hold lieblich' Jungfrau,

        (Schläge)

auf die ich all' mein' Hoffnung bau';
darum ist der Tag so schön blau,

        (Schläge)

als ich anfänglich fand."

        Er springt wütend auf.

Sachs! Seht, ihr bringt mich um!
Wollt ihr jetzt schweigen?

Sachs

                Ich bin ja stumm?
Naturregel-M   Die Zeichen merkt' ich; wir sprechen dann:
derweil lassen die Sohlen sich an.

Beckmesser

        gewahrt, daß Magdalene sich vom Fenster
Erregtheitstriller,   *entfernen will:*
Unmut-M.   Sie entweicht? – Bst! Bst!

Act 2, Scene 6 – Do't not!

VS 300▶7 Why think I of this day   } lute motif, Beckmes-
CD 2/16 2:18   ser's song, chalk
    (Sachs strikes)   stroke motif

it other days doth excel?

    (Beckmesser annoyed)

Now to you all I say it:
I love a young damsel

    (two strokes)

whose father gives me truly,   } Beckmesser's
                                                                     courtship motif
    Sachs nods ironical approval.

assurance full,

    (several little strokes)

I, as her bridegroom shall stand.

    (Strokes, Beckmesser very angrily)   } excitement trill

'Let all who dare,   } anger motif

    (strike)

              now come and stare

    (strike)

here upon the maiden so fair,   } Beckmesser's
                                                                     courtship motif
    (strokes)

with whom I fondly hope to pair
therefore seemeth so bright the air,

    (strokes)

today in all the land."

    He springs forward in a rage.

Sachs! Sachs! you drive me mad!
Will you keep quiet?

Sachs

               Nay, I am dumb?
I am but marking. We'll talk anon: } nature rule motif
Meanwhile, soling your shoes will be done.

Beckmesser

    perceives that Magdalene is going to with-
    draw from the window:

She is gone. – Bst! Bst!

The Mastersingers of Nuremberg

Beckmessers Werbe-M. (in der Laute), Unmut-M.

                    Herr Gott, ich muß!
um die Ecke herum die Faust gegen Sachs ballend.
Sachs, euch gedenk' ich die Ärgernuß!
Er macht sich zum 2. Vers fertig.

SACHS

(mit dem Hammer nach dem Leisten ausholend)

Kreidestrich-M.

Merker am Ort:
fahret fort!

BECKMESSER

Laute-M., Beckmessers Ständchen, Kreidestrich-M.

(immer stärker und atemloser)
„Will heut mir das Herz hüpfen,
(Sachs mit dem Hammer: Schläge)

werben um Fräulein jung,
doch tät der Vater knüpfen
daran ein' Bedingung

Beckmessers Werbe-M.

für den, wer ihn beerben
will, und auch werben
um sein Kindelein fein.
Der Zunft ein bied'rer Meister,
wohl sein' Tochter er liebt,
doch zugleich auch beweist er,
was er auf die Kunst gibt:

Beckmessers Werbe-M.

zum Preise muß es bringen
im Meistersingen,
wer sein Eidam will sein.

Kreidestrich-M., Erregtheitstriller, Ärger-M. (in B. Stimme)

Er stampft wütend mit den Füßen.

Nun gilt es Kunst,
daß mit Vergunst,

Beckmessers Werbe-M., Kreidestrich-M., Erregtheitstriller

ohn' all' schädlich gemeinen Dunst
ihm glücke des Preises Gewunst,
wer begehrt, mit wahrer Inbrunst,

Sachs, welcher kopfschüttelnd es aufgibt, die einzelnen Fehler anzumerken, arbeitet hämmernd fort, um den Keil aus dem Leisten zu schlagen.

Act 2, Scene 6 – Do't not!

> I must, be quick!
> *shaking his fist round the corner at Sachs.*

Beckmesser's courtship motif (in the lute), resentment motif

Sachs, I'll remember this spiteful trick!
He prepares for the second verse.

Sachs

(brandishing his hammer)

Marker at hand:
take your stand!

chalk stroke motif

Beckmesser

(getting louder and more breathless)
„This morning my heart light is,
(Sachs strikes with the hammer)

lute motif, Beckmesser's song, chalk stroke motif

when I look upon,
her father, as his right is
makes one condition
for him who would his heir be
and eke his pair be
of his daughter so sweet.

Beckmesser's courtship motif

His daughter he well loveth,
a Master renowned here,
and at the same time proveth,
that to him art is dear:
the prize first must he bring her,
as Mastersinger,
who'd be a wooer fit.

Beckmesser's courtship motif

He stamps his feet with rage.

Now art is, quoth,
he, what here go'th,

chalk stroke motif, excitement trill, anger motif (in B. Stimme)

free from common and empty froth
as prizeman must he plight his troth
who desires, with a heart unloth,

Beckmesser's courtship motif, chalk stroke motif, excitement trill

Sachs, shaking his head, gives up marking the separate faults, but hammers on to knock the key out of the last.

um die Jungfrau zu frein!" –

SACHS

Unmut-M.,
Schaffenslust-M.

(über den Laden weit herausgelehnt)
Seid ihr nun fertig?

BECKMESSER

(in höchster Angst)
Wie fraget ihr?

SACHS

hält die fertigen Schuhe triumphierend heraus:
Mit den Schuhen ward ich fertig schier. –
während er die Schuhe an den Bändern hoch in der Luft tanzen läßt:

Schusterlied

Das heiß' ich mir echte Merkerschuh':
mein Merkersprüchlein hört dazu! –
(sehr kräftig)

Kreidestrich-M. (in der Singstimme)

Mit lang' und kurzen Hieben
steht's auf der Sohl' geschrieben:

BECKMESSER

der sich ganz in die Gasse zurückgezogen hat und an die Mauer mit dem Rücken sich anlehnt, singt, um Sachs zu übertäuben, mit größter Anstrengung, schreiend und atemlos hastig, während er die Laute wütend nach Sachs zu schwingt.

Beckmessers Ständchen

„Darf ich mich Meister nennen,
das bewähr' ich heut gern,
weil ich nach dem Preis brennen
muß, dursten und hungern.

SACHS

Beckmessers Ständchen

da lest es klar,
und nehmt es wahr,
und merkt's euch immerdar.
Gut Lied will Takt:

Act 2, Scene 6 – Do't not!

as spouse the maid to greet!" –

SACHS

(leaning far out over his door)
        Now have you finished?

resentment motif,
work lust motif

BECKMESSER

(in anguish)
        Why ask you now?

SACHS

holds out the completed shoes in triumph:

With the shoes my work is done, I trow. –
as he dances the shoes high in the air by the strings.

That pair now I call good Marker's shoon:
my Marker's motto hear thereon! –

(very loud)

By long and short strokes beaten,
upon your sole 'tis written:

cobbler's song

chalk stroke motif (in the voice)

BECKMESSER

who has retreated quite into the alley, leans his back against the wall and, to drown Sachs's voice, sings with the greatest vigor, shrieking and breathlessly hurrying, while he shakes the lute at Sachs.

„That I Master was duly,
chosen, I'd shew to her;
to win the prize I truly
burn with thirst and hunger.

Beckmesser's song

SACHS

its truth is sure,
now con it o'er,
and hold it evermore.
Let verses' feet:

Beckmesser's song

199

The Mastersingers of Nuremberg

Beckmessers Ständchen
 Kreidestrich-M. (in der Singstimme)

wer den verzwackt,
dem Schreiber mit der Feder
haut ihn der Schuster aufs Leder. –

BECKMESSER

Beckmessers Werbe-M.

Nun ruf' ich die neun Musen,
daß an sie blusen
mein' dicht'rischen Verstand.
Wohl kenn' ich alle Regeln,
halte gut Maß und Zahl;
doch Sprung und Überkegeln

Beckmessers Werbe-M.

wohl passiert je einmal,
wann der Kopf ganz voll Zagen,
zu frein will wagen
um jung Mägdeleins Hand.

DAVID

hat den Fensterladen, dicht hinter Beckmesser, ein wenig geöffnet und lugt daraus hervor:

Wer Teufel hier? –
Er wird Magdalene gewahr.
             Und drüben gar?
Die Lene ist's, –
           ich seh' es klar!
Herr Je! der war's!
             Den hat sie bestellt.
Der ist's, der ihr besser als ich gefällt!

NACHBARN

erst einige, dann immer mehre, öffnen in der Gasse die Fenster und gucken heraus.

Wer heult denn da? –
           Wer kreischt mit Macht? –
Ist das erlaubt so spät zur Nacht?

SACHS

Nun lauft in Ruh':
habt gute Schuh',
der Fuß euch drin nicht knackt,

Act 2, Scene 6 – Do't not!

fit music's beat,
and lest your pen forget it
upon your shoes I have set it. –

BECKMESSER

The nine Muses I summon,
that they may come on
and my attainments prove.
I've all rules conned profoundly,
measure and beat I know;
and if my song goes roundly
some slips may be let go,
if with heart full of terrors,
he make some errors
who seeks for a maid's love.

DAVID

has opened the window-shutter a little, just behind Beckmesser and peeps out:

Now, who is here? –

He recognizes Magdalene.

            And who up there?
'Tis Lene, sure! –
            I see, 'tis clear!
Good Lord, 'twas he!
            So, she bade him come.
Then she likes him better than me as groom!

NEIGHBOURS

first a few, then more and more, open the windows in the alley and look out.

Who howls then there? –
            Who cries so loud? –
So late at night, is that allowed?

SACHS

Now take your road;
you're rightly shod:
these shoes will fit your feet,

Beckmesser's song

chalk stroke motif (in his voice)

Beckmesser's courtship motif

Beckmesser's courtship motif

The Mastersingers of Nuremberg

Beckmessers Ständchen

ihn hält die Sohl' im Takt! Takt! Takt!

BECKMESSER

verschnauft sich.

Ärger-M.

Beckmessers Werbe-M.

Ein Junggesell',
trug ich mein Fell,
mein' Ehr', Amt, Würd' und Brot zur Stell',
daß euch mein Gesang wohl gefäll',
und mich das Jungfräulein erwähl',
wenn sie mein Lied gut fand." –

DAVID

Nun warte, du kriegst's!
                            Dir streich' ich das Fell!
Er entfernt sich nach innen.

NACHBARN

Gebt Ruhe hier! – 's ist Schlafenszeit. –
Mein', hört nur, wie dort der Esel schreit! –
Ihr da, seid still und schert euch fort! –
Heult, kreischt und schreit an andrem Ort!

Magdalene winkt, da sie David wiederkommen sieht, diesem heftig zurück, was Beckmesser als Zeichen des Mißfallens deutend, zur äußersten Verzweiflung im Gesangsausdrucke bringt.

Act 2, Scene 6 – Do't not!

their soles will mark the beat! beat! beat! — *Beckmesser's song*

BECKMESSER

out of breath.

For, by the muse — *anger motif*
my skin I'd lose,
my office, rank, the goods I use, — *Beckmesser's*
that you the prize shall not refuse, — *courtship motif*
and me the young damsel should choose,
if she my song approve." –

DAVID

Wait till I begin!
      I'll polish your skin!

He goes in.

NEIGHBOURS

Keep quiet, there! – 'Tis sleeping time. –
Ah, hear but how the donkey brays! –
You there! Be still and get you gone! –
Howl, cry and bray some otherwhere!

Magdalene, seeing David return, makes urgent signs to him to go away, which Beckmesser interprets as signs of displeasure, and his singing expresses his despair.

7. Szene – Ach, Himmel! David!

Sachs beobachtet noch eine Zeitlang den wachsenden Tumult, löscht aber alsbald sein Licht aus und schließt den Laden so weit, daß er, ungesehen, stets durch eine kleine Öffnung den Platz unter der Linde beobachten kann. –

Walther und Eva sehen mit wachsender Sorge dem anschwellenden Auflaufe zu; er schließt sie in seinen Mantel fest an sich und birgt sich hart an der Linde im Gebüsch, so daß beide fast ungesehen bleiben. –

Die Nachbarn verlassen die Fenster und kommen nach und nach in Nachtkleidern einzeln auf die Straße herab.

David

ist, mit einem Knüppel bewaffnet, zurückgekommen, steigt aus dem Fenster und wirft sich nun auf Beckmesser.

Lebhaftigkeit-M. — Zum Teufel mit dir, verdammter Kerl!   KA 365 ▸ 1357
CD 2/17 1:17

Beckmesser wehrt sich, will fliehen; David hält ihn am Kragen.

Magdalene

(am Fenster, schreiend)

Prügel-M. — Ach, Himmel! David! Gott, welche Not!
Zu Hilfe! Zu Hilfe! Sie schlagen sich tot!

Scene 7 – Oh, heaven! David!

Sachs watches for a time the growing tumult, but soon puts out his light and so far closes his door that, unseen, he can watch the place under the lime tree through a small opening. –

Walther and Eva observe the gathering uproar with growing anxiety; he folds her in his cloak and holds her close to himself, hiding carefully in the foliage under the lime tree so that both remain almost unperceived. –

The neighbours leave the windows and come one by one to the street in their night clothes.

David

comes back, armed with a cudgel, climbs out of the window and throws himself on Beckmesser.

VS 318▶1
CD 2/17 1:17 The devil take your song, you cursed rogue! *livelihood motif*

Beckmesser defends himself, tries to fly; David holds him by the collar.

Magdalene

(at the window, crying out)

Oh, Heaven! David! Lord, what ill luck!
Oh, stop them. They both will be killed!   *beating motif*

BECKMESSER

Prügel-M.

(zu David)
Verfluchter Bursch! Läßt du mich los?

DAVID

Gewiß! Die Glieder brech' ich dir bloß!

Beckmesser und David balgen sich fortwährend; bald verschwinden sie gänzlich, bald kommen sie wieder in den Vordergrund, immer Beckmesser auf der Flucht, David ihn einholend, festhaltend und prügelnd.

NACHBARN

(an den Fenstern)

Seht nach! – Springt zu! –
          Da würgen sich zwei! –

Sie kommen herab, in die Gasse laut schreiend.

Heda! Herbei! 's gibt Schlägerei.
Da würgen sich zwei.

LEHRBUBEN

Einzeln, dann mehr, kommen von allen Seiten dazu.

Herbei! Herbei! 's gibt Keilerei! –
'sind die Schuster! –
          Nein, 'sind die Schneider! –
Die Trunkenbolde! – Die Hungerleider! –

NACHBARN

Ihr da! Laßt los! Gebt freien Lauf! –
Laßt ihr nicht los, wir schlagen drauf! –

MAGDALENE

Ach, Himmel! Welche Not!
Zu Hilfe! – David! –
          Sie schlagen sich tot! –
David, bist Du toll? –
          Himmel, welche Not!

Act 2, Scene 7 – Oh, heaven! David!

BECKMESSER

(to David) — *beating motif*

Accursed knave! Let me go free?

DAVID

Not yet, till I have broken your bones!

Beckmesser and David continue to wrestle. Now they disappear entirely, now they appear again in the foreground, Beckmesser always attempting to fly and David catching him again, holding him and beating him.

NEIGHBOURS

(at the windows)

Look out! – Come on! –
              There two are at blows! –

They are coming down, calling into the alley loudly.

Halloa! Come on! There's fighting here:
and two are at blows.

PRENTICES

A few, then more, come on from different sides.

Come on! Come on! They're fighting here! –
'Tis the cobblers! –
                  No, 'tis the tailors! –
The drunken wretches! – The staving beggars! –

NEIGHBOURS

Yet there, let go! Now let him go! –
Let go your hold or we fall to! –

MAGDALENE

Oh, Heaven! What ill luck!
Oh, stop them! – David! –
              They both will be killed! –
David, art thou mad? –
                Heaven, what ill luck!

The Mastersingers of Nuremberg

Prügel-M.   Sie schlagen sich noch tot!

NACHBARINNEN

(welche die Fenster geöffnet haben, herausguckend)

Was ist das für Zanken und Streit?
Da gibt's gewiß noch Schlägerei?
Wär' nur der Vater nicht dabei! –
Da ist mein Mann gewiß dabei! –
Ach, welche Not! –
Mein' seht nur dort! – Mein' seht nur hier! –
Der Zank und Lärm! – Der Lärm und Streit! –
's wird einem wahrlich angst und bang!
Heda! Ihr dort unten,
    so seid doch nur gescheit! –
Ei hört, was will die Alte da? –
Seid ihr alle denn nur immer gleich
    zu Streit und Zank bereit?
    So seit doch nur gescheit!

LEHRBUBEN

(von allen Seiten, durcheinander)

Kennt man die Schlosser nicht,
die haben's sicher angericht'! –
Ich glaub', die Schmiede werden's sein. –
Nein, 'sind die Schlosser dort, ich wett'. –
Ich kenn' die Schreiner dort –
Gewiß, die Metzger sind's! –
Hei! Schaut die Schäffler dort beim Tanz! –
Dort seh' die Bader ich im Glanz;
herbei zum Tanz! –
Herbei, herbei, jetzt geht's zum Tanz! –
Immer mehr! 's gibt große Keilerei! –

(jubelnd)

Krämer finden sich zur Hand
mit Gerstenstang' und Zuckerkand;
mit Pfeffer, Zimt, Muskatennuß,
sie riechen schön, doch machen viel Verdruß;
sie riechen schön

Act 2, Scene 7 – Oh, heaven! David!

[3] At last they both be killed!

WOMEN

(have opened the windows and look out)

[1] What is all this brawling and strife?
There's surely fighting close at hand?
If only father were not there! –
My husband surely will be there! –
Ah, what ill luck! –
Ah, look ye there! – Ah, look ye here! –
The strife and noise! – The noise and strife! –
[2] It truly freezes up the blood!
Listen, you below there!
              do have some little sense! –
Now hear! What wants the old one there? –
[3] Are ye then forever all alike,
              so ready for a fight?
              Do have some little sense!

PRENTICES

(from all sides, in confusion)

[1] We know the locksmiths;
surely they have set this brawl afoot! –
I trow the smiths have set it on. –
No, 'tis the locksmiths, I am sure. –
I know the joiners there –
I see the butchers there! –
Hey! See the coopers in the dance! –
I know the barbers at a glance;
[2] they join the dance! –
Come on, come on, and join the dance! –
Still they come! They 'reat it tooth and nail! –
(joyously)
[3] Grocers too, a timid band
with barley-sugar sticks in hand;
with peppercorns and cinnamon!
Tho' good they smell, yet till they oft have done;
Though good they smell

beating motif

Prügel-M. und bleiben gern vom Schuß.

Gesellen

(mit Knitteln bewaffnet, von verschiedenen Seiten dazu)

Heda! Gesellen 'ran!
Dort wird mit Streit und Zank getan;
da gibt's gewiß noch Schlägerei;
Gesellen, haltet euch dabei!
's sind die Weber! – 's sind die Gerber! –
Die Preisverderber! –
Dacht ich mir's doch gleich:
spielen immer Streich' –
Wischt's ihnen aus! – Gebt's denen scharf!
Immer mehr! Die Keilerei wird groß! –
Dort den Metzger Klaus
kenn' ich heraus!
's ist morgen der Fünfte!
      's brennt manchem im Haus!

Nachbarn

(durcheinander, sich stoßend, dann schlagend)

Gleich auseinander da, ihr Leut'! –
Ei seht, auch ihr hier? –
Was sucht ihr hier? –
Geht's euch was an? –
Hat man euch was getan? –
Euch kennt man gut. –
Euch noch viel besser. –
Wieso denn? – Ei, so! –
Esel! – Dummrian! –
Euch gönnt' ich's schon lange! –
Wird euch wohl bange? –
Das für die Klage! –
Lümmel! Seht euch vor, wenn ich schlage! –
Hat euch die Frau gehetzt? –
Schaut, wie es Prügel setzt! –
Lümmel! – Grobian! –
Seid ihr noch nicht gewitzt? –
Nun, schlagt doch! – Das sitzt! –

Act 2, Scene 7 – Oh, heaven! David!

              yet fain they would be gone.   *beating motif*

JOURNEYMEN

(armed with clubs, come on from different sides)

[1] What ho, companions here!
The sound of strife and blows I hear;
Come on, there's fighting close at hand;
ye journeymen, come take your stand!
[2] 'Tis the weavers! – 'Tis the tanners! –
The bargain-spoilers! –
'Tis then as I thought:
ever at their games' –
Now tan them well! – Hit true and hard!
Still they come, the fight is getting hot! –
[3] There is butcher Klaus
plainly I see!
The fifth is tomorrow!
              Then guard you from fire!

NEIGHBOURS

(in confusion, poking each other, then fighting)

[1] At once let one another go! –
How now? What you here? –
What seek you here? –
What's that to you? –
What have they done to you? –
All know you well. –
They know you better. –
[2] How so, then? – Well, so! –
Donkey! – Stupid! –
That long have I owed you! –
Are you afraid, then? –
That for the payment! –
Blockhead! Have a care if I strike you! –
What! Has your wife been cross? –
See how the cudgel falls! –
Blockhead! – Stupid! –
[3] What, not yet found your wits –
Lay on then! – Take that! –

Prügel-M.	Daß dich Halunken gleich ein Donnerwetter träf'!
	MEISTER[1]
	(und älteren Bürger, von verschiedenen Seiten)
Beckmessers Ständchen	Was gibt's denn da für Zank und Streit? Das tost ja weit und breit! Gebt Ruh' und schert euch jeder gleich nach Hause heim,
	MAGDALENE
	(mit größter Anstrengung) Hör doch nur, David! So laß doch nur den Herrn dort los, er hat mir nichts getan! So hör mich doch nur an!
	GESELLEN Herbei! – Hei! Hier setzt's Prügel! – Schneider mit dem Bügel! – Zünfte heraus! – Heut' ist der Fünfte! – 's brennt manchem im Haus! – Nur tüchtig drauf und dran, wir schlagen los! Ihr da, macht! Packt euch fort! – Wir sind hier grad' am Ort! Wolltet ihr etwa den Weg uns hier verwehren? – Macht Platz, wir schlagen drein! – Macht ihr euch selber fort! – Gürtler! – Spengler! – Zinngießer! Leimsieder! – Lichtsieder!
	NACHBARN
	(auf der Gasse durcheinander) Daß dich Halunke! – Wartet, ihr Racker! – Maßabzwacker! –

---

[1] *Die Meister singen nun, unterstützt von Fagotten, Hörnern und Kontrabässen, das Motiv des Beckmesserständchens. Diese Basslinie bietet eine gute Orientierung im allgemeinen Stimmengewirr.*

Act 2, Scene 7 – Oh, heaven! David!

You rascal, let me
catch you then I pay you out!   *beating motif*

MASTERS[1]

(and older citizens arrive from various sides)

What is this sound of brawl and strife?   *Beckmesser's song*
It sounds from far and near!
Now peace! At once
betake yourselves towards your beds,

MAGDALENE

(with great effort)

Hear me now, David!
and let the marker there go free,
he has not done me harm!
Nay, do but hear me speak!

JOURNEYMEN

Come on! – Hey! There go cudgels! –
Tailors with their measures! –
Guilds come ye on! –
Today is the fifth! –
　　　　Then guard you from fire! –
Now gaily let us go and join the fray!
Hallo there, get you gone! –
We get here just in time!
What, would you, then, block
the way by force against us? –
Make room, we come to fight! –
You, clear away yourselves! –
Girdlers! – Tinkers! – Pewterers! –
Glue-boilers! – Wax-boilers!

NEIGHBOURS

(on the alley, in confusion)

What you, you scoundrel! –
Wait there, you rascal! –
Short-weight swindlers! –

---

[1] *The Masters are now singing the motif of the Beckmesser song, supported by bassoons, horns and contrabasses. This bass line provides a good orientation in the general tumult of the voices.*

Prügel-M. Euch gönnt' ich's lang'! –
Racker! – Zwacker! – Wird euch bang? –
Wollt ihr noch mehr? –
Packt euch jetzt heim,
sonst kriegt ihr's von der Frau! –
Geht's euch was an, wenn ich nicht will? –
Was geht's euch an, wenn mir's gefällt? –
Auf, schert euch heim! –
Schickt die Gesellen heim! –
So gut wie ihr bin Meister ich! –
Dummer Kerl – Macht euch fort!

Lehrbuben

Meinst du damit etwa mich? – Halt's Maul! –
Mein' ich damit etwa dich? – Hei! Das sitzt.
Seht nur, der Has'!
Hat überall die Nas'! –
Immer mehr heran! –
Jetzt fängt's erst richtig an! –
Lustig, wacker! Jetzt geht's erst recht an! –
Nur immer heran zu uns! –
Hei! Nun geht's Plauz
hast du nicht gesehn! –
Hast's auf die Schnauz'! –
Ha, nun geht's: Krach!
Hagelwetterschlag! –

Magdalene

Ach! Welche Not!
David! So hör' doch nur einmal!
  (hinabspähend)
Herr Gott, er hält ihn noch!

Nachbarinnen

Mein'! Dort schlägt sich mein Mann! –
Ach! Gott! Säh' ich nur meinen Hans! –
Sind die Köpf' vom Wein euch voll? –
Säh' die Not ich wohl an? –
Ach, sieht man die an?
Seid ihr alle blind und toll? –

Act 2, Scene 7 – Oh, heaven! David!

I've owed that long! –
② Rascal! – Scoundrel! – What, afraid? –
Would you have more? –
Now get you home,
you'll catch it from your wife! –
③ What's that to you, if I don't go? –
What's that to you, if I'm content? –
Up, get you home! –
Send home the journeymen! –
As Master I'm as good as you! –
Stupid ass! – Get you gone!

beating motif

PRENTICES

① Dost thou mean to speak to me? – Be still! –
Do I mean to speak to thee? – Hei! That hit.
See that one there!
② his nose is everywhere! –
Still they're coming on! –
Now first the fun begins! –
Gaily, bravely! Now the fun begins! –
③ Let more and more come on to help! –
Hei! there goes! Crack!
didst thou see it too! –
One for your snout! –
Ha! there goes! Crack!
like a thunder-clap! –

MAGDALENE

① Ah! What ill luck!
② David! But once hear me speak!
(looking below)
③ Good Lord, he holds him still!

WOMEN

There! My man's in the fight! –
① Ah! God! Could I see but my Hans! –
Are your heads all full of wine? –
Oh, alack, what a sight? –
Ah, look, what a sight?
Are ye, then, all gone mad? –

Prügel-M.

Sind euch vom Wein die Köpfe voll? –
Seht dort den Christian,
er walkt den Peter ab! –
Mein'! Dort den Michel seht,
der haut dem Steffen eins! –
Hilfe! Der Vater! Der Vater!
Ach, sie haun ihn tot! –
Jesus! Sie schlagen meinen Jungen tot! –
Jesus! Der Hans hat einen Hieb am Kopf! –
Peter! So höre doch! –
Hans! Ei, so höre doch! –
Gott! Wie sie walken,
wie sie wackeln hin und her! –
Gott steh' uns bei, geht das so weiter fort! –
Gott! Welche Höllennot! –
Hört keines mehr sein Wort! –
Hei! Mein Mann schlägt wacker auf sie drein!

MEISTER

Beckmessers Ständchen

sonst schlag' ein Hageldonnerwetter drein!
Schert euch gleich nach Hause heim!
Ei, so schlag' ein heil'ges
    Hageldonnerwetter drein,
wollt ihr nicht gleich nach Hause heim!
Jetzt schert euch gleich nach Hause heim!
Ei, so schlag' das Donnerwetter drein!
Schert ihr euch nicht gleich nach Hause heim,

MAGDALENE

Mein'! David, ist er toll?
Ah! – Ah! David, hör:
's ist Herr Beckmesser!

NACHBARINNEN

Gott, welche Not! –
Hört keines mehr sein Wort! –
Die Köpf' und Zöpfe wackeln hin und her! –
Franz, sei doch nur gescheit! –
Ach, wie soll das enden? –
Welches Toben! Welches Krachen! –
Gott steh' uns bei, geht das so weiter fort! –

Act 2, Scene 7 – Oh, heaven! David!

[2] Are all your heads, then, still so full of wine? –
Look there at Christian,
beating Peter black and blue! –
My! Look at Michael there!
His club gave Stephen one! –   *beating motif*
[3] Help, for my father! My father!
Ah, they'll murder him! –
Lord! I am certain they will kill my boy! –
Murder! My Hans has got a broken head! –
Peter! Now hear me speak! –
Hans! Hear me speak to thee! –
Lord! How they wrestle,
how they stagger to and fro! –
Lord save us all, if this cannot be stopped! –
Lord! What accursed ill luck! –
My voice I cannot hear! –
Hei! My husband boldly joins the fight!

Masters

[1] or blows will rain like hailstones on your heads!   *Beckmesser's song*
Now at once betake you home!
[2] Ei, then let the blows now rain
            like hailstones on your heads,
or go directly to your beds!
Now get you all at once to bed!
Blows will rain like hailstones on your heads!
Now at once betake you to your beds,

Magdalene

[1] Ha! David, art thou mad?
[2] Ah! – Ah! David, hear
me! 'Tis Beckmesser!

Women

[1] Lord, what ill luck! –
Not one her voice can hear! –
The heads and pigtails waggle up and down! –
Franz, have a little sense! –
Ah how will it finish? –
What a hubbub! What a clatter! –
Lord save us now, if this cannot be stayed! –

The Mastersingers of Nuremberg

Prügel-M.
So hört doch! –
Schon hört man nicht sein eigen Wort! –
Auf, schaffet Wasser her!
Da gießt's auf die Köpf' hinab! –
Wasser ist das allerbest' für ihre Wut:
schafft's nur her!
Auf, schreit um Hilfe: Mord und Zeter, herbei!

Nachbarn

Schert doch ihr euch selber fort! –
Schert euch heim! – Macht euch fort! –
Haltet's Maul! Wir weichen nicht! –
Keiner weiche! –
Tuchscherer! – Leinweber! –
Schlagt sie nieder! –
Stemmt euch hier nicht mehr zuhauf,
oder sonst wir schlagen drein! –
Immer 'ran! Wacker zu! –

Gesellen

Schert euch selber fort –
Wir sind grad' am Ort! –
Nicht gewichen! –
Schlagt sie nieder! Keiner weiche! –
Tuchscherer! Leinweber! –
Immer 'ran! – Wacker zu! – Immer drauf! –
Immer 'ran, wer's noch wagt! –
Schlagt's ihn' hin! – Haltet's Maul! –
Schert euch fort, hier geht's los!
Wir schlagen drauf! Scher' sich jeder heim!
Immer drauf! – Immer drauf und dran! –
Zünfte! Zünfte! Heraus! –
Jetzt gilt's: keiner weiche hier! –
Zünfte heraus!

Meister

Beckmessers Ständchen
schlag' ein Donnerwetter drein!
Stemmt euch hier nicht mehr zuhauf',
oder sonst wir schlagen drein!

218

Act 2, Scene 7 – Oh, heaven! David!

② Now hear me! –
In vain! not one her voice can hear! –
Up! bring us water here,
and pour on their heads below! –
Water is the best of things to cool their rage:
bring it here!
③ Up, call the warder: cry out murder and fire!

beating motif

NEIGHBOURS

① Get you home yourselves! –
Get you home! – Get you gone! –
Hold your noise! We won't give way! –
Never waver! –
② Cloth-cutters! – Flax-weavers! –
Knock them over! –
Do not crowd together there
or we too a part will bear! –
Come ye on! Boldly on! –

JOURNEYMEN

① Get you gone yourselves–
We are just in time! –
Do not waver! –
Knock them over! Never waver! –
② Cloth-cutters! Flax-weavers! –
Come ye on! – Boldly on! – Come ye on! –
Come you on, if you dare! –
③ Give it him! – Hold your noise! –
Get you gone, here we come!
We join the fray! Get you home to bed!
Come ye on! – Keep the fight alive! –
Comrades! Guilds, come ye on! –
'Tis well: Do not waver now! –
Guilds, come ye on!

MASTERS

① blows will' rain upon your heads!
② Do not crowd together there,
or we too a part will bear!

Beckmesser's song

219

Prügel-M.

Beckmessers Ständchen

MEISTER UND NACHBARN

Scher sich jeder gleich nach Hause heim!

LEHRBUBEN

Wo es sitzt, da wächst nichts so bald nach! –
Wo es sitzt, da fleckt's, da wächst kein Gras
so bald nicht wieder nach! –
Der hat's gekriegt! –
Jetzt fährt's hinein wie Hagelschlag!
Bald setzt es blut'ge Köpf', Arm' und Bein'!
Dort der Pfister denkt daran:
hei! Der hat's! –
Der hat genug! –
Scher sich jeder heim, wer nicht mit keilt! –
Tüchtig gekeilt! –

POGNER

ist im Nachtgewand oben an das Fenster getreten:

Um Gott! Eva! Schließ zu!
Ich seh', ob unt' im Hause Ruh'!

Er zieht Magdalenen, welche jammernd die Hände nach der Gasse hinab gerungen, herein und schließt das Fenster.

WALTHER

der bisher mit Eva sich hinter dem Gebüsch verborgen, faßt jetzt Eva dicht in den linken Arm und zieht mit der rechten Hand das Schwert.

Jetzt gilt's zu wagen,
sich durchzuschlagen!

Er dringt mit geschwungenem Schwerte bis in die Mitte der Bühne vor, um sich mit Eva durch die Gasse durchzuhauen.

Da springt Sachs mit einem kräftigen Satze aus dem Laden, bahnt sich mit geschwungenem Knieriemen Weg bis zu Walther und packt diesen beim Arm.

Act 2, Scene 7 – Oh, heaven! David!

MASTERS AND NEIGHBOURS

[3] Get you home at once and go to bed!

beating motif

PRENTICES

Beckmesser's song

[1] Where that fell, the hair won't grow so soon! –
Where that falls it marks, the hair won't grow
upon the place so soon! –
He had one there! –
[2] Like hail stones now the blows come down!
There'll soon be bloody heads, arms and legs!
There the baker thinks it out:
ha! he's down! –
[3] He has enough! –
Let all get them home who will not fight! –
On to the fray! –

POGNER

appears in his nightgown at the window above:

[1] How now! Eva! Come in!
I'll see below if all is safe!

> *He draws Magdalene, who is wringing her hands in distress towards the alley, into the room and closes the window.*

WALTHER

> *who until now has hidden himself with Eva behind the foliage, clasps her in his left arm and with his right hand draws his sword.*

[2] Now comes the time, let
us win our freedom!

> *He presses with drawn sword to the middle of the stage, to cut a way for himself with Eva through the alley.*

> *Sachs thereupon makes a vigorous rush from his door, clears a way to Walther by swinging his stirrup and seizes him by the arm.*

Prügel-M.

Beckmessers Ständchen

Meister und Nachbarn

Gebt Ruh' und scher sich jeder heim!
Sonst schlagen wir Meister
                selbst noch drein!
Jetzt hilft nichts, Meister!
                Schlagt selbst drein!

Nachbarinnen

Schreiet Mord und Zeter!
Wasser her! Auf, schafft nur Wasser her
und gießt's den bösen Buben auf die Köpf'!
Immer toller, wie sie lärmen, toben, schlagen!
Hier hilft einzig Wasser noch!
Hier ans Fenster! –
Hier, an die Fenster her, bringt Wasser nur,
sonst schlagen sie sich tot! – Ah! –
Topf und Hafen! Krug und Kanne,
alles voll, und gießt's ihn' auf den Kopf!

    Die Rauferei ist allgemein geworden, Schreien und Toben.

Lehrbuben

Immer lustig! Heisa, lustig!
Keilt euch wacker! Keiner weiche!
Haltet selbst Gesellen mutig stand!
Wer wich, 's wär' wahrlich eine Schand'!
Hei! Juche!
Immer lustig! Nicht gewichen!
Wacker drauf und dran!
Wir stehen alle wie ein Mann!
Wie ein Mann stehn wir
alle fest zur Keilerei!

Gesellen

Zünfte! Zünfte heraus! –
Jetzt gilt's: keiner weiche hier! –
Alle Zünfte raus! Zünfte!
Zünfte! Heraus!

Act 2, Scene 7 – Oh, heaven! David!

MASTERS AND NEIGHBOURS — *beating motif*
1. Be still, and all at once go home! — *Beckmesser's song*
If not, then we Masters
                    join the fray!
2. Now nought helps, Masters!
                    Join the fray!

WOMEN
1. Cry out murder fire!
Water here! Up, bring ye water here
and pour it on the hot-brained fellows' heads!
Ever madder grows their riot, wrangling, fighting!
Water is our only help!
To the window! –
2. Here, to the window bring us water here,
or they will all be killed! – Ah! –
Bowls and buckets! Pots and pitchers,
fill them full and pour upon their heads!

 The row has become general. Shrieks and blows.

PRENTICES
Ever merry! Hei, be merry!
fight ye bravely! Never waver!
Hold your own though journeymen should come!
If you give way 'twould be a shame!
Hei! Hurrah!
2. Ever merry! Do not waver!
Strike with might and main!
All stand together like one man!
Like one man stand we all,
and fight with might and main!

JOURNEYMEN
2. Comrades! Guilds come ye on! –
'Tis well: do not waver here! –
All the guilds come out!
Comrades! Comrades! Come out!

Nachtwächter

Bläst auf dem Horn. Sogleich mit dem Eintritte des Nachtwächterhornes (3/4 Takt) haben die Frauen aus allen Fenstern starke Güsse von Wasser aus Kannen, Krügen und Becken auf die Streitenden herabstürzen lassen; dieses, mit den besonders starken Tönen des Hornes zugleich, wirkt auf alle mit einem panischen Schrecken: Nachbarn, Lehrbuben, Gesellen und Meister suchen in eiliger Flucht nach allen Seiten hin das Weite, so daß die Bühne sehr bald gänzlich leer wird; die Haustüren werden hastig geschlossen; auch die Nachbarinnen verschwinden von den Fenstern, welche sie zuschlagen.

Pogner

Sommernachtzauber-M.

(auf der Treppe)

He! Lene! Wo bist du?

KA 394 ▸ 1441
CD 2/17 3:15

Sachs

die halb ohnmächtige Eva die Treppe hinaufstoßend:

Ins Haus, Jungfer Lene!

Prügel-M. (sich beruhigend)

Pogner empfängt Eva und zieht sie in das Haus. Sachs, mit dem Knieriemen David eines überhauend und mit einem Fußtritt ihn voran in den Laden stoßend, zieht Walther, den er mit der andren Hand fest gefaßt hält, gewaltsam schnell ebenfalls mit sich hinein und schließt sogleich fest hinter sich zu. –

Prügel-M., Beckmessers Ständchen

Beckmesser, durch Sachs von David befreit, sucht sich, jämmerlich zerschlagen, eilig durch die Menge zu flüchten.

Lebhaftigkeit-M. (ruhiger), Prügel-M., Erregtheitstriller

Als die Straße und Gasse leer geworden und alle Häuser geschlossen sind, betritt der Nachtwächter im Vordergrunde rechts die Bühne, reibt sich die Augen, sieht sich verwundert um, schüttelt den Kopf und stimmt, mit leise bebender Stimme, den Ruf an:

Act 2, Scene 7 – Oh, heaven! David!

NIGHT-WATCHMAN

> *Blows his horn. At the moment of the night-warder's entrance (3/4 time) the women pour out of all windows, from cans jugs and basins, copious streams of water down on to the fighters; this, together with the very loud tone of the horn produces a general panic. Neighbors, Prentices, Journeymen and Masters fly in all directions, so that the stage very soon becomes empty; the doors are closed hastily; the women also disappear and close the windows.*

POGNER

    (on the steps)   } *summer night's*

VS 347▸3
CD 2/17 3:15   Ho! Lene! Where art thou?   } *magic motif*

SACHS

    pushing the almost fainting Eva up the steps:

Go in, mistress Lene!

> *Pogner receives Evan and pulls her by the arm* } *beating motif*
> *into the house. Sachs giving David a stroke* } *(calming down)*
> *with his stirrup and, sending him into the shop*
> *by a kick, draws Walther, whom he has seized*
> *with his other hand, quickly and forcibly with*
> *him into the house which he immediately clos-*
> *es behind him. –*

> *Beckmesser, freed from David by Sachs woe-* } *beating motif,*
> *fully battered, hastily tries to escape through* } *Beckmesser's song*
> *the crowd.*

> *When the street and alley are empty and all* } *livelihood motif*
> *the houses are closed, the night-warder enters* } *(ruhiger), beating*
> *on the right side of the front of the stage, rubs* } *motif, excitement trill*
> *his eyes, looks around in surprise, shakes his*
> *head and sings his verse with a tremulous*
> *voice:*

The Mastersingers of Nuremberg

Lebhaftigkeit-M. (ruhig)

Erregtheitstriller

Sommernachtzauber-M., Prügel-M. (scherzohaft), Lebhaftigkeit-M. (ruhig), Beckmessers Ständchen (mit nachklingender Liebessehnsucht-Sequenz daraus, vor dem Schlussakkord)

Der Nachtwächter

Hört, ihr Leut', und laßt euch sagen,
die Glock' hat eilfe geschlagen:
bewahrt euch vor Gespenstern und Spuk,
daß kein böser Geist eu'r Seel' beruck'!
Lobet Gott, den Herrn!

Hornruf.

Der Vollmond tritt hervor und scheint hell in die Gasse hinein; der Nachtwächter schreitet langsam dieselbe hinab.

Als der Nachtwächter um die Ecke biegt, fällt der Vorhang schnell, genau mit dem letzten Takte.

KA 396 ▶ 1456
CD 2/17 3:53

Act 2, Scene 7 – Oh, heaven! David!

Night-watchman

VS 349 ▶ 4
CD 2/17 3:53

Hear, all folk, the warder's ditty,
eleven strikes in our city:
defend yourselves from spectre and sprite,
that no evil imp your souls affright!
Praise ye God, the Lord!

livelihood motif (calm)

Horn call.

The full moon comes out, and shines brightly into the alley, down which the Night-watchman slowly walks;

As the Night-watchman turns the corner, the curtain falls quickly exactly with the last chord.

summer night's magic motif, beating motif (as a scherzo), livelihood motif (calm), Beckmesser's song (with an echo of its love-longing sequence, just before the final chord)

Wahn-M.,
Wach auf Choral,
Schusterlied¹,
(Tristanmotive),
Taufspruch-M. (Sachs),
Wach auf Choral
(Schluss),
Wahn-M.

3. AUFZUG

1. SZENE – GLEICH, MEISTER! HIER!

In Sachsens Werkstatt. Kurzer Raum. Im Hintergrunde die halbgeöffnete Ladentüre, nach der Straße führend. Rechts zur Seite eine Kammertüre. Links das nach der Gasse gehende

Erregtheitstriller,
Schustermühe-M.

Fenster, mit Blumenstöcken davor, zur Seite ein Werktisch. Sachs sitzt auf einem großen Lehnstuhle an diesem Fenster, durch welches die Morgensonne hell auf ihn hereinscheint; er hat vor sich auf dem Schoße einen großen Folianten und ist im Lesen vertieft.

David-M.

David zeigt sich, von der Straße kommend, unter der Ladentüre; er lugt herein und, da er Sachs gewahrt, fährt er zurück. – Er versichert sich aber, daß Sachs ihn nicht bemerkt, schlüpft herein, stellt seinen mitgebrachten Handkorb auf den hinteren Werktisch beim Laden und untersucht seinen Inhalt; er holt Blumen und Bänder hervor, kramt sie auf dem Tische aus und findet endlich auf dem Grunde eine Wurst und einen Kuchen; er läßt sich an, diese zu verzehren, als Sachs, der ihn fortwährend nicht beachtet, mit starkem Geräusch eines der großen Blätter des Folianten umwendet.

DAVID

Kreidestrich-M.

fährt zusammen, verbirgt das Essen und wendet sich zurück:

Wahn-M.
David-M.

Gleich, Meister! Hier!
Die Schuh' sind abgegeben
in Herrn Beckmessers Quartier. –
Mir war's, als rieft ihr mich eben? –

....
¹ *zweiter Teil, dessen Text das Schusterschicksal besingt (ruhig)*

ACT 3

Scene 1 – Yes, Master! Here!

delusion motif,
awake choral,
cobbler's song¹,
(Tristan motifs),
baptismal verse
(Sachs), awake choral
(end),
delusion motif

In Sachs's workshop. Front scene. At back is the half open door leading to the street. On the right side a chamber door. On the left a window looking on the alley, with flowers before it; on the same side a work bench. Sachs sits in a large arm chair at this window, through which the morning sun shines brightly upon him: he has a large folio on his lap and is absorbed in reading it.

excitement trill,
cobbler's labor motif

David is seen coming from the street. He peeps in and on seeing Sachs starts back. – He is reassured as Sachs does not see him and slips in, places a basket he has brought on the work bench at back by the door, and examines its contents: he takes out flowers and ribbons, lays them out on the table and at last finds at the bottom a sausage and a cake; he prepares to eat thee when Sachs who has not taken notice of him, noisily turns over a leaf of the folio.

David motif

DAVID

starts, hides the food and turns round:

chalk stroke motif

Yes, Master! here!
The shoes were taken early
to Master Beckmesser's house. –
Methought now that you called me? –

delusion motif
David motif

---
¹ *second part, describing the cobbler's fate (calm)*

The Mastersingers of Nuremberg

David-M.	(beiseite) Er tut, als säh' er mich nicht? Da ist er bös', wenn er nicht spricht! –	KA 398 ▸ 1 CD 3/2 0:39
Wahn-M.	*Er nähert sich, sehr demütig, langsam Sachs.*	
	Ach, Meister! Wollt mir verzeihn; kann ein Lehrbub' vollkommen sein? Kennet ihr die Lene wie ich, dann vergäbt ihr mir sicherlich.	
Erregtheitstriller	Sie ist so gut, so sanft für mich und blickt mich oft an so innerlich. Wenn ihr mich schlagt, streichelt sie mich und lächelt dabei holdseliglich; muß ich karieren, füttert sie mich und ist in allem gar liebelich!	

Erregtheitstriller,
Kreidestrich-M.
	Nur gestern,
	              weil der Junker versungen,
	hab' ich den Korb ihr
	                   nicht abgerungen.	

Erregtheitstriller, *Unmut-M., Laute-M.*	Das schmerzte mich: – und da ich fand, daß nachts einer vor dem Fenster stand, und sang zu ihr und schrie wie toll, –	
Prügel-M.	da hieb ich dem den Buckel voll: wie käm' nun da was Großes drauf an? – Auch hat's unsrer Liebe gar wohl getan! –	
David-M.	Die Lene hat mir eben alles erklärt und zum Fest Blumen und Bänder beschert. –	
	Er bricht in größere Angst aus.	
David-M., Kreidestrich-M., Wahn-M.	Ach, Meister! Sprecht doch nur ein Wort! – (Hätt ich nur die Wurst und den Kuchen erst fort!)	

Sachs hat unbeirrt immer weiter gelesen. Jetzt schlägt er den Folianten zu. Von dem starken Geräusch erschrickt David so, daß er strauchelt und unwillkürlich vor Sachs auf die Knie fällt. –

Sachs sieht über das Buch, das er noch auf dem Schoße behält, hinweg, über David, welcher immer auf den Knien, furchtsam nach ihm aufblickt, hin und heftet seinen Blick unwillkürlich auf den hinteren Werktisch.

Act 3, Scene 1 – Yes, Master! Here!

KA 354 ▶ 14
CD 3/2 0:39

(aside)

Today he seems not to see? — *David motif*
He does not speak: then he is cross! —

He approaches Sachs very humbly and slowly. — *delusion motif*

Ah, Master! Will you forgive?
did a faultless prentice e'er live?
If you knew Lene as I,
then your pardon you'd not deny.
She is so good, so sweet to me,
and looks at me oft so tenderly. — *excitement trill*
When you are harsh, then she is kind;
her smiles will drive all care from my mind;
when I am fasting, food she will bring,
and she is lovely in ev'rything!
But last night, — *excitement trill,*
    when she learned the knight's failure, — *chalk stroke motif*
nought would she let me
        take from her basket.
That hurt me sore: – and when I found, — *excitement trill,*
that late, one before her window stood, — *resentment motif,*
and sang to her, and cried like mad, – — *lute motif*
I fell upon him tooth and nail: — *beating motif*
why make so great a matter of that? –
Besides, to our love good has come there from! –
And Magdalene now has made it all clear, — *David motif*
and today flowers and ribbons are from her. –

He breaks out in terror.

Ah, Master! Speak one word I pray! – — *David motif,*
(Were now the cake — *chalk stroke motif,*
         and the sausage away!) — *delusion motif*

Sachs has read on undisturbed. He now closes the book. David starts at the noise so that he stumbles and falls unintentionally on his knees before Sachs.

Sachs looks away over his book, which he still holds on his knees, over David who. still on his knees, looks up to him frightened, and fixes his eyes mechanically on the table. –

The Mastersingers of Nuremberg

SACHS

(sehr leise)

David-M., Hoffnung-M.
Blumen und Bänder seh ich dort?
Schaut hold und jugendlich aus.
Wie kamen mir die ins Haus?

DAVID

(verwundert über Sachs' Freundlichkeit)

Erregtheitstriller
Ei, Meister! 's ist heut festlicher Tag;
da putzt sich jeder so schön er mag.

SACHS

Singkunst-M.
(immer leise, wie für sich)
Wär' heut' Hochzeitsfest?

DAVID

Erregtheitstriller, Singkunst-M.
Ja, käm's erst so weit,
daß David die Lene freit!

SACHS

(immer wie zuvor)

Erregtheitstriller
's war Polterabend, dünkt mich doch?

DAVID

(Polterabend?... Da krieg ich's wohl noch? –)
Hoffnung-M.
Verzeiht das, Meister; ich bitt', vergeßt!
Wir feiern ja heut Johannisfest.

Singkunst-M.
SACHS
Johannisfest?

DAVID

(Hört er heut schwer?)

SACHS

David-M.
Kannst du dein Sprüchlein, so sag es her!

Act 3, Scene 1 – Yes, Master! Here!

SACHS

(very softly)
Flowers and ribbons there I see?
Right fresh and fair they appear.
Then tell me, how came they there?

David motif,
hope motif

DAVID

(surprised at Sachs's friendliness)
Ah, Master! today's festival day,
and each one decks him as best he may.

excitement trill

SACHS

(still softly, as to himself)
Is it wedding day?

singing art motif

DAVID

Aye, would that it were!
that I might wed Lene fair!

excitement trill,
singing art motif

SACHS

(as before)
Wedding eve! Then, now for the fight?

excitement trill

DAVID

(Wedding eve!?... The, now for the fight? –)
Forgive that, Master, forget, I pray!
The feast of St. John we keep today.

hope motif

SACHS
Midsummer day?

singing art motif

DAVID

(Deaf must he be?)

SACHS
Know'st thou thy verses? then sing to me!

David motif

233

David

ist allmählich wieder zu stehen gekommen.

David-M.
Mein Sprüchlein? Denk', ich kann's gut. –
('setzt nichts!
　　　　　　der Meister ist wohlgemut.) –
(stark und grob)

Beckmessers Ständchen
Kreidestrich-M.
„Am Jordan Sankt Johannes stand"…

Sachs

Wa… was?

David

(lächelnd)
　　　　　Verzeiht das Gewirr!
Prügel-M., Erregtheitstriller
Mich machte der Polterabend irr'.
Er sammelt und stellt sich gehörig auf.

Taufchoral
„Am Jordan Sankt Johannes stand,
all' Volk der Welt zu taufen;
kam auch ein Weib aus fernem Land,
aus Nürnberg gar gelaufen:
sein Söhnlein trug's zum Uferrand,
empfing da Tauf' und Namen;
doch als sie dann sich heimgewandt,
nach Nürnberg wieder kamen,
Erregtheitstriller, Singkunst-M. ②
in deutschem Land gar bald sich fand's,
daß, wer am Ufer des Jordans
Johannes ward genannt,
　　　　　an der Pegnitz hieß der Hans." –
(sich besinnend)

Erregtheitstriller
Hans?… Hans!…
　　　　　Herr – Meister!
　　　　　　　's ist heut eu'r Namenstag!
David-M.
Nein! Wie man so was vergessen mag!
Hier! Hier die Blumen sind für euch, –
die Bänder, und was nur alles noch gleich?
Ja, hier, schaut! Meister, herrlicher Kuchen!
Möchtet ihr nicht auch
　　　　　　　die Wurst versuchen? –

Act 3, Scene 1 – Yes, Master! Here!

VS 360 ▶ 3
CD 3/2 3:48

DAVID

has gradually come into position.

My verses well do I know. – } *David motif*
('Tis nought! }
                His anger is gone, I trow.) – }
(loudly and roughly)
„St. John baptized in Jordan's tide"…   *Beckmesser's song*

SACHS   *chalk stroke motif*

Wha… what?

DAVID

(simling)
                Forgive me again!
The wedding eve tune was in my brain.   *beating motif,*
  He collects himself and stands up becomingly.   *excitement trill*

VS 360 ▶ 16
CD 3/3 0:01

„St. John baptized in Jordan's tide
all folk of ev'ry nation;   *choral of baptism*
from Nüremberg a woman hied,
to seek from him salvation:
her little son was by her side,
and took both name and blessing.
To Nüremberg, with mother's pride,
her pilgrim's path retracing,   *excitement trill,*
right soon she found in German's lands,   *singing art motif ②*
that ev'ry babe who on Jordan's
far shore Johannes hight,
      on the Pegnitz changed to Hans." –
  (considering)
Hans?… Hans!…   *excitement trill*
          Ah – Master!
              Why: 'Tis your name-day, too?
Nay! but to think that I never knew!   } *David motif*
Here! here, the flowers take from me, – }
the flowers, I pray you, all that you see. }
This cake I hid for fear you should spy it! }
Here, too, a sausage, }
              would you but try it? – }

The Mastersingers of Nuremberg

David-M.

SACHS
immer ruhig, ohne seine Stellung zu verändern:
Schön' Dank, mein Jung'! Behalt's für dich!
Doch heut auf die Wiese begleitest du mich;

Entzückung-M.
König-David-M.
mit Blumen und Bändern putz dich fein:
sollst mein stattlicher Herold sein!

DAVID
Sollt' ich nicht lieber Brautführer sein?
Meister, ach! Meister,
                      ihr müßt wieder frein.

SACHS
Hättst wohl gern eine Meistrin im Haus?

DAVID
Ich mein', es säh' doch viel stattlicher aus.

SACHS
Wer weiß? Kommt Zeit, kommt Rat.

DAVID

David-M.
                              's ist Zeit.

SACHS
Dann wär' der Rat wohl auch nicht weit?

DAVID
Gewiß! Gehn schon Reden hin und wieder;
den Beckmesser, denk' ich,

Beckmessers Werbe-M.
                      sängt ihr doch nieder?
Ich mein', daß der heut
                    sich nicht wichtig macht!

SACHS
Wohl möglich;
            hab' mir's auch schon bedacht. –
Jetzt geh und stör mir den Junker nicht.
Komm wieder, wann du schön gericht'!

Act 3, Scene 1 – Yes, Master! Here!

SACHS *(David motif)*

still quietly, without changing his position:

Good thanks, my boy! I leave it thee!
But out to the meadow shalt thou go with me;
With flowers and ribbons make thee gay: *delight motif*
thou my herald shalt be today!   *king David motif*

DAVID

Might I not be your groomsman, beside?
Master, ah! Master,
                you must win the bride.

SACHS

Would'st thou have, then, a mistress about?

DAVID

The house were statelier so, without doubt.

SACHS

Who knows? With time comes thought.

DAVID

                Time's past.   *David motif*

SACHS

Perchance the thought will come at last?

DAVID

In sooth, all around have had such fancies;
and, if you sing,
        gone are Beckmesser's chances!   *Beckmesser's court-*
Metinks that today   *ship motif*
        he will come to nought!

SACHS

'Tis likely;
        that I also have thought. –
Now go; in peace let the knight remain.
When thou art dressed, then come again!

The Mastersingers of Nuremberg

David-M.   *David küßt Sachs gerührt die Hand.*   KA 417 ▶ 286
CD 3/3 2:35

DAVID

(für sich)

– So war er noch nie, wenn sonst auch gut! –
Unmut-M.   (Kann mir gar nicht mehr denken,
                 wie der Knieriemen tut!)
Er packt seine Sachen zusammen und geht in die Kammer ab. –

Wahn-M.   *Sachs, immer noch den Folianten auf dem Schoße, lehnt sich, mit untergestütztem Arm,*
David-M.   *sinnend darauf: es scheint, daß ihn das Gespräch mit David gar nicht aus seinem Nachdenken gestört hat.*

SACHS

Wahn! Wahn!   KA 418 ▶ 305
Überall Wahn!   CD 3/4 0:01
Wohin ich forschend blick'
in Stadt- und Weltchronik,
den Grund mir aufzufinden,
warum gar bis aufs Blut
die Leut' sich quälen und schinden
Wahn-M.   in unnütz toller Wut?
Hat keiner Lohn
noch Dank davon:
in Flucht geschlagen,
wähnt er zu jagen;
hört nicht sein eigen Schmerzgekreisch,
wenn er sich wühlt ins eigne Fleisch,
wähnt Lust sich zu erzeigen! –
               Wer gibt den Namen an? –

(kräftig)

's ist halt der alte Wahn,
ohn' den nichts mag geschehen,
Lenzesgebot-M.   's mag gehen oder stehen!
Steht's wo im Lauf,
er schläft nur neue Kraft sich an:
Leidenschaft-M.   gleich wacht er auf, –

Act 3, Scene 1 – Yes, Master! Here!

David, touched, kisses Sachs's hand. — *David motif*

DAVID

(aside)

– He ne'er was like this though ever kind! –
(Now the feel of his stirrup-strap
                has gone from my mind!) — *resentment motif*

He puts his things together and goes into the chamber. –

Sachs, still with the folio on his lap, leans with his arms resting upon it; his talk with David does not seem to have disturbed his meditation. — *delusion motif*

SACHS

Craze! Craze!
Ev'rywhere craze!
In vain my looks I cast
O'er present things and past,
the reasons ever seeking,
why men so fiercely fight;
each one his malice wreaking
in aimless frenzied spite?
He wins no wage
for all his woe:
and fleeing, dreams he
chases his foe; his
outcry of pain he doth not hear,
when he himself his flesh doth tear,
exulting in his anguish! –
            Ah, who shall tell his name? – — *delusion motif*

(loud)

the craze is still the same:
nought happens here without is,
howe'er we go about it,
stayed in its course, — *springtime's behest motif*
in sleep returns its strength again:
and with new force, – — *passion motif*

The Mastersingers of Nuremberg

Wahn-M.	dann schaut, wer ihn bemeistern kann!...
Nürnberg-M.	Wie friedsam treuer Sitten,
	getrost in Tat und Werk,
Entzückung-M.	liegt nicht in Deutschlands Mitten
	mein liebes Nürenberg! –

Er blickt mit freudiger Begeisterung ruhig vor sich hin.

Doch eines Abends spat,
ein Unglück zu verhüten
bei jugendheißen Gemüten,

Nürnberg-M. geht über in Beckmessers Werbe-M.

ein Mann weiß sich nicht Rat;
ein Schuster in seinem Laden
zieht an des Wahnes Faden:
wie bald auf Gassen und Straßen
fängt der da an zu rasen!
Mann, Weib, Gesell' und Kind
fällt sich da an wie toll und blind;

Lebhaftigkeit-M., Prügel-M., Kreidestrich-M.

und will's der Wahn gesegnen,
nun muß es Prügel regnen,
mit Hieben, Stoß' und Dreschen
den Wutesbrand zu löschen. –

Sommernachtzauber-M., Beckmessers Ständchen, Prügel-M. (scherzohaft), Beckmessers Werbe-M.

Gott weiß, wie das geschah? –
– Ein Kobold half wohl da: –
ein Glühwurm fand sein Weibchen nicht; –
der hat den Schaden angericht'. –
Der Flieder war's: – Johannisnacht! – –
Nun aber kam Johannistag! –

Johannistag-M., Preislied (Stollen) ②, Nürnberg-M.

Jetzt schaun wir, wie Hans Sachs es macht,
daß er den Wahn fein lenken kann,
ein edler Werk zu tun:
denn läßt er uns nicht ruhn,
selbst hier in Nürenberg,

Entzückung-M.

so sei's um solche Werk',
die selten vor gemeinen Dingen,
und nie ohn' ein'gen Wahn gelingen.

KA 420 ▶ 335
CD 3/4 2:25

Act 3, Scene 1 – Yes, Master! Here!

it wakes – ah, who can hold it then!...   *delusion motif*
With peaceful ways contented,   *Nuremberg motif*
and helpful work in hand,
my Nüremberg lies planted   *delight motif*
amidst our fatherland! –

> *He gazes before him in joyful enthusiasm.*

But on an evening late,
to safeguard from disaster,
and youthful passion to master,
a man, fighting with fate;   *Nuremberg motif,*
a shoemaker at his leather   *transitioning into*
pulls at the craze's tether: *Beckmesser's courts-*
then soon his neighbors awaken,   *hip motif*
by rage and passion shaken!
Man, wife, and youth and child,
blindly fall as though gone wild;
and madness brings the blessing,   *livelihood motif,*
of strife and blows unceasing,   *beating motif,*
repeating, aye, the story,   *chalk stroke motif*
to quell the raging fury. –
God knows how that befel? –   *summer night's magic*
– A kobold wove the spell: –   *motif, Beckmesser's*
In rain his mate a glow-worm sought; –   *song, beating motif*
'twas he who all this tumult wrought. –   *(scherzo-like),*
The elder 'twas: – Midsummer eve! – –   *Beckmesser's courts-*
    hip motif
But now has dawned Midsummer day! –   *Midsummer day motif,*
We'll see what spell Hans Sachs can weave,   *prize song (stanza) ②,*
that he the craze may turn the way,   *Nuremberg motif*
that leads to noble works:
and if this craze yet lurks,
e'en here in this our town,
then let its worth be shown!   *delight motif*
For work has never virtue in it,
unless some help from craze begin it.

2. Szene – Grüss Gott, mein Junker!

Traum-M.

Walther tritt unter der Kammertüre ein. Er bleibt einen Augenblick dort stehen und blickt auf Sachs. Dieser wendet sich und läßt den Folianten auf den Boden gleiten.

Freundschaft-M.

Sachs

Grüß Gott, mein Junker! Ruhtet ihr noch?   KA 428 ▶ 438
Ihr wachtet lang, nun schlieft ihr doch?   CD 3/5 0:01

Walther

(sehr ruhig)
Ein wenig, aber fest und gut.

Sachs

So ist euch nun wohl baß zu Mut?

Walther

(immer sehr ruhig)

Traum-M.   Ich hatt' einen wunderschönen Traum.

Sachs

Preislied (Stollen) ②,   Das deutet Gut's: erzählt mir den!
verwischt und geht
über in Werbe-M.   **Walther**

Ihn selbst zu denken, wag' ich kaum:
ich fürcht', ihn mir vergehn zu sehn. –

Act 3, Scene 2 – Sir knight, I greet you!

Scene 2 – Sir knight, I greet you!

Walther enters by the chamber door. He pauses there for a moment and looks at Sachs, who turns and lets the book slide to the floor.

dream motif

Sachs

} *friendship motif*

VS 374▶12
CD 3/5 0:01
Sir knight, I greet you! Lay you till now?
Though late to bed, you slept, I trow?

Walther

(very quietly)
A little, but my sleep was good.

Sachs

So then you rise in hopeful mood?

Walther

(still very quietly)
A dream I have had, of beauty rare.

dream motif

Sachs

An omen good! tell me your dream!

} *prize song (stanza)* ②, *fading and transitioning into courtship motif*

Walther

Thereon to think I scarcely dare:
in fear lest it should fade I seem. –

243

The Mastersingers of Nuremberg

Sachs

Freundschaft-M.   Mein Freund! Das grad' ist Dichters Werk,
daß er sein Träumen deut' und merk'.
Glaubt mir, des Menschen wahrster Wahn
wird ihm im Traume aufgetan: –
Eva-M.   all' Dichtkunst und Poeterei
ist nichts als Wahrtraumdeuterei.
Was gilt's, es gab der Traum euch ein,
Eva-M.   wie heut ihr sollet Meister sein?

Walther

(sehr ruhig)

Werbe-M.   Nein, von der Zunft und ihren Meistern
wollt' sich mein Traumbild nicht begeistern.

Sachs

Doch lehrt' es wohl den Zauberspruch,
Eva-M.   mit dem ihr sie gewännet?

Walther

Freundschaft-M.   Wie wähnt ihr doch nach solchem Bruch,
wenn ihr noch Hoffnung kennet!

Sachs

Die Hoffnung lass' ich mir nicht mindern,
Werbe-M.   nichts stieß sie noch übern Haufen;
wär's nicht, glaubt,
             statt eure Flucht zu hindern,
wär' ich selbst mit euch fortgelaufen! –
Drum bitt' ich, laßt den Groll jetzt ruhn!
Ihr habt's mit Ehrenmännern zu tun;
die irren sich und sind bequem,
daß man auf ihre Weise sie nähm': –
wer Preise erkennt und Preise stellt,
der will am End' auch, daß man ihm gefällt.
Eu'r Lied, das hat ihnen bang gemacht;
und das mit Recht: denn wohlbedacht,
mit solchem Dicht'- und Liebesfeuer
Eva-M.   verführt man wohl Töchter zum Abenteuer; –
Freundschaft-M.   doch für liebseligen Ehestand

Act 3, Scene 2 – Sir knight, I greet you!

SACHS

My friend! just that is poet's work; *friendship motif*
to find in dreams what meanings lurk.
Believe! our deepest wisdom here
is oft in dreams to us made clear. –
All poems that the world has known *Eva motif*
are nought but truths our dreams have shown.
Perchance your dream may show the way
to win the Master's prize today! *Eva motif*

WALTHER

(very quietly)

Nay, from your guild and all its Masters, *courtship motif*
my dream would bring me new disasters.

SACHS

Yet might it teach the magic spell
that makes the mastersinger? *Eva motif*

WALTHER

How bold your heart, since what befel, *friendship motif*
if in it hope still linger!

SACHS

With hope my heart is ever beating,
and thence hope shall not be driven; *courtship motif*
were't not so,
        ne'er had I stayed your flitting,
but myself as your guide had given! –
So, pray you, let your anger go!
you have with men of homour to do:
mistakes they make, and each we'd find,
in other men the thoughts of his mind: –
and fair 'tis that they who grant a prize,
should ask what seemeth goodly in their eyes.
Your song has filled them with dark dismay;
and with good cause, for, truth to say,
a song so full of poet's passion
may kindle our maidens in evil fashion; – *Eva motif*
but if song calm wedded life shall speed, *friendship motif*

Freundschaft-M.	man andre Wort' und Weisen fand.	KA 435 ▶ 521 CD 3/5 3:43

WALTHER

(lächelnd)

Freundschaft-M., Die kenn' ich nun auch seit dieser Nacht:
Beckmessers es hat viel Lärm auf der Gasse gemacht.
Ständchen

SACHS

(lachend)

Singkunst-M. ② Ja, ja! Schon gut! Den Takt dazu
(karikiert) hörtet ihr auch! Doch laßt dem Ruh',
und folgt meinem Rate, kurz und gut:
faßt zu einem Meisterliede Mut!

WALTHER

Werbe-M.
mit Übergang in Ein schönes Lied, – ein Meisterlied:
Singkunst-M. ② wie fass' ich da den Unterschied?

SACHS

Jugendzeit-M. Mein Freund, in holder Jugendzeit,   KA 437 ▶ 543
wenn uns von mächt'gen Trieben   CD 3/6 0:01
zum sel'gen ersten Lieben
die Brust sich schwellet hoch und weit,
ein schönes Lied zu singen,
mocht' vielen da gelingen:
Leidenschaft-M., der Lenz, der sang für sie.
Werbe-M. (ungestüm) Kam Sommer, Herbst und Winters Zeit,
viel Not und Sorg' im Leben,
manch' eh'lich Glück daneben:
Kindtauf', Geschäfte, Zwist und Streit: –
Jugendzeit-M. denen's dann noch will gelingen,
Leidenschaft-M. ein schönes Lied zu singen,
Meistersinger-M. ② seht: Meister nennt man die!

WALTHER

zart und begeistert anschwellend:

Ich lieb' ein Weib, und will es frein,
mein dauernd Eh'gemahl zu sein.

Act 3, Scene 2 – Sir knight, I greet you!

KA 379 ▶ 8　then other words and tunes we need.　　　*friendship motif*
CD 3/5 3:43

WALTHER

　　(smiling)

And those, too, I know since yesternight:　　*friendship motif,*
if in the alley I heard them aright.　　　　　　*Beckmesser's song*

SACHS

　　(laughing)

Aye, aye! 'Tis true! My beat also　　　　　　*singing art motif ②*
you heard thereto! But let that go,　　　　　　*(caricatured)*
and mark well my counsel:
fit now to a Mastertone your mood!

WALTHER

A beauteous song, – a Mastertone:　　　　　*courtship motif*
I thought of old that they were one?　　　　　*transitioning into*
　　　　　　　　　　　　　　　　　　　　　　　singing art motif ②

SACHS

VS 380 ▶ 17　My friend, when youth's desires compel,　　*youth motif*
CD 3/6 0:01　and 'twards the goal of loving
the soul is surely moving,
when hearts with passion beat and swell,
the boon of song by Heaven
to many then is given:
'tis spring that sings, not they.　　　　　　　　*passion motif,*
through summer, fall and winter's spell,　　　*courtship motif*
when life hath brought its burden,　　　　　　*(impetuosly)*
with marriage joy as guerdon:
children, misfortune, strife as well: –
they to whom then still by Heaven,　　　　　　*youth motif*
the grace of song is given,　　　　　　　　　　*passion motif*
as Masters live for aye!　　　　　　　　　　　　　*mastersinger motif ②*

WALTHER

　　tendering and fervently, crescendo:

I love a maid and fain would prove,
in lasting wedlock all my love.

Sachs

Jugendzeit-M.

Die Meisterregeln lernt beizeiten,
daß sie getreulich euch geleiten
und helfen, wohl bewahren,
was in der Jugend Jahren

Leidenschaft-M.
Werbe-M.

mit holdem Triebe
Lenz und Liebe
euch unbewußt ins Herz gelegt,
daß ihr das unverloren hegt!

Walther

Leidenschaft-M.

Stehn sie nun in so hohem Ruf,
wer war es, der die Regeln schuf?

Sachs

Das waren hochbedürft'ge Meister,
von Lebensmüh' bedrängte Geister:
in ihrer Nöten Wildnis

Leidenschaft-M.

sie schufen sich ein Bildnis,
daß ihnen bliebe
der Jugendliebe
ein Angedenken, klar und fest,

Lenzesgebot-M.

dran sich der Lenz erkennen läßt. –

Walther

Leidenschaft-M.
Entzückung-M.

Doch, wem der Lenz schon lang entronnen,
wie wird er dem im Bild gewonnen?

Sachs

Freundschaft-M.,
Eva-M.,
Leidenschaft-M.
Entzückung-M.
Jugendzeit-M.,
Freundschaft-M.

Er frischt es an, so gut er kann:
drum möcht' ich, als bedürft'ger Mann,
will ich die Regeln euch lehren,
sollt ihr sie mir neu erklären. –
Seht, hier ist Tinte, Feder, Papier:
ich schreib's euch auf, diktiert ihr mir!

Walther

Wie ich's begänne, wüßt' ich kaum.

Act 3, Scene 2 – Sir knight, I greet you!

SACHS

Then let the Master-rules now speed you, — *youth motif*
that they may ever truly lead you,
and help to keep untainted
what spring and youth have planted
amidst youth's pleasures; — *passion motif*
so the treasures, — *courtship motif*
deep in the heart in secret laid,
through might of song shall never fade!

WALTHER

Tell me, then, if so high they stand,
by whom of old the rules were planned? — *passion motif*

SACHS

By masters worn with woe of living,
with world's distress and anguish striving:
by heavy cares o'erweighted,
a vision they created,
amid their sadness,
of youth and gladness;
remembrance clear of love to bring,
and make again their vanished spring. – — *springtime's behest motif*

WALTHER

Yet, when the time of spring is over, — *passion motif*
can empty dreams its life recover? — *delight motif*

SACHS

Upon such dreams the heart may feed. — *friendship motif,*
I pray you, then, as one in need, — *Eva motif,*
safe on my counsel leaning, — *passion motif*
give you to our rules new meaning. – — *delight motif*
Pen, ink and paper ready you see: — *youth motif,*
I'll write the words you sing to me! — *friendship motif*

WALTHER

I know not how to start aright.

The Mastersingers of Nuremberg

	SACHS	KA 446 ▸ 624 CD 3/6 3:30
Freundschaft-M., *Jugendzeit-M.*	Erzählt mit euren Morgentraum.	
	WALTHER	
Leidenschaft-M. *(„verwischend")*	Durch eurer Regeln gute Lehr' ist mir's, als ob verwischt er wär'.	
	SACHS	
Freundschaft-M.	Grad' nehmt die Dichtkunst jetzt zur Hand: mancher durch sie das Verlor'ne fand.	
Werbe-M. *mit Übergang in* *Singkunst-M.* ②	**WALTHER** So wär's nicht Traum, doch Dichterei?	
	SACHS	
Freundschaft-M.	'sind Freunde beid', stehn gern sich bei.	
	WALTHER	
	Wie fang' ich nach der Regel an?	
	SACHS	
Traum-M.	Ihr stellt sie selbst und folgt ihr dann. Gedenkt des schönen Traums am Morgen: für's andre laßt Hans Sachs nur sorgen.	
	WALTHER	
	hat sich zu Hans Sachs am Werktisch gesetzt, *wo dieser das Gedicht Walthers nachschreibt.*	KA 448 ▸ 652 CD 3/7 0:01
Preislied (Stollen) *Singkunst-M.* ② *Werbe-M.*	„Morgenlich leuchtend in rosigem Schein, von Blüt' und Duft geschwellt die Luft, voll aller Wonnen nie ersonnen, ein Garten lud mich ein, Gast ihm zu sein." –	
	SACHS	
	Das war ein „Stollen"; nun achtet wohl, daß ganz ein gleicher ihm folgen soll.	

Act 3, Scene 2 – Sir knight, I greet you!

SACHS *(VS 387 ▶ 7 / CD 3/6 3:30)*

Think only of your dream this night.   *friendship motif, youth motif*

WALTHER

Through all the rules that you have taught,
meseems the dream has come to nought.   *passion motif (fading)*

SACHS

The poet's art, then, try betimes;
words that are lost oft are found in rhymes.   *friendship motif*

WALTHER

Then 'twere no dream, but poetry?   *courtship motif transitioning into singing art motif ②*

SACHS

Good friends are they, ne'er far apart   *friendship motif*

WALTHER

But how by the rules shall I begin?

SACHS

First make your rules, and keep them then.   *dream motif*
Think only on your vision's beauty:
to guide well shall be by duty.

WALTHER

(VS 389 ▶ 1 / CD 3/7 0:01) has placed himself by the working bench near Sachs who writes down Walther's poem.

„Bathed in the sunlight at dawn of the day,   *prize song (stanza)*
when blossoms rare
made sweet the air,   *singing art motif ②*
with beauties teeming,
past all dreaming,   *courtship motif*
a glorious garden lay,
cheering my way." –

SACHS

That was a „Stanza", and take good heed;
another like it must now succeed.

251

WALTHER

Warum ganz gleich?

SACHS

                    Damit man seh',
Ihr wähltet euch gleich ein Weib zur Eh'.

WALTHER

Preislied (Stollen)   „Wonnig entragend dem seligen Raum,
Singkunst-M. ②   bot gold'ner Frucht
                     heilsaft'ge Wucht,
Werbe-M.   mit holdem Prangen
                     dem Verlangen,
                     an duft'ger Zweige Saum,
                     herrlich ein Baum." –

SACHS

Ihr schlosset nicht im gleichen Ton:
das macht den Meistern Pein;
doch nimmt Hans Sachs die Lehr' davon,
Hoffnung-M.   im Lenz wohl müss' es so sein. –
Nun stellt mir einen „Abgesang".

WALTHER

Was soll nun der?

SACHS

                    Ob euch gelang,
Entzückung-M.   ein rechtes Paar zu finden,
das zeigt sich an den Kinden;
den Stollen ähnlich, doch nicht gleich,
an eignen Reim' und Tönen reich;
daß man's recht schlank und selbstig find',
das freut die Eltern an dem Kind;
und euren Stollen gibt's den Schluß,
daß nichts davon abfallen muß. –

Singkunst-M.   **WALTHER**

Preislied
(Liebesthema)   „Sei euch vertraut,
welch hehres Wunder mir geschehn:

Act 3, Scene 2 – Sir knight, I greet you!

WALTHER

Wherefore alike?

SACHS

      To make it plain,
to all men that you wed are fain.

WALTHER

„High o'er the garden a tree then did rise; } *prize song (stanza)*
the golden store   *singing art motif* ②
its branches bore
so richly thronging,   *courtship motif*
woke my longing,
when, sparkling there, my eyes
looked on the prize." –

SACHS

You ended in another key:
that Masters blame, you know;
but I, Hans Sachs, your meaning see;
in spring it needs must be so. –   *hope motif*
An „Aftersong" now sing as well.

WALTHER

What meaneth that?

SACHS

      The child will tell,
if true and fitly mated,   } *delight motif*
the pair by you created;
though like the stanzas; yet its own
and new must be both rhyme and tone.
Let it be shapely found and neat;
such children parents gladly greet;
your stanzas so will find an end,
and all things together will blend. –

WALTHER   *singing art motif*

„How shall I name   *prize song*
the radiant wonder there revealed?   *(love theme)*

Preislied (Liebesthema) Eva-M.	an meiner Seite stand ein Weib, so hold und schön ich nie gesehn: gleich einer Braut	KA 452 ▶ 707 CD 3/7 2:58
Entzückung-M.	umfaßte sie sanft meinen Leib; mit Augen winkend, die Hand wies blinkend, was ich verlangend begehrt, die Frucht so hold und wert vom Lebensbaum."	

Traum-M.

SACHS

*Wahn-M.
(bricht ab)*

(gerührt)

Das nenn' ich mir einen Abgesang!
Seht, wie der ganze Bar gelang!
Nur mit der Melodei
seid ihr ein wenig frei:
doch sag' ich nicht, daß das ein Fehler sei;
nur ist's nicht leicht zu behalten, –

Hohn-M., Kreidestrich-M.

und das ärgert unsre Alten!
Jetzt richtet mir noch einen zweiten Bar,
damit man merk', welch' der erste war.
Auch weiß ich noch nicht,
                        so gut ihr's gereimt,

Traum-M.

was ihr gedichtet, was ihr geträumt.

WALTHER

*Preislied (Stollen)
Singkunst-M. ②*

„Abendlich glühend in himmlischer Pracht
verschied der Tag,
wie dort ich lag:

Werbe-M.

aus ihren Augen
Wonne saugen,
Verlangen einz'ger Macht
in mir nur wacht'.

Preislied (Stollen)

Nächtlich umdämmert
                      der Blick mir sich bricht:

Singkunst-M. ②

wie weit so nah,
beschienen da

Werbe-M.

zwei lichte Sterne
aus der Ferne,
durch schlanker Zweige Licht,

Act 3, Scene 2 – Sir knight, I greet you!

A woman fair my vision blessed; *prize song (love theme)*
her peer no mortal e'er beheld: *Eva motif*
bride-like she came,
and folded me fast on her breast; *delight motif*
then gently raising
her hand, and gazing
where gleamed the fruit's golden hue,
she shewed the place where grew
the tree of life."

SACHS *dream motif*

(moved) *delusion motif (breaks off)*

In sooth, I call that an Aftersong!
See how the verse now flows along!
But with the melody
are you a little free.
Yet say I not that's a fault with me;
but for the ear 'tis perplexing, –
and to old men that is vexing! *scorn motif,*
A second verse must you now compose, *chalk stroke motif*
to fix in mind how the first one goes.
And still I know now,
⠀⠀⠀⠀⠀⠀⠀⠀though clear was your theme,
but half your poem, and half your dream. *dream motif*

WALTHER

„Sunset was gilding with heavenly light *prize song (stanza)*
the dying day,
as there I lay; *singing art motif ②*
my heart on fire
one desire, *courtship motif*
from eyes so wondrous bright,
to drink delight.
Night closes round me *prize song (stanza)*
⠀⠀⠀⠀⠀⠀⠀⠀and darkens the place:
afar yet near, *singing art motif ②*
two stars appear,
in day's declining, *courtship motif*
softly shining,
where branches interlace,

The Mastersingers of Nuremberg

Preislied (Liebes-
thema)

Eva-M.

Entzückung-M.

hehr mein Gesicht.
Lieblich ein Quell
auf stiller Höhe dort mir rauscht;
jetzt schwellt er an sein hold Getön',
so stark und süß ich's nie erlauscht:
leuchtend und hell,
wie strahlten die Sterne da schön!
Zu Tanz und Reigen
in Laub und Zweigen,
der gold'nen sammeln sich mehr,
statt Frucht ein Sternenheer
im Lorbeerbaum."

KA 456 ▶ 767
CD 3/7 5:55

Traum-M.

Wahn-M., Entzü-
ckung-M., Preislied
(Stollen) ②

Traum-M.

SACHS

(sehr gerührt)

Freund, – euer Traumbild wies euch wahr:
gelungen ist auch der zweite Bar. –
Wolltet ihr noch einen dritten dichten,
des Traumes Deutung würd' er berichten. –

WALTHER

Leidenschaft-M.
(Beginn)

steht schnell auf:
Wo fänd' ich die? – Genug der Wort'!

SACHS

Freundschaft-M.,
Nürnberg-M., Preislied
(Liebesthema)

erhebt sich ebenfalls und tritt mit freundlicher
Entschiedenheit zu Walther:

Dann Tat und Wort
am rechten Ort! –
Drum bitt' ich, merkt mir wohl die Weise:
gar lieblich drin sich's dichten läßt.
Und singt ihr sie in weit'rem Kreise,
so haltet mir auch das Traumbild fest.

WALTHER

Was habt ihr vor?

Nürnberg-M.,
Stolzing-M.

SACHS

                Eu'r treuer Knecht

Act 3, Scene 2 – Sir knight, I greet you!

VS 396 ▶ 9 down on my face.
CD 3/7 5:55
There on a height, — *prize song (love theme)*
a bubbling fountain at my feet,
from earth outpours its limpid stream,
with swelling tone, so full and sweet. — *Eva motif*
Sparkling and bright,
new gathering stars on me beam, — *delight motif*
as, gainly dancing,
through branches glancing,
their golden lustre they shed;
not fruit but stars o'erspread
the laurel tree."

SACHS — *dream motif*

(much moved) — *delusion motif, delight motif, prize song (stanza) ②*

Friend, – your vision told you true,
and bravely goes verse the second, too. –
Make a third one, ere your work is over; — *dream motif*
the vision's meaning let that discover. –

WALTHER

rises quickly: — *passion motif (beginning)*
Ah, what were that? – Enough of words!

SACHS

rises at te same time and approaches Walther — *friendship motif, Nuremberg motif, prize song (love theme)*
with friendly decision:

Then word and deed
let fortune speed! –
I pray you, well the tune remember,
right well it suits with such a theme,
and, when before the folk you sing it
hold fast in your mind that morning dream.

WALTHER

What would you do? — *Nuremberg motif, Stolzing motif*

SACHS

                    Your trusty squire

The Mastersingers of Nuremberg

Nürnberg-M., fand sich mit Sack und Tasch' zurecht: KA 460 ▶ 822
Stolzing-M. die Kleider, drin am Hochzeitsfest CD 3/7 8:35
 daheim ihr wolltet prangen,
Hoffnung-M. die ließ er her zu mir gelangen:
Traum-M. ein Täubchen zeigt' ihm wohl das Nest,
 darin sein Junker träumt'.
Stolzing-M., Drum folgt mir jetzt ins Kämmerlein:
Nürnberg-M., mit Kleidern, wohl gesäumt,
Zunftideal-M., sollen beide wir gezieret sein,
Erregtheitstriller wenn's Stattliches zu wagen gilt.
 Drum kommt, seid ihr gleich mir gewillt.

Preislied (Liebes- *Walther schlägt in Sachsens Hand ein; so ge-*
thema) *leitet ihn dieser, ruhig festen Schrittes, zur*
 Kammer, deren Türe er ihm ehrerbietig öffnet,
 und dann ihm folgt.

Act 3, Scene 2 – Sir knight, I greet you!

VS 399 ▶ 14
CD 3/7 8:35

bearing your packs, with that attire:
where in to grace your wedding-feast
at home you meant to prink you,
has found his way to me, how think you?
Some bird, sure, must have shewn the nest
wherein his master dreams.
Then with me to your chamber go;
for raiment gay beseems
such a task as lies before us now;
by daring deeds to reach your ends.
So come, if you and I are friends.

> *Nuremberg motif,*
> *Stolzing motif*
>
> *hope motif*
> *dream motif*
>
> *Stolzing motif, Nuremberg motif, guild ideal motif, excitement trill*

Walther grasps Sachs's hand, who leads him with a quiet, firm step to the chamber door, opening it for him respectfully and then following him.

3. Szene – Ein Werbelied! Von Sachs!

Beckmessers Ständchen,
Prügel-M.

Man gewahrt Beckmesser, welcher draußen vor dem Laden erscheint, in großer Aufgeregtheit hereinlugt und, da er die Werkstatt leer findet, hastig hereintritt.

Kreidestrich-M.,
Wahn-M.

Missgunst-M.,
Kreidestrich-M.,
Unmut-M.

Er ist sehr aufgeputzt, aber in sehr leidendem Zustande. – Er blickt sich erst unter der Türe nochmals genau in der Werkstatt um. Dann hinkt er vorwärts, zuckt aber zusammen und und streicht sich den Rücken. Er macht wieder einige Schritte, knickt aber mit den Knien und streicht nun diese.

Unmut-M.,
Laute-M.,
Missgunst-M.,
Prügel-M.

Beckmessers Ständchen

Er setzt sich auf den Schusterschemel, fährt aber schnell schmerzhaft wieder auf. Er betrachtet sich den Schemel und gerät dabei in immer aufgeregteres Nachsinnen. Er wird von den verdrießlichsten Erinnerungen und Vorstellungen gepeinigt; immer unruhiger beginnt er, sich den Schweiß von der Stirn zu wischen. –

Laute-M., Beckmessers
Werbe-M., Prügel-M.,
Kreidestrich-M.

Er hinkt immer lebhafter umher und starrt dabei vor sich hin. – Als ob er von allen Seiten verfolgt wäre, taumelt er fliehend hin und her. – Wie um nicht umzusinken, hält er sich an dem Werktisch, zu dem er hingeschwankt war, an und starrt vor sich hin.

Missgunst-M.

Ärger-M., Stolzing-M.

Matt und verzweiflungsvoll sieht er um sich; – sein Blick fällt endlich durch das Fenster auf Pogners Haus; er hinkt mühsam an dasselbe heran und, nach dem gegenüberliegenden Fenster ausspähend, versucht er, sich in die Brust zu werfen, als ihm sogleich der Ritter

SCENE 3 – A TRIAL SONG! BY SACHS!

Beckmesser appears outside the shop window, looking in, in great perturbation. Finding the shop empty he enters hastily.	Beckmesser's song, beating motif
He is dressed very richly, but seems very miserable. He peeps again carefully round the shop from the doorway. He then limps forwards, winces in pain and rubs his back. After a few more steps forward his knees give way. He rubs them.	chalk stroke motif, delusion motif / envy motif, chalk stroke motif, resentment motif
He sits on the cobbler's stool, but starts up again in pain. He contemplates the stool and his thoughts appear to become increasingly agitated. He is distressed by the most grievous memories and fancies; getting ever more uneasy, he begins to wipe the perspiration from his brow. –	resentment motif, lute motif, envy motif, beating motif

Beckmesser's song |
| He limps round more and more restlessly, staring before him. – As if pursued from all sides, he stumbles hither and thither as in flight. – As though to save himself from falling he holds on to the table, to which he has tottered, and stares before him. | lute motif, Beckmesser's courtship motif, beating motif, chalk stroke motif |
| Weak and in despair he looks around; – at length his glance falls on Pogner's house through the window to which he limps with difficulty, and looking at the opposite window tries to assume a bold manner as he thinks of Walther. | envy motif

anger motif, Stolzing motif |

The Mastersingers of Nuremberg

Ärger-M., Stolzing-M., Prügel-M.	Walther einfällt. Ärgerliche Gedanken entstehen ihm dadurch, gegen die er mit schmeichelndem Selbstgefühle anzukämpfen sucht. KA 468 ▶ 925 CD 3/7 12:39
Kreidestrich-M., Missgunst-M., Prügel-M., Beckmessers Werbe-M.	Die Eifersucht übermannt ihn; er schlägt sich vor den Kopf. Er glaubt die Verhöhnung der Weiber und Buben auf der Gasse zu vernehmen, wendet sich wütend ab und schmeißt das Fenster zu.
Kreidestrich-M., Wahn-M., Beckmessers Ständchen, Ärger-M.	Sehr verstört wendet er sich mechanisch wieder dem Werktische zu, indem er, vor sich hinbrütend, nach einer neuen Weise zu suchen scheint.
Preislied (Stollen), Singkunst-M. ②	Sein Blick fällt auf das von Sachs zuvor beschriebene Papier; er nimmt es neugierig auf, überfliegt es mit wachsender Aufregung und bricht endlich wütend aus: KA 470 ▶ 952 CD 3/8 0:01

BECKMESSER

Singkunst-M. ② Unmut-M., Beckmesser-M.	Ein Werbelied! – Von Sachs! – Ist's wahr? – Ha! Jetzt wird mir alles klar! –
Freundschaft-M. übergehend in Nürnberg-M., Unmut-M.	*Da er die Kammertüre gehen hört, fährt er zusammen und steckt das Papier eilig in die Tasche. – Sachs, im Festgewande, tritt ein, kommt vor und hält an, als er Beckmesser gewahrt.*

SACHS

Unmut-M.	Sieh da, Herr Schreiber: auch am Morgen? Euch machen die Schuh' doch nicht mehr Sorgen?

Erregtheitstriller	**BECKMESSER**
Kreidestrich-M. Missgunst-M. (abrutschend)	Zum Teufel! So dünn war ich noch nie beschuht; fühl' durch die Sohl'
Unmut-M., Prügel-M., Missgunst-M., Laute-M.	den kleinsten Kies! **SACHS** Mein Merkersprüchlein wirkte dies; trieb sie mit Merkerzeichen so weich.

Act 3, Scene 3 – A trial song! By Sachs!

VS 405 ▸ 16
CD 3/7 12:39

Angry thoughts arise in consequence which he tries to fight down by an assumption of self-confidence.

anger motif, Stolzing motif, beating motif

Jealousy overcomes him. He strikes his forehead. He fancies that he hears again the mocking of the women and boys in the alley; turns away in a rage and slams the window shut.

chalk stroke motif, envy motif, beating motif, Beckmesser's courtship motif

Much disturbed he turns mechanically again to the work-table which he contemplates as he appears to be seeking a new tune.

chalk stroke motif, delusion motif, Beckmesser's song, anger motif

VS 407 ▸ 1
CD 3/8 0:01

His looks fall on the paper written by Sachs; he takes it up with curiosity; runs over it in growing excitement and at length breaks out in fury:

prize song (stanza), singing art motif ②

BECKMESSER

A trial song! – by Sachs! – Is't so? –
Ha! Now ev'rything I know! –

singing art motif ②
resentment motif, Beckmesser motif

He hears the chamber door open, starts and hurriedly puts the paper in his pocket. – Sachs, dressed for the festival, comes forward and stops on seeing Beckmesser.

friendship motif transitioning into Nuremberg motif, resentment motif

SACHS

What you, Sir Marker! Here so early?
The shoes do not still
                give trouble, surely?

resentment motif

BECKMESSER

The devil!
    so thin never were shoes before;
through them I feel
               the smallest stone!

excitement trill

chalk stroke motif
envy motif (sliding)

resentment motif, beating motif, envy motif, lute motif

SACHS

My Marker's proverb that has done;
marking your faults has made them so thin.

The Mastersingers of Nuremberg

Unmut-M., Prügel-M., Missgunst-M. (abrutschend), Erregtheitstriller, Laute-M.

BECKMESSER
Schon gut der Witz,
        und genug der Streich'!
Glaubt mir, Freund Sachs:
        jetzt kenn' ich euch!
Der Spaß von dieser Nacht,
der wird euch noch gedacht.
Daß ich euch nur nicht im Wege sei,
schuft ihr gar Aufruhr und Meuterei!

Unmut-M., Erregtheitstriller, Laute-M., Prügel-M., Beckmessers Werbe-M. Kreidestrich-M., Missgunst-M. (abrutschend)

SACHS
's war Polterabend, laßt euch bedeuten;
eure Hochzeit spukte unter den Leuten:
je toller es da hergeh',
je besser bekommt's der Eh'!

BECKMESSER
   (wütend)

Erregtheitstriller Schaffenslust-M.

Oh, Schuster voll von Ränken
und pöbelhaften Schwänken!
Du warst mein Feind von je:
nur hör, ob hell ich seh'! –

Wut-M.

Die ich mir auserkoren,
die ganz für mich geboren,
zu aller Witwer Schmach
der Jungfer stellst du nach.
Daß sich Herr Sachs erwerbe
des Goldschmieds reiches Erbe,
im Meisterrat zur Hand
auf Klauseln er bestand,
ein Mägdlein zu betören,
das nur auf ihn sollt' hören,
und andren abgewandt
zu ihm allein sich fand.

Missgunst-M., Unmut-M.

Darum! Darum! –
Wär' ich so dumm? –
Mit Schreien und mit Klopfen
wollt' er mein Lied zustopfen,
daß nicht dem Kind werd' kund,
wie auch ein andrer bestund. –

Act 3, Scene 3 – A trial song! By Sachs!

BECKMESSER

Enough of jets!
           Though your wit is keen,
trust me, friend Sachs:
                   your guile is seen!
Your trick of yesterday
you will not soon forget.
So that I should not obstruct your way,
uproar and fighting astir you set!

*resentment motif,
beating motif,
envy motif (sliding),
excitement trill,
lute motif*

SACHS

'Twas wedding eve, let me remind you;
and a bride today the folk have assigned you:
the madder the fun, you see,
the better your luck will be!

*resentment motif,
excitement trill,
lute motif,
beating motif, Beckmesser's courtship motif
chalk stroke motif,
envy motif (sliding)*

BECKMESSER

(furiously)

Oh, cobbler full of cunning,
with brain on tricks e'er running!
You ever were my foe,
and now your craft I know! –
The maid for whom I've waited,
for me alone created,
all widowers to shame,
on her you fix your aim.
'Tis Master Sachs's pleasure,
to win the goldsmith's treasure,
and so before the guild,
our ears with stuff he filled,
a maidens fancy fooling,
that she might heed his schooling,
and, to the shame of all,
her choice on him might fall.
And so! And so! –
ah now I know –
With voice and hammer ringing,
you sought to drown my singing,
lest she should understand,
another stood there at hand. –

*excitement trill
work lust motif*

rage motif

*envy motif,
resentment motif*

Kreidestrich-M., *Missgunst-M.,* *Prügel-M.*	Ja, ja! Haha! Hab' ich dich da? – Aus seiner Schusterstuben hetzt' endlich er den Buben mit Knüppeln auf mich her, daß meiner los er wär'!	
Missgunst-M.	Au, au! Au, au!	
Beckmesser-M.	Wohl grün und blau. zum Spott der allerliebsten Frau, zerschlagen und zerprügelt, daß kein Schneider mich aufbügelt!	
Wut-M.	Gar auf mein Leben war's angegeben! Doch kam ich noch so davon, daß ich die Tat euch lohn': zieht heut nur aus zum Singen,	
Kreidestrich-M., *Unmut-M.,* *Wut-M.*	merkt auf, wie's mag gelingen! Bin ich gezwackt auch und zerhackt, euch bring' ich doch sicher aus dem Takt.	

SACHS

Wut-M. *(abflauend)*	Gut Freund, ihr seid in argem Wahn; glaubt, was ihr wollt, daß ich getan; gebt eure Eifersucht nur hin; zu werben kommt mir nicht in Sinn.

Wut-M. (wieder *aufflackernd),* *Missgunst-M.*	**BECKMESSER** Lug und Trug! Ich kenn' es besser.

SACHS

Wut-M. *(abflauend)*	Was fällt euch nur ein, Meister Beckmesser! Was ich sonst im Sinn, geht euch nicht an; doch, glaubt, ob der Werbung seid ihr im Wahn.

BECKMESSER

Ihr sängt heut nicht?

SACHS

Nicht zur Wette.

Act 3, Scene 3 – A trial song! By Sachs!

VS 412▶7
CD 3/8 2:32

Aye, aye! Ho, ho!   *chalk stroke motif,*
'tis even so? –   *envy motif,*
Directed by your cunning,   *beating motif*
the boys in packs came running,
with cudgels for the fray,
to drive me from your way!
And now through you,   *envy motif*
         I'm black and blue,
and shamed before the maiden too!   *Beckmesser motif*
With tooth and nail they tore me:
ne'er a tailor could restore me!
Suspicions fill me,   *rage motif*
they meant to kill me!
Yet by luck I got away,
that I my debt might pay.
Go forth when all assemble,
today your voice may tremble!   *chalk stroke motif,*
Though I am thwacked,   *resentment motif,*
         laugh not too soon,   *rage motif*
for I will yet put you out of tune.

SACHS

Good friend, your wits are overcast.   *rage motif*
Think what you will of what is past: *(waning)*
be not through jealousy so blind;
for wooing never crossed my mind.

BECKMESSER

'Tis not true! I know you better.   *rage motif (flaring up again),*
     envy motif

SACHS

What fancy in this, Master Beckmesser!   *rage motif*
What I have in mind concerns you not: *(waning)*
but trust,
         that no wooing is in my plot.

BECKMESSER

You will not sing?

SACHS

         Not as suitor.

The Mastersingers of Nuremberg

BECKMESSER
Kein Werbelied?

KA 480 ▶ 1067
CD 3/8 4:05

SACHS
       Gewißlich, nein!

BECKMESSER

Meistersinger-M. ⑤
Missgunst-M.

Wenn ich aber drob ein Zeugnis hätte?
 (Er greift in die Tasche.)

SACHS
 (auf den Werktisch blickend)

Preislied
(Liebesthema)

Das Gedicht?… hier ließ ich's.
       Stecktet ihr's ein?

KA 481 ▶ 1073
CD 3/9 0:01

BECKMESSER
 (das Blatt hervorziehend)
Ist das Eure Hand?

SACHS
       Ja, war es das?

BECKMESSER

Freundschaft-M.
(Beginn)

Ganz frisch noch die Schrift?

SACHS
     Und die Tinte noch naß!

BECKMESSER
's wär' wohl gar ein biblisches Lied?

SACHS
Der fehlte wohl, wer darauf riet'!

BECKMESSER
Nun denn?

SACHS
    Wie doch?

Act 3, Scene 3 – A trial song! By Sachs!

VS 415 ▶ 12
CD 3/8 4:05

BECKMESSER
Not sing, today?

SACHS
You need not fear!

BECKMESSER
But what if I have a proof you mean to? } *mastersinger motif* ⑤
   (He feels in his pocket.) } *envy motif*

SACHS
   (looking on the table)

VS 416 ▶ 6
CD 3/9 0:01

Ah, the song?… You took it? } *prize song*
I left it here. } *(love theme)*

BECKMESSER
   (producing the paper)
Is this not your hand?

SACHS
Ah, was it that?

BECKMESSER
The writing is fresh? } *friendship motif (be-*
  } *ginning)*

SACHS
And the ink still is wet!

BECKMESSER
May be, 'tis a biblical song?

SACHS
Who counts on that, indeed is wrong!

BECKMESSER
Well then?

SACHS
How now?

BECKMESSER
Freundschaft-M.   Ihr fragt?

SACHS
                                                Was doch?

BECKMESSER
Beckmesser-M.   Daß ihr mit aller Biederkeit
                                 der ärgste aller Spitzbuben seid!

SACHS
Freundschaft-M.,
Beckmesser-M.   Mag sein doch hab' ich noch nie entwandt,
                                 was ich auf fremden Tischen fand:
Unmut-M.   und daß man von euch
Erregtheitstriller   auch nicht Übles denkt,
                                 behaltet das Blatt, es sei euch geschenkt.

BECKMESSER
                                      (in freudigem Schreck aufspringend)
                                 Herr Gott! –
                                        Ein Gedicht? Ein Gedicht von Sachs?...
Beckmesser-M.   Doch halt, –
                                        daß kein neuer Schad' mir erwachs'! –
Freundschaft-M.,   Ihr habt's wohl schon recht gut memoriert?
Beckmesser-M.

SACHS
Seid meinethalb doch nur unbeirrt!

BECKMESSER
Ihr laßt mir das Blatt?

SACHS
                                                Damit ihr kein Dieb.

BECKMESSER
Und, macht' ich Gebrauch?

SACHS
                                                Wie's euch belieb'.

Act 3, Scene 3 – A trial song! By Sachs!

BECKMESSER

You ask? ⎫ *friendship motif*

SACHS

What more?

BECKMESSER

That you with all your probity *Beckmesser motif*
the worst of rogues for ever will be!

SACHS *friendship motif,*
Beckmesser motif
May be; but yet I was never known
to take up things I did not own.
And men for this action *resentment motif*
  might call you thief! *excitement trill*
To save you from that, I give you the leaf.

BECKMESSER

(springing up in joyful surprise)
Good Lord! –
  A song? A song by you?…
Yet stay, – *Beckmesser motif*
  lest mishap should cross me anew! –
The song you have, no doubt, got by heart? *friendship motif,*
Beckmesser motif

SACHS

Fear not that my claim your plan will thwart!

BECKMESSER

You give me the song?

SACHS

  Lest thief you should be.

BECKMESSER

The song may I sing?

SACHS

  I leave you free.

The Mastersingers of Nuremberg

Freundschaft-M.,
Beckmesser-M.

BECKMESSER
Doch sing' ich das Lied?

KA 484 ▶ 1117
CD 3/9 1:39

SACHS
               Wenn's nicht zu schwer.

BECKMESSER
Und, wenn ich gefiel'?

SACHS
               Das – wunderte mich sehr!

BECKMESSER

(ganz zutraulich)

Da seid ihr nun wieder zu bescheiden;
ein Lied von Sachs, –

(gleichsam pfeifend)

               das will was bedeuten! –

Missgunst-M.,
Beckmessers
Werbe-M.

Und seht nur, wie mir's ergeht,
wie's mit mir Ärmsten steht!
Erseh' ich doch mit Schmerzen,
das Lied, das nachts ich sang, –
dank euren lust'gen Scherzen! –

Missgunst-M.,
Beckmessers
Werbe-M.

es machte der Pognerin bang. –
Wie schaff' ich mir nun zur Stelle
ein neues Lied herzu?
Ich armer, zerschlag'ner Geselle,
wie fänd' ich heut dazu Ruh'!
Werbung und eh'lich Leben,
ob das mir Gott beschied,
muß ich nun grad' aufgeben,

Beckmesser-M.

hab' ich kein neues Lied.
Ein Lied von euch, dess' bin ich gewiß,

Kreidestrich-M.
Entzückung-M.

mit dem besieg' ich jed' Hindernis:
soll ich das heute haben,
vergessen, begraben

Erregtheitstriller,
Kreidestrich-M.

sei Zwist, Hader und Streit,
und was uns je entzweit'.

Act 3, Scene 3 – A trial song! By Sachs!

BECKMESSER

The song I may sing?

friendship motif, Beckmesser motif

SACHS

If you know how.

BECKMESSER

And if I succeed?

SACHS

'Twould startle me, I trow!

BECKMESSER

(with complete trust)

Ah, now you fail to prize yourself duly.
A song by Sachs, –
   (whistling)
         That means something truly! –
And look you! sad is my plight,
since the ills of the night,
with heart aching and doubting,
when e'er I think of my lay. –
Thanks to your foolish flouting, –
the maiden was filled with dismay. –
How can I, with all my learning,
now make anew my song?
With anger and pain I am burning!
In sooth 'twould take me too long.
Wedlock and wooing tender,
though they have come my way,
must I at once surrender,
failing a song today.
A song by Sachs! Ah, surely I know,
with that each hindrance right now will go.
Let this gift make our peace, then,
and happily cease,
then, our jars, quarrels and strife,
that made us foes for life!

envy motif, Beckmesser's courtship motif

envy motif, Beckmesser's courtship motif

Beckmesser motif

chalk stroke motif

delight motif

excitement trill, chalk stroke motif

The Mastersingers of Nuremberg

Preislied (Stollen)   *Er blickt seitwärts in das Blatt; plötzlich runzelt sich seine Stirne.*

Missgunst-M., Kreidestrich-M.
Und doch! Wenn's nur eine Falle wär'? –
Noch gestern wart ihr mein Feind: –
Wie käm's, daß nach so großer Beschwer'
ihr's freundlich heut mit mir meint?

Freundschaft-M.

SACHS

Ich macht' euch Schuh' in später Nacht:
hat man je so einen Feind bedacht?

BECKMESSER

Ja, ja! Recht gut! Doch eines schwört:
wo und wie ihr das Lied auch hört,
daß nie ihr euch beikommen laßt,
zu sagen, das Lied sei von euch verfaßt.

SACHS

Das schwör' ich und gelob' es euch:
nie mich zu rühmen, das Lied sei von mir.

BECKMESSER

     (sich vergnügt die Hände reibend)
Was will ich mehr?
                 Ich bin geborgen:
jetzt braucht sich Beckmesser
                  nicht mehr zu sorgen.

Beckmessers Werbe-M.

SACHS

Doch, Freund, ich führ's euch zu Gemüte,
und rat' es euch in aller Güte:

Lebhaftigkeit-M.
studiert mir recht das Lied;
sein Vortrag ist nicht leicht;
ob euch die Weise geriet',
und ihr den Ton erreicht.

BECKMESSER

Freund Sachs, ihr seid ein guter Poet;
doch was Ton und Weise betrifft, gesteht,

Kreidestrich-M.
da tut mir's keiner vor.

Act 3, Scene 3 – A trial song! By Sachs!

KA 422 ▶ 10
CD 3/9 3:02

He looks sideways at the paper; suddenly he wrinkles his forehead.   *prize song (stanza)*

And yet, if 'twere but a trap, at last? –   *envy motif, chalk*
Since foes we have been for aye: –   *stroke motif*
how comes it, after all that has passed,
a friend I find you today?

SACHS   *friendship motif*

Till late at night I made your shoes;
is't so that men ever serve their foes?

BECKMESSER

Ay, ay! 'Tis true! Yet one thing swear,
that whenever this song you hear,
you never will bring me to shame,
and, though I should win, you will make no claim.

SACHS

My promise and my oath I give;
ne'er will I claim it, so long as I live.

BECKMESSER

(rubbing his hands with delight)
What would I more?
      Ill-luck is over:
Beckmesser now will
     henceforth live in, clover.   *Beckmesser's courtship motif*

SACHS

But, friend now deem me not a scoffer,
if counsel good to you I offer:
to con the song with heed;   *livelihood motif*
not easy 'tis to sing.
The „mode" may fail at your need,
the „tone" may falsely ring.

BECKMESSER

Friend Sachs, as poet, first is your place,
but when „tones" and „modes" are in hand, confess,
that I need have no fear.   *chalk stroke motif*

	Drum spitzt nur fein das Ohr, –
	und: „Beckmesser!
	Keiner besser!" –
	Darauf macht euch gefaßt,
Lebhaftigkeit-M.,	wenn ihr mich ruhig singen laßt. –
Beckmessers	Doch nun memorieren,
Werbe-M.	schnell nach Haus:
	ohne Zeit zu verlieren
	richt' ich das aus. –
	Hans Sachs, mein Teurer,
	ich hab' euch verkannt;
	durch den Abenteurer
	war ich verrannt: –
	(sehr zutraulich)
	(so einer fehlte uns bloß! –
	Den wurden wir Meister doch los[1]! –)
	Doch mein Besinnen
Lebhaftigkeit-M.,	läuft mir von hinnen!
Beckmessers	Bin ich verwirrt
Werbe-M.	und ganz verirrt? –
	Die Silben, die Reime,
	die Worte, die Verse!
	Ich kleb' wie am Leime,
	und brennt doch die Ferse.
	Ade! Ich muß fort:
	an andrem Ort
	dank' ich euch inniglich,
	weil ihr so minniglich;
	für euch nun stimme ich,
	kauf' eure Werke gleich,
	mache zum Merker euch,
	doch fein mit Kreide weich,
	nicht mit dem Hammerstreich! –
Kränzlein-M.,	Merker! Merker! Merker Hans Sachs!
Erregtheitstriller,	Daß Nürnberg schusterlich blüh' und wachs'!
Beckmessers Werbe-M.	

KA 493 ▶ 1223
CD 3/9 4:34

Beckmesser nimmt tanzend von Sachs Abschied, taumelt und poltert der Ladentüre zu; plötzlich glaubt er, das Gedicht in seiner Tasche vergessen zu haben, läuft wieder vor, sucht ängstlich auf dem Werktische, bis er es

---

[1] *diese klassische Kadenz benutzte Beckmesser im 1. Akt (Seite 94) zu „Von Melodei nicht eine Spur". Sie wird später von Sachs (292) wieder aufgegriffen, als er sich freut, dass er in Walther "den Rechten fand".*

Act 3, Scene 3 – A trial song! By Sachs!

VS 425 ▶ 19
CD 3/9 4:34

Then open well your ear, –
and: „Beckmesser!
Tone-professor!" –
And all your doubt will cease,
if you let me but sing in peace. – *livelihood motif,*
But now I must learn it *Beckmesser's courts-*
well by heart: *hip motif*
that no time may be wasted,
I must depart. –
Hans Sachs, my comrade,
your heart is misread;
by the knight of Stolzing
I was mislead: –

    (very confidentially)

(we well can spare such as he! –
We Masters from him now are free[1]! –)
But all my senses
scatter and leave me! *livelihood motif,*
Are my wits dazed *Beckmesser's courts-*
and all I astray? – *hip motif*
The stanzas, the accents,
the measure, the verses!
I stay here and chatter,
with feet all on fire.
Farewell! I must go:
we meet again.
Thanks in sincerity
take for your friendliness;
you shall my vote command,
all of your works I buy,
you shall our Marker be,
but only chalk we use;
mark not with hammer blows! –
Marker! Marker! Marker Hans Sachs! *chaplet motif,*
That Nürnberg ever may bloom and wax! *excitement trill,*
    Beckmesser's courts-
    Beckmesser, dancing about, takes leave of *hip motif*
    Sachs and hurries stumbling to the door; sud-
    denly he thinks he has forgotten to pocket
    the song, comes forward again and anxiously
    seeks it on the table, until he discovers it in his

---

[1] *this classic cadenza Beckmesser used in act 1 (page 95) for „of melody not even a trace". It will be later quoted by Sachs (293) when he is glad having found in Walther "the right one".*

The Mastersingers of Nuremberg

Prügel-M.,
Kränzlein-M.,
Entzückung-M.,
Beckmessers Werbe-M.

in der eigenen Hand gewahr wird: darüber KA 497 ▸ 1300
scherzhaft erfreut, umarmt er Sachs nochmals CD 3/9 6:07
voll feurigen Dankes und stürzt dann, hinkend
und strauchelnd, geräuschvoll durch die La-
dentür ab.

Unmut-M.

SACHS

sieht Beckmesser gedankenvoll lächelnd nach.

So ganz boshaft doch keinen ich fand;
er hält's auf die Länge nicht aus:
vergeudet mancher oft viel Verstand,
doch hält er auch damit haus;

Erregtheitstriller,
Beckmesser-M.
Nürnberg-M.,
Johannistag-M.,
Werbe-M.

die schwache Stunde kommt für jeden;
da wird er dumm und läßt mit sich reden.
Daß hier Herr Beckmesser ward zum Dieb,
ist mir für meinen Plan gar lieb.

Eva nähert sich auf der Straße der Ladentüre.
Sachs wendet sich und gewahrt Eva.

Sieh, Ev'chen! Dacht ich's doch, wo sie blieb'! KA 499 ▸ 1356
CD 3/10 0:01

Act 3, Scene 3 – A trial song! By Sachs!

VS 430 ▶ 1
CD 3/9 6:07

hand; delighted thereat, he again embraces Sachs, in fervent gratitude, and then rushes, limping and stumbling noisily, through the shop door.

beating motif,
chaplet motif,
delight motif,
Beckmesser's court-
ship motif

Sachs

resentment motif

follows Beckmesser with his eyes, thoughtfully smiling.

So rank malice ne'er yet I have known;
ere long he will meet with his meed:
tough many squander wits that they own,
yet keep enough for their need,
the hour of weakness comes to cheat them;
then are they fools, and so we defeat them.
That Master Beckmesser stole the song,
in truth will help my plan along.

excitement trill,
Beckmesser motif
Nuremberg motif,
Midsummer day motif,
courtship motif

Eva approaches the shop door from the street. Sachs turns and sees Eva.

VS 432 ▶ 12
CD 3/10 0:01
See, Ev'chen! Where, methought, can she be!

4. Szene – Grüss Gott, mein Evchen!

Anmut-M.

Eva, reich geschmückt, in glänzend weißer Kleidung, auch etwas leidend und blaß, tritt zum Laden herein und schreitet langsam vor.

Sachs

Grüß Gott, mein Evchen! Ei, wie herrlich
und stolz du's heute meinst!
Du machst wohl Alt und Jung begehrlich,

Werbe-M.

wenn du so schön erscheinst!

Eva

Resignation-M.[1]

Meister, 's ist nicht so gefährlich:
und ist's dem Schneider geglückt,
wer sieht dann, wo's mir beschwerlich,
wo still der Schuh mich drückt?

Sachs

Der böse Schuh'! 's war deine Laun',
daß du ihn gestern nicht probiert.

Eva

Resignation-M.

Merk' wohl, ich hatt' zu viel Vertraun;
im Meister hatt' ich mich geirrt.

Sachs

Ei, 's tut mir leid! Zeig her, mein Kind,
daß ich dir helfe gleich geschwind.

---

[1] *Das Motiv ist ein traurig wirkendes Fragment des Sommernachtzauber-Motivs, das sich beim Erscheinen Walthers wieder in das vollständige Original zurück verwandelt.*

Scene 4 – Good day, my Ev'chen!

Eva, richly dressed in gleaming white, rather sad and pale, enters the shop and comes slowly forward.

grace motif

Sachs

Good day, my Evchen! Ei, art arming thyself with weavons fine,
both old and young by beauty charming,
that thou so bright dost shine?

courtship motif

Eva

Master, 'tis not so alarming:
though all be well with a dress,
some fault yet the foot may be harming,
unseen the shoe may press.

resignation motif[1]

Sachs

The wicked shoe! The fault was thine,
that yesterday thou triedst them not.

Eva

Mark you, too firm a faith was mine!
The master was not all I thought.

resignation motif

Sachs

If grieves me sore, come here to me,
that I may help thee, let me see.

---

[1] *The motif is a fragment of the summer night's magic motif with a sad connotation, that will turn back to its full original when Walther appears in this scene.*

The Mastersingers of Nuremberg

EVA

Resignation-M. Sobald ich stehe, will es gehn;
Unmut-M. doch, will ich gehn, zwingt mich's zu stehn.

SACHS

Hier auf den Schemel streck den Fuß:
der üblen Not ich wehren muß. –

Resignation-M. *Sie streckt einen Fuß auf dem Schemel am Werktisch aus.*

Was ist mit dem?

EVA

Unmut-M. Ihr seht, zu weit!

SACHS

Kind, das ist pure Eitelkeit;
der Schuh ist knapp.

EVA

Das sagt' ich ja:
Resignation-M. drum drückt er mich an den Zehen da.

SACHS

Hier links?

EVA

Nein, rechts.

SACHS

Wohl mehr am Spann?

EVA

Hier mehr am Hacken.

SACHS

Kommt der auch dran?

EVA

Ach, Meister! Wüßtet ihr besser als ich,
wo der Schuh mich drückt?

Act 3, Scene 4 – Good day, my Ev'chen!

EVA

Whene'er I stand, it will away; *resignation motif*
but when I move it makes me stay. *resentment motif*

SACHS

Upon the stool here place the shoe:
and I will see what I can do. –

> *She places one foot on the stool near the table.* *resignation motif*

What's wrong with that?

EVA

Too broad, you see! *resentment motif*

SACHS

Child, that is nought but vanity;
the shoe fits close.

EVA

Yes, there, I know:
'tis on my toes that it hurts me so. *resignation motif*

SACHS

Here left?

EVA

No, right.

SACHS

Here at the heel?

EVA

More on the instep.

SACHS

What there as well?

EVA

Ah, Master! Know you, then, better than I,
where the shoe doth pinch?

SACHS

Ei! 's wundert mich,
daß er zu weit, und doch drückt überall!

Sommernachtzauber-M.

Walther, in glänzender Rittertracht, tritt unter die Türe der Kammer. Eva stößt einen Schrei aus und bleibt, unverwandt auf Walther blickend, in ihrer Stellung, mit dem Fuße auf dem Schemel. – Sachs, der vor ihr niedergebückt steht, bleibt mit dem Rücken der Türe zugekehrt, ohne Walthers Eintritt zu beachten.

Aha! – Hier sitzt's: nun begreif' ich den Fall. –
Kind, du hast recht: 's stak in der Naht.
Nun warte, dem Übel schaff' ich Rat:
bleib nur so stehn; ich nehm' dir den Schuh
eine Weil' auf den Leisten,
                dann läßt er dir Ruh'!

Resignation-M.

Walther, durch den Anblick Evas festgebannt, bleibt ebenfalls unbeweglich unter der Türe stehen. Sachs hat Eva sanft den Schuh vom Fuße gezogen; während sie in ihrer Stellung verbleibt, macht er sich am Werktisch mit dem Schuh zu schaffen und tut, als beachte er nichts anderes.

(bei der Arbeit)

Immer schustern, das ist nun mein Los;
des Nachts, des Tags, komm' nicht davon los.
Kind, hör zu: ich hab' mir's überdacht,
was meinem Schustern ein Ende macht:
am besten, ich werbe doch nun um dich;
da gewänn' ich doch was als Poet für mich. –
Du hörst nicht drauf? So sprich doch jetzt;

Resignation-M.

hast mir's ja selbst in den Kopf gesetzt? –
Schon gut! – ich merk': –

Unmut-M.

          „mach deinen Schuh'!"– –
Säng' mir nur wenigstens einer dazu! –

Preislied (Stollen) ②

Hörte heut gar ein schönes Lied: –
wem dazu wohl
                ein dritter Vers geriet'? –

Act 3, Scene 4 – Good day, my Ev'chen!

SACHS

          I wonder why,
if 'tis too broad, it still pinches you so!

> *Walther, in shining knightly costume enters by the chamber door. Eva utters a cry, and remains in the same position, her foot on the stool, looking at Walther. – Sachs who stands bent down before her, remains with his back turned to the door, without taking notice of Walther's entrance.*

summer night's magic motif

Aha! – 'Tis found! Now the reason I know. –
Child, thou art right, something is wrong.
Be patient, the fault I'll mend ere long:
stand so awhile; the shoe on the last
I will place for a moment,
          thy pain will be past!

> *Walther, held fast by Eva's look, also remains standing motionless in the doorway. Sachs had gently drawn Eva's shoe from her foot; she remains in the same position, as he takes the shoe to the work-table and works at it as if taking note of nothing else*

resignation motif

(working

Cobbling always, that now is my lot;
by night, by day, my toil ceases not.
Child, give heed, and hear what I've thought:
my cobbling must to an end be brought;
and haply 'twere best to venture for thee;
then some profit as poet were won for me. –
Thou hear'st me not? Now speak a word;
for first the plan from thy lips I heard. –   *resignation motif*
'Tis well! – I see: –
          „Make but thy shoes!" – –   *resentment motif*
If I could only summon my muse! –
Lately a beauteous song I heard: –   *prize song (stanza)* ②
would but some one now
          sing me verse the third? –

WALTHER

den begeisterten Blick unverwandt auf Eva geheftet:

Preislied (Stollen)
„Weilten die Sterne im lieblichen Tanz?
So licht und klar
im Lockenhaar,
vor allen Frauen
hehr zu schauen,
lag ihr mit zartem Glanz
ein Sternenkranz."

SACHS

(immer fort arbeitend)

Werbe-M.
Lausch, Kind! Das ist ein Meisterlied.

WALTHER

„Wunder ob Wunder nun bieten sich dar:
zwiefachen Tag
ich grüßen mag;
denn gleich zwei'n Sonnen
reinster Wonnen,
der hehrsten Augen Paar
nahm ich da wahr."

SACHS

(beiseite zu Eva)

Derlei hörst du jetzt bei mir singen.

WALTHER

Preislied
(Liebesthema)
„Huldreichstes Bild,
dem ich zu nahen mich erkühnt!
Den Kranz, von zweier Sonnen Strahl

Eva-M.
zugleich geblichen und ergrünt,

Sachs hat den Schuh zurückgebracht und ist jetzt darüber her, ihn Eva wieder an den Fuß zu ziehen.

minnig und mild
Entzückung-M.
sie flocht ihn um das Haupt dem Gemahl:
dort huldgeboren,

Act 3, Scene 4 – Good day, my Ev'chen!

WALTHER

gazing in rapture on Eva:

„Lured from their dances the stars glided down,   *prize song (stanza)*
and sparkled fair
about her hair;
on her attending
beauty lending,
and round her head there shone
a starry crown."

SACHS

(still working)
Hark, child! that is a Mastersong.   *courtship motif*

WALTHER

„Wonder on wonder was born on the height:
ere night was gone
a twofold dawn
was rising o'er me
as before me,
like suns, her eyes so bright
greeted my sight."

SACHS

(aside to Eva)
Such songs are heard now in my dwelling.

WALTHER

„Oh, hallowed scene,   *prize song (love*
that like a spell my footsteps drew!   *theme)*
Lit up by sunbeams richly shed
the wreath grew pale and bloomed anew,   *Eva motif*

Sachs has brought back the shoe and is now occupied in fitting it again on Eva's foot.

tender her mien,
as her hand wove its leaves round my head: *delight motif*
where love hath bound me,

Preislied *(Liebesthema)*	nun ruhmerkoren, gießt paradiesische Lust sie in des Dichters Brust – im Liebestraum!"

Sachs

Nun schau, ob dazu mein Schuh geriet?
Mein' endlich doch, – es tät mir gelingen?
Versuch's, – tritt auf!
Sag, drückt er dich noch?

Wahn-M.,
Schaffenslust-M.,
Erregtheitstriller

> *Eva, die wie bezaubert, regungslos gestanden, gesehen und gehört hat, bricht jetzt in heftiges Weinen aus, sinkt Sachs an die Brust und drückt ihn schluchzend an sich. – Walther ist zu ihnen getreten; er drückt begeistert Sachs die Hand. Längeres Schweigen leidenschaftlicher Ergriffenheit. – Sachs tut sich endlich Gewalt an, reißt sich wie unmutig los und läßt dadurch Eva unwillkürlich an Walthers Schulter sich anlehnen.*

Sachs

Schusterlied, Wahn-M.
(in den Hörnern),
Schustermühe-M.

Hat man mit dem Schuhwerk nicht seine Not!
Wär' ich nicht noch Poet dazu,
ich machte länger keine Schuh'!
Das ist eine Müh', ein Aufgebot!
Zu weit dem einen, dem andern zu eng;
von allen Seiten Lauf' und Gedräng':
da klappt's,
da schlappt's;

Resignation-M.

hier drückt's,
da zwickt's; –
der Schuster soll auch alles wissen,

Schusterlied

flicken, was nur immer zerrissen:
und ist er gar Poet dazu,
da läßt man am End' ihm auch da keine Ruh'
und ist er erst noch Witwer gar,
zum Narren hält man ihn fürwahr: –

Resignation-M.,
Meistersinger-M. ④,
Eva-M.

die jüngsten Mädchen, ist Not an Mann,
begehren, er hielte um sie an;
versteht er sie, versteht er sie nicht, –
all eins, ob ja, ob nein er spricht, –

Act 3, Scene 4 – Good day, my Ev'chen!

there fame hath crowned me,
I drink from her radiant eyes *prize song (love*
all joys of paradise – *theme)*
in loves fair dream!"

SACHS

Now see if as well my shoe will pass.
At last, I trow, my labour has prospered?
Now try, stand up!
Say, how is it now?

> *Eva, who has stood motionless as if enchantet,*
> *gazing and listening, now passionately bursts* *delusion motif,*
> *into tears, sinks on Sachs's breast and presses* *work lust motif,*
> *herself to him, sobbing. – Walther has come* *excitement trill*
> *to them; he presses Sachs's hand. – Sachs at*
> *length controls himself and tears himself mood-*
> *ily away; and so leaves Eva involuntarily leaning*
> *on Walther's shoulder.*

SACHS

A shoemaker's life is aye full of care! *cobbler's song, delusi-*
were I not a poet too, *on motif (horns),*
henceforth I ne'er would make a shoe! *cobbler's labor motif*
No rest; ever culled, now here, now there!
Too wide for this one, for that one too small.
To all his neigh boundsman and thrall:
Too loose,
too tight,
too thick,
too slight. – *resignation motif*
The cobbler must have wit unending,
patching all the holes that need mending: *cobbler's song*
and if he be a poet too,
no rest can he find then, but toil ever new;
should he a widower chance to be;
to fool him well then all agree: –
the youngest maidens, when wooers fail, *resignation motif,*
expect him to tell the lover's tale; *mastersinger motif ④,*
and if he know, or know not their ways, – *Eva motif*
all one, if yes, or no he says. –

289

The Mastersingers of Nuremberg

Unmut-M. am End'– riecht er doch nach Pech
Hohn-M. und gilt für dumm, tückisch und frech. –
Ei! 's ist mir nur um den Lehrbuben leid;
der verliert mir allen Respekt:
Eva-M., die Lene macht ihn schon nicht recht gescheit,
Resignation-M. daß aus Töpf' und Tellern er leckt.
Wo Teufel er jetzt nur wieder steckt! –

EVA

indem sie Sachs zurückhält und von neuem an sich zieht:

Wahn-M. O Sachs! Mein Freund! Du teurer Mann!
Wie ich dir Edlem lohnen kann!
Eva-M. Was ohne deine Liebe,
was wär' ich ohne dich? –
Ob je auch Kind ich bliebe,
erwecktest du mich nicht?
Durch dich gewann ich,
was man preist;
durch dich ersann ich,
was ein Geist;
durch dich erwacht',
durch dich nur dacht'
ich edel, frei und kühn;
Eva-M. du ließest mich erblühn!
Ja, lieber Meister, schilt mich nur;
ich war doch auf der rechten Spur.
Eva-M. Denn, hatte ich die Wahl,
nur dich erwählt' ich mir;
du warest mein Gemahl,
(Tristanmotive) den Preis reicht' ich nur dir. –
Eva-M. Doch nun hat's mich gewählt
zu nie gekannter Qual;
(Tristanmotive) und werd' ich heut vermählt,
so war's ohn' alle Wahl: –
das war ein Müssen, war ein Zwang!
Euch selbst, mein Meister, wurde bang.

SACHS

Mein Kind, von Tristan und Isolde

Act 3, Scene 4 – Good day, my Ev'chen!

VS 446 ▶ 13
CD 3/11 1:40

They smell pitch about the place!   *resentment motif*
they call him dull, knavish and base. –   *scorn motif*
Ah! I am grieved for the prentice, I say:
all respect he loses for me:
for Lene spoils him by night and by day,   *Eva motif,*
and a lazy glutton is he.   *resignation motif*
The devil now knows where he can be! –

EVA

as she holds Sachs back and again draws him to her:

O Sachs! My friend! My only friend!   *delusion motif*
All I shall owe thee till the end!
What but for thy love's keeping,   *Eva motif*
what were I but for thee? –
In childhood's dream yet sleeping,
hads't thou not wakened me.
Through thee my wisdom
I have won;
through thee my spirit
I have known;
through thee I live,
through thee I strive:
and, noble, brave and free
thy spirit grew in me!   *Eva motif*
Aye, dearest Master, chide at will;
my fancy was the right one still:
and if I had a voice,   *Eva motif*
and were my heart my own;
'tis thou would'st be my choice,
the prize were thine alone. –   *(Tristan motifs)*
But now I feel a power   *Eva motif*
that tears my will in twain;
and were I wed this hour,   *(Tristan motifs)*
all choice would be in vain: –
to stem the flood that surges here,
e'en you, my Master, would not dare.

SACHS

My child, of Tristan and Isolde

The Mastersingers of Nuremberg

(Tristanmotive)	kenn' ich ein traurig Stück: –	KA 525 ▶ 1601
	Hans Sachs war klug, und wollte	CD 3/11 4:48
Erregtheitstriller	nichts von Herrn Markes Glück. –	
	's war Zeit, daß ich den Rechten fand,	
	wär' sonst am End' doch hineingerannt.[1] –	
	Aha! Da streicht die Lene schon ums Haus:	
	nur herein! He! David! Kommst nicht heraus?	

> *Magdalene, in festlichem Staate, tritt durch die Ladentüre herein. David, ebenfalls im Festkleid, mit Blumen und Bändern sehr reich und zierlich ausgeputzt, kommt zugleich aus der Kammer heraus.*

Resignation-M.	Die Zeugen sind da, Gevatter zur Hand:
(fröhlich),	jetzt schnell zur Taufe! Nehmt euren Stand!
Meistersinger-M. ④	

> *Alle blicken ihn verwundert an.*

Taufchoral	Ein Kind ward hier geboren:	KA 527 ▶ 1625
	jetzt sei ihm ein Nam' erkoren!	CD 3/12 0:01
	So ist's nach Meisterweis' und Art,	
	wenn eine Meisterweise geschaffen ward,	
	daß die einen guten Namen trag',	
	dran jeder sie erkennen mag. –	
Erregtheitstriller,	Vernehmt, respektable Gesellschaft,	
Meistersinger-M. ①	was euch hier zur Stell' schafft. –	
	Eine Meisterweise ist gelungen,	
	von Junker Walther gedichtet und gesungen:	
	der jungen Weise lebender Vater	
Taufchoral	lud mich und die Pognerin zu Gevatter.	
Erregtheitstriller	Weil wir die Weise wohl vernommen,	
	sind wir zur Taufe hierher gekommen;	
	auch daß wir zur Handlung Zeugen haben,	
Taufchoral	ruf' ich Jungfer Lene und meinen Knaben.	
	Doch da's zum Zeugen kein Lehrbube tut,	
	und heut auch den Spruch er gesungen gut,	
	so mach' ich den Burschen	
	gleich zum Gesell'.	
Kreidestrich-M.	Knie nieder, David, und nimm diese Schell'!	

> *David ist niedergekniet; Sachs gibt ihm eine starke Ohrfeige.*

Kunst-M.	Steh auf, Gesell, und denk an den Streich:
Taufchoral	du merkst dir dabei die Taufe zugleich. –

---

[1] *musikalisch ein Zitat aus der 3. Szene (276: „Den wurden wir Meister doch los"). Dort zeigte sich Beckmesser zufrieden, Walther los zu sein. Hier freut sich Sachs darüber, dass er in Walther "den Rechten fand".*

Act 3, Scene 4 – Good day, my Ev'chen!

VS 452 ▶ 4 CD 3/11 4:48 a grievous tale I know: –	*(Tristan motifs)*
Hans Sachs was wise and would not	
endure king Marke's woe.. –	} *excitement trill*
To find the man before too late,	
I sought, or else that had been my fate.¹ –	
Aha! Already Lene is about:	
come you in! Ho! David! Thou too, come out.	

Magdalene, in festal array, enters through the shop door. David, also dressed for the festival, decked out with flowers and ribbons comes out of the chamber at the same time.

The witnesses here, and sponsors at hand!	} *resignation motif*
So, for the christ'ning, take now your stand!	} *(joyful),*
All look at him in surprise.	*mastersinger motif* ④
VS 453 ▶ 11 A child, newly created,	} *choral of baptism*
CD 3/12 0:01 with a name shall now be mated!	
This is by use the Masters' right	
whene'er a Mastermode has been brought to light,	
the strain by a goodly name they call,	
and so henceforth 'tis known to all. –	
Now know, worthy people, who hear me,	} *excitement trill,*
why I call you near me. –	*mastersinger motif* ①
Here a „Mastermode" was fashioned newly,	
and by this knight has been sung before us duly:	
he asks that we our aid now may lend him	
and straight at its baptism here attend him.	*choral of baptism*
As to his song our ears have listened,	} *excitement trill*
we hither come that it may be christened.	
That we who have heard attest its fitness,	
let David and Lene now stand to witness.	*choral of baptism*
But as no prentice a witness may be,	
and right well today he has sung to me,	
a journeyman I will	
make of him now.	
David, and, on thy knees, take this blow.	*chalk stroke motif*

David has knelt; Sachs gives him a smart box on his ear.

Arise, the blow thou wilt not forget:	*art motif*
the baptism that will fix in thy pate. –	*choral of baptism*

---
¹ melodically, a quote from scene 3 (page 277: „We Masters from him now are free"). There, Beckmesser was happy to have gotten rid of Walther. Here Sachs is glad having found in Walther „the right one".

293

Kunst-M., Taufchoral	Fehlt sonst noch was, uns keiner schilt; wer weiß, ob's nicht gar einer Nottaufe gilt. Daß die Weise Kraft behalte zum Leben, will ich nur gleich den Namen ihr geben: –	KA 532 ▶ 1668 CD 3/12 2:18
Traum-M. (ohne Harfe) Erregtheitstriller	Die „selige Morgentraum-Deutweise" sei sie genannt zu des Meisters Preise. –	KA 532 ▶ 1675 CD 4/1 0:01
Taufspruch-M. (Sachs)	Nun wachse sie groß, ohn' Schad' und Bruch. Die jüngste Gevatterin spricht den Spruch.	

Er tritt aus der Mitte des Halbkreises, der von den übrigen um ihn gebildet worden war, auf die Seite, so daß nun Eva in der Mitte zu stehen kommt.

Eva

Taufspruch-M. (Eva)	Selig, wie die Sonne meines Glückes lacht, Morgen voller Wonne, selig mir erwacht; Traum der höchsten Hulden, himmlisch' Morgenglühn: Deutung euch zu schulden, selig süß' Bemühn!
Preislied (Stollen)	Einer Weise, mild und hehr, sollt' es hold gelingen, meines Herzens süß' Beschwer' deutend zu bezwingen. Ob es nur ein Morgentraum? Selig deut' ich mir es kaum.
Taufspruch-M. (Eva)	Doch die Weise, was sie leise mir vertraut,
Entzückung-M. Erregtheitstriller	hell und laut, in der Meister vollem Kreis, deute sie auf den höchsten Preis.

Sachs

Preislied (Stollen)	Vor dem Kinde, lieblich hold, mocht' ich gern wohl singen: doch des Herzens süß' Beschwer' galt es zu bezwingen: 's war ein schöner Morgentraum;

Act 3, Scene 4 – Good day, my Ev'chen!

If aught should lack what blame indeed? — *art motif,*
Perchance 'tis „half-baptism" we now may need. — *choral of baptism*
That the mode's good-luck may last unbroken,
before you, let its name be spoken: –
The mode of „Morning dream-story" — *dream motif (without the harp)*
so be it called, to its Master's glory. – — *excitement trill*
And let it both far and wide be heard. — *baptismal verse*
I leave to the godmother now the word. — *(Sachs)*

> *He moves from the middle of the half-circle which the others have formed round him, so that Eva stands now in the middle.*

Eva

Brightly as the sun — *baptismal verse (Eva)*
upon my fortune breaks,
so this gladsome dawn with
blissful promise wakes.
Dream of dazzling glory,
Heavens morning glow:
who should tell thy story?
who thy meaning shew?
☐ In this sweet and holy strain, — *prize song (stanza)*
lies a secret hidden,
☐ stilling all the welcome pain
that fills my heart unbidden.
Is it but a morning dream?
Dare I try to rede its theme?
☐ But the strain, yet — *baptismal verse (Eva)*
once again, though
whispered here,
loud and clear, — *delight motif*
mid the Masters' guild shall rise, — *excitement trill*
there to win the highest prize.

Sachs

☐ To the maid I fain would sing, — *prize song (stanza)*
              of my secret hidden:
But to tell my heart's sweet pain,
              now it is forbidden.
'Twas a lovely morning dream;

The Mastersingers of Nuremberg

	dran zu deuten wag' ich kaum.
Taufspruch-M. *(Eva)*	Diese Weise, was sie leise mir anvertraut, im stillen Raum, sagt mir laut: auch der Jugend ew'ges Reis grünt nur durch des Dichters Preis.

WALTHER

Preislied (Stollen)	Deine Liebe ließ mir es gelingen, meines Herzens süß' Beschwer' deutend zu bezwingen: ob es noch der Morgentraum? Selig deut' ich mir es kaum.
Taufspruch-M. *(Eva)*	Doch die Weise, was sie leise dir vertraut, im stillen Raum, hell und laut in der Meister vollem Kreis, werbe sie um den höchsten Preis.

DAVID

Preislied (Stollen)	Wach' oder träum' ich schon so früh? Das zu erklären, macht mir Müh': 's ist wohl nur ein Morgentraum? Was ich seh', begreif' ich kaum.
Taufspruch-M. *(Eva)*	Ward zur Stelle gleich Geselle? Lene Braut? – Im Kirchenraum wir gar getraut? 's geht der Kopf mir wie im Kreis, daß ich Meister bald heiß'! Meister, Meister bald, gar bald ich heiß'!

MAGDALENE

Preislied (Stollen)	Wach' oder träum' ich schon so früh? Das zu erklären, macht mir Müh': 's ist wohl nur ein Morgentraum?

Act 3, Scene 4 – Good day, my Ev'chen!

hardly dare I rede its theme.
    But this strain,   *baptismal verse*
    yet once again,   *(Eva)*
    though whispered here,
    now in my ear,
    telleth clear
    that the crown that never dies
    blooms but through the poems prize.

WALTHER

Through thy love I found the secret hidden,   *prize song (stanza)*
stilling all the pain that filleth
                    my heart unbidden.
Is it still the morning dream?
    Dare I try to rede its theme!
    But this strain,   *baptismal verse*
    yet once again,   *(Eva)*
    Though whispered here
    to greet thine ear
    loud and clear,
    'mid the Masters' guild shall rise
    thereto win me the highest prize.

DAVID

Am I awake or dreaming still?   *prize song (stanza)*
How to be sure I cannot tell:
but a morning dream is this?
    Dare I try to rede its miss.
    School is over?   *baptismal verse*
    I her lover?   *(Eva)*
    Lene bride? –
    before the altar
    at my side?
    Yes my fortunes soon will rise,
    to a Master's prize!
    Master! Master! I shall win the prize!

MAGDALENE

Am I awake or dreaming still?   *prize song (stanza)*
How to be sure I cannot tell:
but a morning dream is this?

The Mastersingers of Nuremberg

Taufspruch-M.
(Eva)

Was ich seh', begreif' ich kaum.
Er zur Stelle
gleich Geselle?
Ich die Braut,
im Kirchenraum
wir gar getraut?
Ja! Wahrhaftig, 's geht! Wer weiß,
daß ich Meistrin bald heiß'?
Ja, wahrhaftig! 's geht: bald, bald
                ich Frau Meistrin heiß'!

Preislied (Stollen),
Taufspruch-M.
(Eva)

SACHS

(zu den übrigen sich wendend)

Preislied
(Liebesthema)

Jetzt all' am Fleck'!

    KA 540 ▸ 1730
    CD 4/1 5:30

(zu Eva)

                Den Vater grüß!
Auf, nach der Wies', – schnell auf die Füß'! –

Eva und Magdalene gehen.

(zu Walther)

Nürnberg-M.

Nun, Junker, kommt! Habt frohen Mut! –
David, Gesell': schließ den Laden gut!

Als Sachs und Walther ebenfalls auf die Straße gehen, und David über das Schließen der Ladentür sich hermacht, wird im Proszenium ein Vorhang von beiden Seiten zusammengezogen, so daß er die Szene gänzlich verschließt.

Act 3, Scene 4 – Good day, my Ev'chen!

[3] Dare I try to rede its miss.
School is over? *} baptismal verse (Eva)*
free my lover?
I a bride,
before the altar
at his side?
Yes my fortunes soon will rise,
with a Master for prize!
Yes my fortunes rise:
           my Master will win the prize! *} prize song (stanza),*
baptismal verse (Eva)

Sachs

(turning to the others)

VS 463 ▶ 4 Now all go forth! *} prize song*
CD 4/1 5:30 *(love theme)*
   (to Eva)
                    thy father greet!
Off to the field! There will we meet! –

Eva and Magdalene go.

(to Walther)

Now, come, Sir knight! Your ills are past! – *} Nuremberg motif*
David, lock up: leave all safe and fast!

As Sachs and Walther go together into the street and David sets himself to lock up the shop doors, a curtain is drawn from both sides in the Proscenium closing in the scene.

5. Szene – Sankt Krispin, lobet ihn! KA 545 ▶ 1781
CD 4/1 6:30

Nürnberg-M.,
Erregtheitstriller,
Johannistag-M.,
Kunst-M.,
Meistersinger-M.

Die Vorhänge sind nach der Höhe aufgezogen worden; die Bühne ist verwandelt.

Diese stellt einen freien Wiesenplan dar, im ferneren Hintergrunde die Stadt Nürnberg. Die Pegnitz schlängelt sich durch den Plan: der schmale Fluß ist an den nächsten Punkten praktikabel gehalten.

Buntbeflaggte Kähne setzen unablässig die ankommenden, festlich gekleideten Bürger der Zünfte, mit Frauen und Kindern, an das Ufer der Festwiese über. Eine erhöhte Bühne, mit Bänken und Sitzen darauf, ist rechts zur Seite aufgeschlagen; bereits ist sie mit den Fahnen der angekommenen Zünfte ausgeschmückt; im Verlaufe stecken die Fahnenträger der noch ankommenden Zünfte ihre Fahnen ebenfalls um die Sängerbühne auf, so daß diese schließlich nach drei Seiten hin ganz davon eingefaßt ist. – Zelte mit Getränken und Erfrischungen aller Art begrenzen im übrigen die Seiten des vorderen Hauptraumes.

Resignation-M.
(fröhlich)

Vor den Zelten geht es bereits lustig her: Bürger, mit Frauen, Kindern und Gesellen, sitzen und lagern daselbst. – Die Lehrbuben der Meistersinger, festlich gekleidet, mit Blumen und Bändern reich und anmutig geschmückt, üben mit schlanken Stäben, die ebenfalls mit Blumen und Bändern geziert sind, in lustiger Weise das Amt von Herolden und Marschällen aus.

Scene 5 – Saint Crispin! Saint Crispin!

The curtains have been drawn up and the scene has been transformed.

It represents a an open meadow with the town of Nuremberg in the distance. The Pegnitz winds its way through the meadow: the narrow stream is kept practicably at the nearest points.

From gaily decorated boats which arrive continually at the bank, Burghers of the guilds, with women and children in festival costume, land on the meadow. A raised platform with chairs and benches on it has been erected on the right, decked with the banners of those Guilds which have already arrived. As new Guilds come on, their banner-bearers also plant their banners around the platform so as finally to close it in entirely on three sides. Tents with drinks and refreshments of all kinds on sides of stage.

In front of the tents there is merry making: Burghers with women and children and Journeymen sit and lie about there. – Prentices of the Mastersingers, richly decked with flowers and ribbons, with slender staves similarly adorned, merrily act the parts of heralds and marshals.

Nuremberg motif, excitement trill, Midsummer day motif, art motif, mastersinger motif

resignation motif (joyful)

The Mastersingers of Nuremberg

Meistersinger-M. ⑦   *Sie empfangen die am Ufer Aussteigenden,* KA 545 ▶ 1788
ordnen die Züge der Zünfte und geleiten diese CD 4/2 0:01
*nach der Singerbühne, von wo aus, nachdem
der Bannerträger die Fahne aufgepflanzt, die
Zunftbürger und Gesellen nach Belieben sich
unter den Zelten zerstreuen. – Soeben, nach
der Verwandlung, werden in der angegebe-
nen Weise die Schuster am Ufer empfangen
und nach dem Vordergrund geleitet.*

DIE SCHUSTER

(ziehen mit fliegender Fahne auf)

Unmut-M.,   Sankt Krispin,
Schaffenslust-M.   lobet ihn!
War gar ein heilig Mann,
zeigt', was ein Schuster kann.

Erregtheitstriller   Die Armen hatten gute Zeit,
macht' ihnen warme Schuh';
und wenn ihm keiner 's Leder leiht',
so stahl er sich's dazu.
Der Schuster hat ein weit Gewissen,
macht Schuhe selbst mit Hindernissen;
Unmut-M.,   und ist vom Gerber das Fell erst weg,
Schaffenslust-M.   dann streck, streck, streck!
Leder taugt nur am rechten Fleck!

*Die Stadtwächter ziehen mit Trompeten und
Trommeln den Stadtpfeifern, Lautenmachern
u.s.w. voraus.*

DIE SCHNEIDER

(mit fliegender Fahne aufziehend)

Als Nürenberg belagert war,
und Hungersnot sich fand,
wär' Stadt und Land verdorben gar,
Erregtheitstriller   war nicht ein Schneider,
  ein Schneider, ein Schneider zur Hand,
der viel Mut hatt' und Verstand.
Hat sich in ein Bocksfell eingenäht,
auf dem Stadtwall da spazieren geht
und macht wohl seine Sprünge

Act 3, Scene 5 – Saint Crispin! Saint Crispin!

VS 468 ▶ 1
CD 4/2 0:01

They receive the new arrivals on the shore, order the processions of Guilds and lead them to the singers' platform, whence, after the banner-bearers have planted the banners, the Burghers and Journeymen disperse as they please at the booths. – As the curtains rise the Shoemakers are being thus received at the bank and conducted to the front.

⎬ *mastersinger motif*
⎬ ⑦

THE SHOEMAKERS

(Advancing with flying banner)

Saint Crispin,
Saint Crispin!
He was a holy man,
did all a cobbler can.
The poor had then a merry time;
well shod from toe to heel;
if leather lacked, he thought no crime,
and stole what he could steel.
A cobbler's conscience is not queasy,
and trifles make it not uneasy;
when from the tanner the skin we get,
then beat, beat, beat!
Leather serves but to shoe our feet.

⎬ *resentment motif,*
⎬ *work lust motif*

⎬ *excitement trill*

⎬ *resentment motif,*
⎬ *work lust motif*

The town watchmen, with trumpets and drums come on, followed by the town pipers, lute makers etc.

THE TAILORS

(Advancing with flying banner)

When Nüremberg a siege withstood,
and famine filled the land,
undone had been our town for good,
were not a tailor,
           a tailor, a tailor at hand.
Boldly then this trick he planned.
In a goatskin safe himself he sews,
on the wall to take a walk he goes,
and there so gaily springing,

excitement trill

gar lustig guter Dinge.
Der Feind, der sieht's und zieht vom Fleck:
Der Teufel hol' die Stadt sich weg,
hat's drin noch so lustige Meck-meck-meck!
Me-e-e-e-eck! Me-e-e-e-eck! Me-e-e-e-eck!
Wer glaubt's, daß ein Schneider,
      ein Schneider, ein Schneider –
           im Bocke steck'!

DIE BÄCKER

(mit fliegender Fahne aufziehend)

Erregtheitstriller

Hungersnot! Hungersnot!
Das ist ein greulich Leiden:
gäb' euch der Bäcker nicht täglich Brot,
müßt' alle Welt verscheiden.
Bäck! Bäck! Bäck!
Täglich auf dem Fleck,
nimm uns den Hunger weg,
nimm uns den Hunger weg!

*Die Schuster, welche ihre Fahne aufgesteckt,
begegnen beim Herabschreiten von der Sängerbühne den Bäckern.*

DIE SCHUSTER

Schaffenslust-M.

Streck! Streck! Streck!
Leder taugt nur am rechten Fleck!

DIE SCHNEIDER

Me-e-e-e-eck! Me-e-e-e-eck! Me-e-e-e-eck!
Wer meint, daß ein Schneider
           im Bocke steck'!

Johannistag-M.
(Beginn)

Ein bunter Kahn mit jungen Mädchen in reicher bäuerischer Tracht kommt an. Die Lehrbuben laufen nach dem Gestade.

LEHRBUBEN

Herr Je! Herr Je! Mädel von Fürth!
Stadtpfeifer, spielt! Daß's lustig wird!

*Sie heben währenddem die Mädchen aus dem
Kahn. – Das Charakteristische des folgenden*

Act 3, Scene 5 – Saint Crispin! Saint Crispin!

VS 476▸6
CD 4/2 2:18
he sets the welkin ringing.
The foe make off with flying feet:
the town they deem the devil's seat,
where goats yet so merrily bleat bleat bleat!
ble-e-e-eat! ble-e-e-eat! ble-e-e-eat!
Who'd think that
                a tailor, a tailor, a tailor –
                    would have such wit?

THE BAKERS

(coming on with their flying banner)

Famine dread! Famine dread!   *excitement trill*
From that may God defend us!
bakers must bring us our daily bread,
or hunger soon would end us.
Wheat, wheat, wheat,
makes the bread we eat:
so hunger we defeat,
so hunger, hunger we defeat!

The shoemakers, who have plated their banner, step back from the singing-stage, meeting the bakers as they do so.

THE SHOEMAKERS

Beat, beat, beat!   *work lust motif*
Leather serves but to shoe our feet.

THE TAILORS

Ble-e-e-eat! ble-e-e-eat! ble-e-e-eat!
Who'd think that a tailor
                would have such wit?

A decorated boat arrives full of young girls in   *Midsummer day motif*
rich peasants dresses. The prentices run to the   *(beginning)*
bank.

PRENTICES

Good Lord! Good Lord! Maidens from Fürth!
Town-pipers play! And make us gay!

*The prentices lift the girls out of the boat.
– The peculiarity of the following dance*

Tanzes, mit welchem die Lehrbuben und Mädchen zunächst nach dem Vordergrund kommen, besteht darin, daß die Lehrbuben die Mädchen scheinbar nur am Platz bringen wollen; sowie die Gesellen zugreifen wollen, ziehen die Buben die Mädchen aber immer wieder zurück, als ob sie sie anderswo unterbringen wollten, wobei sie meistens den ganzen Kreis, wie wählend, ausmessen und somit die scheinbare Absicht auszuführen anmutig und lustig verzögern.

DAVID

kommt vom Landungsplatz vor und sieht mißbilligend dem Tanze zu:

Ihr tanzt? Was werden die Meister sagen?

Die Lehrbuben drehen ihm Nasen.

Hört nicht? –
           Lass' ich mir's auch behagen!

Er nimmt sich ein junges, schönes Mädchen und gerät im Tanze mit ihr schnell in großes Feuer. Die Zuschauer freuen sich und lachen.

LEHRBUBEN

winken David:

David! David! Die Lene sieht zu!

David, erschrocken, läßt das Mädchen schnell fahren, um welches die Lehrbuben sogleich tanzend einen Kreis schließen; da er Lene nirgends gewahrt, merkt David, daß er nur geneckt worden, durchbricht den Kreis, erfaßt sein Mädchen wieder und tanzt nun noch feuriger weiter.

DAVID

Ach! laßt mich mit euren Possen in Ruh'!

Die Buben suchen, ihm das Mädchen zu entreißen; er wendet sich mit ihr jedesmal glücklich ab, so daß nun ein ähnliches Spiel entsteht wie zuvor, als die Gesellen nach dem Mädchen faßten.

Act 3, Scene 5 – Saint Crispin! Saint Crispin!

VS 484 ▶ 6
CD 4/3 0:01

with which, the prentices and girls come to the front, is this: the prentices apparently only wish to bring the girls to the open place, but, as the journeymen keep trying to seize the girls, the prentices draw them away as if seeking to take them away to another place, whereby they make the tour of the whole stage, continually delaying their original purpose in good-natured fun.

David

comes forward from the landing place and looks disapprovingly at the dancing:

You dance? Beware lest the Masters hear it?

The prentices make fun of him.

You laugh? –
                    Well then, I too will dare it!

He seizes a pretty young girl and joins in the dance with great ardour. The onlookers laugh.

Prentices

making signs to David:

David! David! Thy Lene looks on!

David, startled, quickly lets the girl go. The prentices directly dance in a circle round her. As David does not see Lene anywhere, he realizes that he has been fooled, and, breaking through the circle, he seizes the girl again and dances on more ardently.

David

Ah! Cease fooling now, and leave me alone!

The prentices try to pull the girl away from him; he always manages to evade them, so that a similar performance takes rise to that above described, where the journeymen try to seize the girls.

The Mastersingers of Nuremberg

GESELLEN

(vom Ufer her)
Die Meistersinger! –

LEHRBUBEN

Die Meistersinger!
Sie unterbrechen schnell den Tanz und eilen dem Ufer zu.

DAVID

Herr Gott! – Ade, ihr hübschen Dinger!
Er gibt dem Mädchen einen feurigen Kuß und reißt sich los. – Die Lehrbuben reihen sich zum Empfang der Meister: das Volk macht ihnen willig Platz. – Die Meistersinger ordnen sich am Landungsplatze zum festlichen Aufzuge.

{ *Meistersinger-M.*

{ *Erregtheitstriller*

Kothner kommt mit der Fahne im Vordergrunde an. – Die geschwungene Fahne, auf welcher König David mit der Harfe abgebildet ist, wird von allem Volk mit Hutschwenken begrüßt.

{ *König-David-M.,*
{ *Erregtheitstriller*

{ *Kunst-M.,*
{ *Erregtheitstriller,*
{ *Meistersinger-M.*

Der Zug der Meistersinger ist auf der Singerbühne, wo Kothner die Fahne aufpflanzt, angelangt: – Pogner, Eva an der Hand führend, diese von festlich geschmückten und reich gekleideten jungen Mädchen, unter denen auch Magdalene, begleitet, voran.

Als Eva, von den Mädchen umgeben, den mit Blumen geschmückten Ehrenplatz eingenommen, und alle übrigen, die Meister auf den Bänken, die Gesellen hinter ihnen stehend, ebenfalls Platz genommen haben, treten die Lehrbuben, dem Volke zugewendet, feierlich vor der Bühne in Reih und Glied.

{ *König-David-M.*

LEHRBUBEN

Silentium! Silentium!
Macht kein Reden und kein Gesumm!

{ *Erregtheitstriller*

Act 3, Scene 5 – Saint Crispin! Saint Crispin!

JOURNEYMEN
VS 488▶4
CD 4/3 2:26

(at the river bank)

The Mastersingers! –

PRENTICES

The Mastersingers!

They immediately stop dancing and hurry to the bank.

DAVID

Farewell! – ye bonny wenches!

He gives the girl an ardent kiss and tears himself away. – The prentices arrange themselves to receive the Mastersingers: the people freely make way for them. – At the landing-place the Mastersingers arrange themselves for a grand procession. } *mastersinger motif*

Kothner reaches the front with the banner bearing the portrait of king David with his harp, at sight of which the people wave their hats.
excitement trill
} *king David motif, excitement trill*

The procession of the Mastersingers has now reached the platform, where Kothner plants the banner: – Pogner, leading forward Eva by the hand. She is accompanied by girls richly dressed; among them is Magdalene. } *art motif, excitement trill, mastersinger motif*

When Eva, surrounded by the girls, has taken the flower strewn place of honour and all the rest are in their places, the Masters on the benches, the journeymen standing behind them, the prentices advance to the platform in proper order and turn round to the people. } *king David motif*

PRENTICES

VS 493▶1 Silentium! Silentium!
CD 4/4 0:01 Speak no word, let no sound be heard!   *excitement trill*

309

The Mastersingers of Nuremberg

Meistersinger-M. ④   *Sachs erhebt sich und tritt vor. Bei seinem An-*   KA 574 ▶ 2146
blick stößt sich alles an; Hüte und Mützen wer-   CD 4/4 0:20
den abgezogen: alle deuten auf ihn.

VOLK

Ha! Sachs! 's ist Sachs!
Seht, Meister Sachs!
Stimmt an! Stimmt an!

ALLE

Außer Sachs singen alle Anwesenden diese Strophe mit. Alle Sitzenden erheben sich; die Männer bleiben mit entblößtem Haupte. Beckmesser bleibt, mit dem Memorieren des Gedichtes beschäftigt, hinter den anderen Meistern versteckt, so daß er bei dieser Gelegenheit der Beobachtung des Publikums entzogen wird.

Wach auf Choral   „Wach' auf, es nahet gen den Tag;
ich hör' singen im grünen Hag
ein' wonnigliche Nachtigall,
ihr' Stimm' durchdringet Berg und Tal;
die Nacht neigt sich zum Okzident,
der Tag geht auf von Orient,

Erregtheitstriller   die rotbrünstige Morgenröt'
her durch die trüben Wolken geht."

Das Volk nimmt wieder eine jubelnd bewegte Haltung an. Der Chor des Volkes singt wieder allein; die Meister auf der Bühne sowie die andren vorigen Teilnehmer am Gesange der Strophe geben sich dem Schauspiele des Volksjubels hin.

Kunst-M.   Heil! Heil! Sachs!
Heil Nürnbergs Sachs!
Heil Nürnbergs teurem Sachs!
Heil dir, Hans Sachs!

König-David-M.   Heil! Heil!

Sachs, der unbeweglich, wie geistesabwesend, über die Volksmenge hinweggeblickt hatte, richtet endlich seine Blicke vertrauter

Act 3, Scene 5 – Saint Crispin! Saint Crispin!

VS 494 ▶ 1
CD 4/4 0:20

Sachs rises and comes forward. At the sight of him, all press forward, hats and caps are doffed. All point to him.

PEOPLE

Ha! Sachs! 'Tis Sachs!
See! Master Sachs!
Begin! begin!

ALL

All present except Sachs join in this strophe, taking parts according to their voices. All those sitting rise; the men standing with bared heads. Beckmesser, hidden behind the other Masters, is busy trying to learn the song by heart, unobserved by the public.

„Awake! The dawn of day draws near: } *awake choral*
from deepest woods I hear
a soul-gladdening nightingale;
his voice sounds o'er hill and dale;
the night sinks in western skies,
the day from the east doth rise,
the red glow of the dawn awakes } *excitement trill*
and through the cloud-bank breaks."

The people resume their jubilation. The chorus of people sings alone again; the Masters and other characters take part in the rejoicing of the people.

Hail! Hail! Sachs! } *art motif*
Hail Nürnberg's Sachs!
Hail Nürnberg's poet Sachs!
Hail to thee, Hans Sachs!
Hail! Hail! } *king David motif*

Sachs, who motionless, as if wrapt in thought, has been gazing far away over the crowd, at length turns his eyes with kindly expression on

311

	auf sie und beginnt mit ergriffener, schnell aber sich festigender Stimme:

SACHS

Wahn-M.	Euch macht ihr's leicht,
	mir macht ihr's schwer,
	gebt ihr mir Armen zu viel Ehr'.
	Soll vor der Ehr' ich bestehn,
Freundschaft-M.	sei's mich von euch geliebt zu sehn.
	Schon große Ehr' ward mir erkannt,
Erregtheitstriller Kreidestrich-M.	ward heut ich zum Spruchsprecher ernannt.
	Und was mein Spruch euch künden soll,
	glaubt, das ist hoher Ehren voll. –
Zunftberatung-M., Zunftideal-M., Zunftgesetz-M.	Wenn ihr die Kunst so hoch schon ehrt,
	da galt es zu beweisen,
	daß, wer ihr selbst gar angehört,
	sie schätzt ob allen Preisen.
	Ein Meister, reich und hochgemut,
	der will heut euch das zeigen:
	sein Töchterlein, sein höchstes Gut,
	mit allem Hab und Eigen,
	dem Singer, der im Kunstgesang
	vor allem Volk den Preis errang,
Johannistag-M., Kunst-M.	als höchsten Preises Kron'
	er bietet das zum Lohn. –
	Darum, so hört, und stimmt mir bei:
	die Werbung steh' dem Dichter frei.
	Ihr Meister, die ihr's euch getraut,
	euch ruf' ich's vor dem Volke laut: –
Kunst-M., Zunftberatung-M., Singkunst-M.	erwägt der Werbung selt'nen Preis,
	und wem sie soll gelingen,
	daß der sich rein und edel weiß,
	im Werben wie im Singen,
Werbe-M., Zunftgesetz-M.	will er das Reis erringen,
	das nie, bei Neuen noch bei Alten,
	ward je so herrlich hoch gehalten,
	als von der lieblich Reinen,
	die niemals soll beweinen,
Nürnberg-M., Zunftideal-M.	daß Nürenberg mit höchstem Wert
	die Kunst und ihre Meister ehrt!

Act 3, Scene 5 – Saint Crispin! Saint Crispin!

KA 500 ▶ 7
CD 4/5 0:01

them and begins in a voice at first veiled by emotion but quickly becoming firmer:

SACHS

Words light to you, bow me to earth:	*delusion motif*
your praise is far beyond my worth.	
What I must prize all else above,	
is your esteem and honest love,	*friendship motif*
The highest honour you proclaimed,	
for me, when as spokesman I was named.	*excitement trill*
and all my speech, now heed it well!	*chalk stroke motif*
sooth, shall a tale of honour tell. –	
If art so high is prized by you,	*Zunftberatung-M.,*
I fain would show you clearly,	*guild ideal motif,*
that one who lives her servant true	*guild law motif*
o'er all doth love her dearly.	
A Master rich and high in worth,	
his love now lets you measure:	
his daughter fair, his best on earth,	
with all his gold and treasure,	
he offers here before you all	
to him on whom your choice shall fall:	
that art of song alone,	*Midsummer day*
may gain the highest crown. –	*motif, art motif*
Then lend your ears and hearts to me:	
this trial be to singers free.	
Ye Masters who will sing today,	
to you before all folk I say: –	
think well how rare a prize is here,	*art motif,*
that each may surely bring her	*guild council motif,*
a heart and voice both pure and clear,	*singing art motif*
as suitor and as singer.	
Let this your hearts embolden;	*courtship motif,*
that ne'er in present times or olden,	*guild law motif*
was crown so nobly high upholden,	
as by this maiden tender;	
may fate from harm defend her,	
that Nüremberg her voice may raise	*Nuremberg motif,*
for Art, and in her Masters' praise!	*guild ideal motif*

The Mastersingers of Nuremberg

{ Johannistag-M.

Große Bewegung unter allen. Sachs geht auf Pogner zu.

KA 588 ▸ 2278
CD 4/5 4:02

POGNER

(Sachs gerührt die Hand drückend)

{ Kunst-M.,
{ Zunftberatung-M.

O Sachs, mein Freund! Wie dankenswert! –
Wie wißt ihr, was mein Herz beschwert!

SACHS

(zu Pogner)

's war viel gewagt; – jetzt habt nur Mut! –

(zu Beckmesser)

Herr Merker! Sagt, wie steht's? Gut?

{ Zunftberatung-M.,
{ Kunst-M. (nervös
{ abgebrochen),
{ Zunftgesetz-M.

Beckmesser, zu dem sich jetzt Sachs wendet, hat schon während des Einzuges, und dann fortwährend, eifrig das Blatt mit dem Gedicht herausgezogen, memoriert, genau zu lesen versucht und oft verzweiflungsvoll sich den Schweiß getrocknet.

BECKMESSER

O! Dieses Lied!... Werd' nicht draus klug,
und hab' doch dran studiert genug!

SACHS

Mein Freund, 's ist euch nicht aufgezwungen.

{ Missgunst-M.

BECKMESSER

Was hilft's?

{ Kreidestrich-M.

    Mit dem meinen ist doch versungen:
's war eure Schuld! Jetzt seid hübsch für mich:
's wär schändlich, ließt ihr mich in Stich!

SACHS

{ Missgunst-M.
{ (abrutschend)

Ich dächt', ihr gäbt's auf.

BECKMESSER

                    Warum nicht gar?
Die andren sing' ich alle zu paar;

Act 3, Scene 5 – Saint Crispin! Saint Crispin!

Great and general commotion. Sachs goes up to Pogner. — *Midsummer day motif*

POGNER

(pressing Sachs's hand with emotion)
Oh Sachs, my friend! What thanks I owe! –
The weight upon my heart you know!

art motif, guild council motif

SACHS

(to Pogner)
In faith, 'twas bold; – yet we'll not fail! –
(to Beckmesser)
Sir Marker! Say, is all well?

Beckmesser, to whom Sachs now turns, has all through been constantly taking the poem from his pocket and trying to learn it by heart, often wiping the sweat from his brow in despair.

guild council motif, art motif (nervously breaking off), guild law motif

BECKMESSER

Oh! What a song!... 'Tis hazy stuff,
and yet I've studied it enough!

SACHS

May friend, you are not forced to choose it.

BECKMESSER

With mine
              all is over. I cannot use it.
The fault was yours! Help me the to win:
to leave me now would be a sin!

envy motif

chalk stroke motif

SACHS

I thought you'd give up.

envy motif (slipping off)

BECKMESSER

              And why, I pray?
The others will not stand in my way;

The Mastersingers of Nuremberg

Missgunst-M.
(abrutschend)

wenn ihr nur nicht singt.

KA 591 ▶ 2305
CD 4/5 5:05

SACHS

So seht, wie's geht!

BECKMESSER

Kunst-M.
(abgebrochen)

Das Lied, bin's sicher, zwar niemand versteht;
doch bau' ich auf eure Popularität.

SACHS

Singkunst-M. ②

Nun denn, wenn's Meistern und Volk beliebt,
zum Wettgesang man den Anfang gibt.

KA 592 ▶ 2309
CD 4/6 0:01

KOTHNER

(hervortretend)

Ihr ledig' Meister! Macht euch bereit!
Der Ältest' sich zuerst anläßt!
Herr Beckmesser, ihr fangt an: 's ist Zeit!

Meistersinger-M.
(meckernd),
Erregtheitstriller

Die Lehrbuben führen Beckmesser zu einem kleinen Rasenhügel vor der Singerbühne, welchen sie zuvor festgerammelt und reich mit Blumen überdeckt haben.

BECKMESSER

strauchelt darauf, tritt unsicher und schwankt:

Zum Teufel! Wie wackelig!
               Macht das hübsch fest!

Die Buben lachen unter sich und stopfen lustig an dem Rasen. Das Volk stößt sich gegenseitig an.

Spott-M.,
Erregtheitstriller,
Meistersinger-M.
(meckernd)

VOLK

Wie? – Der? – Der wirbt? –
           Scheint mir nicht der Rechte! –
An der Tochter Stell' ich den nicht möchte! –
Seid still! 's ist gar ein tücht'ger Meister! –
Still! Macht keinen Witz!
Der hat im Rate Stimm' und Sitz. –
Ach! der kann ja nicht mal stehn! –

Act 3, Scene 5 – Saint Crispin! Saint Crispin!

if you do not sing. — *envy motif (sliding off)*

SACHS

                'tis not that I would!

BECKMESSER

The song by none will be understood; — *art motif*
but I build upon your favor with the crowd. — *(breaking off)*

SACHS

Then now, if Masters and people will, — *singing art motif ②*
at once the singers may prove their skill.

KOTHNER

  (advancing)

Unmarried Masters, be ye prepared!
The oldest man shall first be heard!
Friend Beckmesser, you begin: 'tis time!

  The prentices lead Beckmesser to a small — *mastersinger motif*
  mound of turf in front of the platform which — *(nagging),*
  they have previously made and firmly rammed — *excitement trill*
  down and decorated with flowers.

BECKMESSER

  stumbles on it and stands tottering and inse-
  curely:

The devil! How rickety!
                Just make that firm!

  The prentices laugh among themselves and
  ram down the turf. The people humourously
  nudge one another.

PEOPLE

What? – He? – He woos? – — *mockery motif,*
          Surely she'll refuse him! – — *excitement trill,*
In the maiden's place I would not choose him! – — *mastersinger motif*
Be still! 'tis sure, a great professor! – — *(nagging)*
Still! and make no jest!
He has in council vote and seat. –
Ah, he cannot keep his feet! –

Spott-M., *Erregtheitstriller,* *Meistersinger-M.* *(meckernd)*	Wie soll es mit dem gehn? – Er fällt fast um! – Gott, ist der dumm! – Stadtschreiber ist er, Beckmesser heißt er. –	KA 597 ▸ 2359 CD 4/6 1:16

Viele lachen.

König-David-M. **DIE LEHRBUBEN**

(in Aufstellung)

Erregtheitstriller Silentium! Silentium!
Macht kein Reden und kein Gesumm!

KOTHNER

Erregtheitstriller Fanget an!

BECKMESSER

Beckmessers
Werbe-M.,
Missgunst-M.

Laute-M.

der sich endlich mit Mühe auf dem Rasenhügel festgestellt hat, macht eine erste Verbeugung gegen die Meister, eine zweite gegen das Volk, dann gegen Eva, auf welche er, da sie sich abwendet, nochmals verlegen hinblinzelt; große Beklommenheit erfaßt ihn; er sucht, sich durch ein Vorspiel auf der Laute zu ermutigen.

Beckmessers
Ständchen

Beckmessers
Werbe-M.

„Morgen ich leuchte in rosigem Schein,
von Blut und Duft
geht schnell die Luft;
wohl bald gewonnen,
wie zerronnen;
im Garten lud ich ein
garstig und fein."

Er richtet sich wieder ein, besser auf den Füßen zu stehen.

DIE MEISTERSINGER

(leise unter sich)

Missgunst-M. (abge- *brochen),* *Meistersinger-M.* ④ *(meckernd)*	Mein! Was ist das? – Sonderbar! – Ist er von Sinnen? Woher mocht' er solche Gedanken gewinnen? –	① ②

Act 3, Scene 5 – Saint Crispin! Saint Crispin!

VS 514 ▶ 7 How will he bear the test? –
CD 4/6 1:16 He'll tumble soon! –
Lord! what a loon! –
Town-writer is he,
Master Beckmesser. –

Several laugh.

mockery motif,
excitement trill,
mastersinger motif
(nagging)

THE PRENTICES

(in position)

Silentium! Silentium!
Speak no word! Let no sound be heard!

king David motif

excitement trill

KOTHNER

Now begin!

excitement trill

BECKMESSER

who with trouble has at length found firm footing on the mound, bows first to the Masters, the to the people and then to Eva, at whom, when she turns away, he again blinks with embarrassment; he tries to calm his uneasiness by a prelude on the lute.

Beckmesser's courtship motif,
envy motif
lute motif

„Bathing in sunlight at dawning of day,
with bosom bare,
to greet the air;
my beauty steaming,
faster dreaming;
a garden roundelay
wearied my way."

Beckmesser's song

Beckmesser's courtship motif

He again attempts to gain a better footing.

MASTERSINGERS

(softly to each other)

① Ah! What is that? –
   It is strange! – He's lost his senses?
② But where has he ever discovered such fancies? –

envy motif (breaking off),
mastersinger motif ④
(nagging)

The Mastersingers of Nuremberg

Missgunst-M. (abgebrochen), Meistersinger-M. ④ (meckernd)	Höchst merkwürd'ger Fall! 　　　　　Was kommt ihm bei?	KA 602 ▸ 2408 CD 4/6 3:30

VOLK

(leise unter sich)

Sonderbar! – Hört ihr's? – Wen lud er ein? –
Verstand man recht? – Wie kann das sein? –
Garstig und fein lud er bei sich ein? –

Wahn-M.

BECKMESSER

zieht das Blatt verstohlen hervor und lugt eifrig hinein: dann steckt er es ängstlich wieder ein.

Beckmessers Ständchen

„Wohn' ich erträglich im selbigen Raum,
hol' Geld und Frucht,
Bleisaft und Wucht…

Erregtheitstriller, Missgunst-M.

Er lugt in das Blatt.

Beckmessers Werbe-M.

Mich holt am Pranger
der Verlanger
auf luft'ger Steige kaum,
häng' ich am Baum."

Kreidestrich-M.

Er wackelt wieder sehr: sucht im Blatt zu lesen, vermag es nicht; ihm schwindelt. Angstschweiß bricht aus.

VOLK

Missgunst-M.

Schöner Werber! Der find't wohl seinen Lohn.
Bald hängt er am Galgen!
　　　　　Man sieht ihn schon!

DIE MEISTERSINGER

Was soll das heißen? – Wie? Ist er nur toll? –
Sein Lied ist ganz von Unsinn voll!

BECKMESSER

Erregtheitstriller, Ärger-M. Laute-M. Beckmessers Werbe-M.

rafft sich verzweiflungsvoll und ingrimmig auf:

„Heimlich mir graut,
weil es hier munter will hergehn:
an meiner Leiter stand ein Weib;

320

Act 3, Scene 5 – Saint Crispin! Saint Crispin!

VS 518 ▶ 2 CD 4/6 3:30 This case is full strange!	envy motif (abgebro-
What can he mean?	chen), mastersinger motif ④ (meckernd)

PEOPLE

(softly to each other)

It is strange! – Heard you? – What roundelay? –
Can that be right? – How can that be? –
Garden roundelay wearied his way? –

BECKMESSER   *delusion motif*

secretly draws the paper forth and hurriedly looks into it: then pockets it again anxiously.

„Sigh for the bard, on a tree he did rise,   *Beckmesser's song*
a golden sore,
its branches tore…

He peeps into the paper.   *excitement trill, envy motif*

With midges thronging   *Beckmesser's courts-*
broke my longing,   *hip motif*
when, dark and bare, the prize,
hooked on my eyes."

He totters again: tries to read the paper, but is unable. He becomes giddy and perspires with anxiety.   *chalk stroke motif*

PEOPLE

Dainty wooer! His due he soon will get.   *envy motif*
He'll end on the gallows!
                            Yes that is clear!

MASTERSINGERS

What is the meaning? – What? Is he gone mad?
Quite full of nonsense is his song!

BECKMESSER

rouses himself with despair and rage: *excitement trill,*
„What is her name,   *anger motif*
what radiant thunder here clearly pealed?   *lute motif*
A woman's hair in fashion dressed: *Beckmessers courtship motif*

The Mastersingers of Nuremberg

Beckmessers
Ständchen,
Erregtheitstriller,
Laute-M., Beck-
messers Werbe-M.

sie schämt und wollt' mich nicht besehn;
bleich wie ein Kraut
umfasert mir Hanf meinen Leib;
mit Augen zwinkend –
der Hund blies winkend,
was ich vor langem verzehrt,
wie Frucht so Holz und Pferd
vom Leberbaum!"

KA 608 ▸ 2442
CD 4/6 5:27

Alles bricht in ein dröhnendes Gelächter aus.

BECKMESSER

verläßt wütend den Hügel und stürzt auf Sachs zu:

Hohn-M., Wut-M.

Verdammter Schuster, das dank' ich dir! –
Das Lied, es ist gar nicht von mir:
vom Sachs, der hier so hoch verehrt,
von eurem Sachs ward mir's beschert.
Mich hat der Schändliche bedrängt,
sein schlechtes Lied mir aufgehängt.

Er stürzt wütend fort und verliert sich unter dem Volke.

VOLK

Mein! Was soll das sein?

Lebhaftigkeit-M.
(Variation)

                Jetzt wird's immer bunter!
Von Sachs das Lied?
                Das nähm' uns doch Wunder!

KOTHNER

(zu Sachs)

Lebhaftigkeit-M.

Erklärt doch, Sachs!

NACHTIGAL

(zu Sachs)

                Welch ein Skandal!

VOGELGESANG

(zu Sachs)

Act 3, Scene 5 – Saint Crispin! Saint Crispin!

VS 524 ▶ 11
CD 4/6 5:27

with clear immortal air it swelled.
Bridling she came,
and folded me there in a chest;
intently gazing, –
her hound was grazing
and gleaned the roots old an new:
she sowed the space with rue,
the seed of strife!"

Beckmesser's song, excitement trill, lute motif, Beckmesser's courtship motif

All break out into mocking laughter.

BECKMESSER

in fury leaves the mound and rushes toward Sachs:

Accursed cobbler, yours the design! –
The song, in sooth, is none of mine:
'twas Sachs whom ye so much revere,
that wrote the song I sang you here!
Now through his shameful trick I see
his worthless stuff he puts on me.

scorn motif, rage motif

He rushes away in fury and loses himself in the crowd.

PEOPLE

Hey! What can that mean?
                       No one can conceive it!
By Sachs the song?
                       We cannot believe it!

livelihood motif (variation)

KOTHNER

(to Sachs)

Explain, then, Sachs!

livelihood motif

NACHTIGAL

(to Sachs)

                       What a disgrace!

VOGELGESANG

(to Sachs)

The Mastersingers of Nuremberg

        Von euch das Lied?

Lebhaftigkeit-M.   **ORTEL UND FOLTZ**
(beruhigt sich)
                        Welch eigner Fall!

    SACHS

        hat ruhig das Blatt, welches ihm Beckmesser
        hingeworfen, aufgenommen:
    Das Lied, fürwahr, ist nicht von mir:
    Herr Beckmesser irrt, wie dort so hier.
Freundschaft-M.   Wie er dazu kam, mag selbst er sagen;
    doch möcht' ich nie mich zu rühmen wagen,
    ein Lied, so schön wie dies erdacht,
    sei von mir, Hans Sachs, gemacht.

    DIE MEISTERSINGER

Missgunst-M.   Wie? Schön? Das Lied wär' schön,
(Beginn)   dieser Unsinnswust?

    VOLK

    Hört! Sachs macht Spaß!
                      Er sagt es nur zur Lust.

    SACHS

    Ich sag' euch Herrn, das Lied ist schön;
    nur ist's auf den ersten Blick zu ersehn,
    daß Freund Beckmesser es entstellt.
    Doch schwör' ich, daß es euch gefällt,
    wenn richtig Wort' und Weise[1]
    hier einer säng' im Kreise;
    und wer dies verstünd', zugleich bewies',
    daß er des Liedes Dichter,
    und gar mit Rechte Meister hieß',
    fänd' er gerechte Richter. –
Erregtheitstriller,   Ich bin verklagt, und muß bestehn:
Zunftgesetz-M., Preis-   drum laßt mich meinen Zeugen ausersehn. –
lied (Liebesthema)   Ist jemand hier, der Recht mir weiß?
    Der tret' als Zeug' in diesen Kreis!

Stolzing-M.   *Walther tritt aus dem Volke hervor und be-*
        grüßt Sachs, sodann nach beiden Seiten

---

[1] Zu dieser Melodie sang Sachs in der 2. Szene des 3. Akts "ein rechtes Paar zu finden, das zeigt sich an den Kinden", als er Walther zur Dichtung des Abgesangs ermunterte

Act 3, Scene 5 – Saint Crispin! Saint Crispin!

VS 528 ▶ 3
CD 4/6 6:21
By you the song?

ORTEL AND FOLTZ

                How strange the case!

livelihood motif
(calming down)

SACHS

    has quietly taken up the paper which Beckmesser threw down:

VS 528 ▶ 10
CD 4/7 0:01
Not mine the song! that I declare.
Friend Beckmesser errs, both here and there.
Let him now to all tell where he got it;
for myself, I dare not boast I wrote it;
nor yet that aught so nobly fine
as this song could e'er be mine.

friendship motif

MASTERSINGERS

What? Fine? The song is fine?
                All that senseless trash?

envy motif
(beginning)

PEOPLE

Hear! Sachs makes fun!
                He says it but in jest.

SACHS

I tell you, Sirs, that the song is fine;
but at first it is not hard to divine
that friend Beckmesser sang it wrong.
Yet swear I, ye will like the song,
if now, by one among you[1]
the words be rightly sung you;
and he who that truth can bring to light,
will prove himself the poet
and Mastersinger, too, by right:
all who have ears will know it. –
I am accused, and take my stand:
my witness let me call, then, here at hand. –
If one to prove my words be here,
let him as witness now appear!

excitement trill,
guild law motif,
prize song
(love theme)

    Walther steps forward from the crowd, greets the Masters and the people in turn, with

Stolzing motif

---
[1] *Sachs sang with this melody in the 2nd scene of the 3rd act "if true and fitly mated, the pair by you created", when he asked Walther to create the Aftersong*

The Mastersingers of Nuremberg

hin die Meister und das Volk mit ritterlicher KA 618 ▸ 2563
Freundlichkeit. Es entsteht sogleich eine an- CD 4/7 2:25
genehme Bewegung; alles weilt einen Augenblick schweigend in seiner Betrachtung.

Entzückung-M., So zeuget, das Lied sei nicht von mir;
Vogelweid-M. und zeuget auch, daß, was ich hier
vom Lied hab' gesagt,
zu viel nicht sei gewagt.

DIE MEISTERSINGER

Stolzing-M. Wie fein! Ei, Sachs, ihr seid gar fein!
Doch mag es heut geschehen sein.

SACHS

Der Regel Güte
 daraus man erwägt,
daß sie auch mal 'ne Ausnahm' verträgt.

VOLK

Ein guter Zeuge, stolz und kühn;
mich dünkt, dem kann was Gut's erblühn.

SACHS

Entzückung-M., Meister und Volk sind gewillt
Eva-M. zu vernehmen, was mein Zeuge gilt.
Herr Walther von Stolzing, singt das Lied! –
Ihr Meister, lest, ob's ihm geriet.

Er übergibt Kothner das Blatt zum Nachlesen.

DIE LEHRBUBEN

(in Aufstellung)

Alles gespannt! 's gibt kein Gesumm:
da rufen wir auch nicht „Silentium!"

Preislied (Stollen) ②, *Walther beschreitet festen Schrittes den klei-*
Traum-M. *nen Blumenhügel.*

WALTHER

Preislied (Stollen) „Morgenlich leuchtend im rosigen Schein, KA 624 ▸ 2610
von Blüt' und Duft CD 4/8 0:01
geschwellt die Luft,

Act 3, Scene 5 – Saint Crispin! Saint Crispin!

knightly courtesy. A movement of pleasure takes place. All remain silent for a short time, observing him.

Bear witness this song is none of mine;   *delight motif, Vogel-*
and witness, too, the song is fine;   *weid-M.*
that all may declare,
my praise went not too far.

MASTERSINGERS

How keen! Ah Sachs, your wit is keen!   *Stolzing motif*
But you today again will win.

SACHS

Those rules are best that
                         will stand wear and tear,
and, now and then, exceptions will bear.

PEOPLE

A goodly witness, proud and bold!
methinks, from him some good may come;.

SACHS

Masters and folk give their word   *delight motif,*
that my witness fairly shall be heard.   *Eva motif*
Sir Walther of Stolzing, sing the song! –
Ye Masters, see if he goes wrong.

He gives Kothner the paper to follow the song.

THE PRENTICES

(in position)

None speaks a word, but all are dumb;
then we need not call out „Silentium!"

Walther firmly steps on the mound.   *prize song (stanza) ②,*
   dream motif

WALTHER

„Bathed in the sunlight at dawning of day,   *prize song (stanza)*
while blossoms rare
made sweet the air,

The Mastersingers of Nuremberg

An dieser Stelle läßt Kothner das Blatt, in welchem er mit andren Meistern nachzulesen begonnen, vor Ergriffenheit unwillkürlich fallen; er und die übrigen hören nur teilnahmvoll zu.

Preislied (Stollen)
voll aller Wonnen,
nie ersonnen,
ein Garten lud mich ein,

(wie entrückt)

dort unter einem Wunderbaum,
von Früchten reich behangen,
zu schaun in sel'gem Liebestraum,
was höchstem Lustverlangen
Erfüllung kühn verhieß,

Erregtheitstriller
das schönste Weib: Eva, – im Paradies!"

VOLK

(leise flüsternd)

Das ist was andres,

Preislied (Stollen) ②
                                    wer hätt's gedacht;
was doch recht Wort und Vortrag macht!

DIE MEISTERSINGER

(leise flüsternd)

Ja wohl, ich merk', 's ist ein ander Ding,
ob falsch man oder richtig sing'.

SACHS

Zeuge am Ort,
fahret fort!

WALTHER

Preislied (Stollen)
„Abendlich dämmernd
                      umschloß mich die Nacht;
auf steilem Pfad
war ich genaht
zu einer Quelle
reiner Welle,
die lockend mir gelacht: –
dort unter einem Lorbeerbaum,
von Sternen hell durchschienen,

Act 3, Scene 5 – Saint Crispin! Saint Crispin!

Kothner, who with the other masters had begun to follow the written words of the song, deeply moved, here lets the paper fall. He and the rest listen with interest.

with beauties teeming, *prize song (stanza)*
past all dreaming,
a garden round me lay,

(in ecstasy)

and there beneath a wondrous tree,
where fruits were richly thronging,
my blissful dream revealed to me
the goal of all my longing,
and life's most glorious prize,
a woman fair: Eva, – in Paradise!" *excitement trill*

PEOPLE

(murmuring softly)

Who would have thought it?
                Who could have known? *prize song (stanza) ②*
How much lies hid in words and „tone"!

MASTERSINGERS

(murmuring softly)

Ah yes, I see 'tis another thing,
if you wrongly or rightly sing.

SACHS

Witness attend!
make an end!

WALTHER

„Darkness had fallen *prize song (stanza)*
           and night closed me round;
on stony road
my footsteps trod,
where on a mountain
rose a fountain
that lured my feet with its sound: –
there underneath a laurel tree,
where stars like fruit were gleaming

Preislied (Stollen)

> ich schaut' im wachen Dichtertraum,
> von heilig holden Mienen,
> mich netzend mit dem edlen Naß,
> das hehrste Weib, die Muse des Parnaß!"

VOLK

Preislied (Stollen) ②

So hold und traut, wie fern es schwebt,
doch ist es grad',
        als ob man selber alles miterlebt!

DIE MEISTERSINGER

Preislied (Stollen) ②

's ist kühn und seltsam, das ist wahr;
doch wohlgereimt und singebar.

SACHS

Zeuge, wohl erkiest!
Fahret fort, und schließt!

WALTHER

(sehr feurig)

Preislied (Liebesthema)

Eva-M.

Entzückung-M.

> „Huldreichster Tag,
> dem ich aus Dichters Traum erwacht!
> Das ich erträumt, das Paradies,
> in himmlisch neu verklärter Pracht,
> hell vor mir lag,
> dahin lachend nun der Quell
>   den Pfad mir wies;
> die, dort geboren,
> mein Herz erkoren,
> der Erde lieblichstes Bild,
> als Muse mir geweiht,
> so heilig ernst als mild,
> ward kühn von mir gefreit;
> am lichten Tag der Sonnen,
> durch Sanges Sieg gewonnen
> Parnaß und Paradies!" –

VOLK

Gewiegt wie in den schönsten Traum,
hör' ich es wohl, doch fass' es kaum.

Act 3, Scene 5 – Saint Crispin! Saint Crispin!

VS 543▶1
CD 4/8 2:42
in poet's dream there smiled on me,
with holy sweetness beaming, *prize song (stanza)*
my muse, who from the sacred fount
bedewed my head, on high Parnassus mount!"

PEOPLE

How sweet the strain, how high its theme! *prize song (stanza) ②*
and yet it seems to us
    as though we lived within the dream!

MASTERSINGERS

'Tis daring, that is true; *prize song (stanza) ②*
but good are rhymes and singing too!

SACHS

Witness whom I chose;
sing you on, and close!

WALTHER

(ardently)

„Oh, hallowed day, *prize song (love*
on which my poet's dream took flight! *theme)*
That Paradise my vision shewed,
revealed anew in Heavens light, *Eva motif*
shining now lay;
thereto pointing the path, *delight motif*
    a laughing streamlet flowed,
and gleaming yonder,
a radiant wonder,
the garden's maiden so fair,
as Muse before me stood
in holy calmness there.
That maid I boldly wooed;
and there in light of Heaven,
the prize of song was given,
Parnassus and Paradise!" –

PEOPLE

Enchanted by this beauteous strain,
scarce can I rede its meaning plain.

DIE MEISTERSINGER

Preislied (Liebesthema)

(sich erhebend)

Ja, holder Sänger, nimm das Reis;
dein Sang erwarb dir Meisterpreis!
Reich das Reis, sein der Preis:
Keiner so, wie nur er, zu werben weiß,
wie er so hold zu werben weiß.

VOLK

(zu Eva)

Reich ihm das Reis, sein sei der Preis!
Keiner wie er so hold zu werben weiß!

POGNER

(mit großer Rührung und Ergriffenheit zu Sachs sich wendend)

O Sachs! Dir dank' ich Glück und Ehr':
vorüber nun all' Herzbeschwer!

Walther ist auf die Stufen der Singerbühne geleitet worden und läßt sich dort vor Eva auf ein Knie nieder.

EVA

zu Walther, indem sie ihn mit einem Kranz aus Lorbeer und Myrte bekränzt, sich hinabneigend:

Erregtheitstriller Keiner wie du so hold zu werben weiß!

Wahn-M. ## SACHS

zum Volk gewandt, auf Walther und Eva deutend:

Den Zeugen, denk' es, wählt' ich gut:
tragt ihr Hans Sachs drum üblen Mut?

VOLK

bricht schnell und heftig in jubelnde Bewegung aus:

Hans Sachs! Nein! Das war schön erdacht!

Act 3, Scene 5 – Saint Crispin! Saint Crispin!

MASTERSINGERS

(rising)

Yes, gracious singer, take thy own!
Thy song hath won the Master's crown!
Grant his own; his the crown:
Right so clear none hath shown,
such right none here hath shown.

prize song (love theme)

PEOPLE

(to Eva)

Grant his own; his be the crown:
No-one but he so clear a right hath shown!

POGNER

(turning to Sachs with deep emotion)

O Sachs! Thou bring'st me peace at last:
now all my heart's distress is past!

Walther has been conducted to the steps of the platform and there kneels on one knee before Eva.

EVA

to Walther, as he stoops down and crowns him with a wreath of laurels and myrtles:

No-one but thou so clear a right hath shown!

excitement trill

SACHS

delusion motif

turning to the people and pointing to Walther and Eva:

The witness, grant me, well I chose:
then you ans Sachs no more are foes?

PEOPLE

break forth in demonstrations of joy:

Hans Sachs! No! That was finely planned!

Das habt ihr einmal wieder gut gemacht.

DIE MEISTERSINGER

(feierlich sich zu Pogner wendend)

König-David-M.   Auf, Meister Pogner! Euch zum Ruhm,
meldet dem Junker sein Meistertum!

POGNER

mit einer goldenen Kette, dran drei große Denkmünzen, zu Walther:

Werbe-M.   Geschmückt mit König Davids Bild,
nehm' ich euch auf in der Meister Gild'!

WALTHER

(mit schmerzlicher Heftigkeit abweisend)

Kreidestrich-M.   Nicht Meister! – Nein! –
Er blickt zärtlich auf Eva.

Taufspruch-M.
(Eva)   Will ohne Meister selig sein!
Alles blickt mit großer Betroffenheit auf Sachs.

SACHS

Meistersinger-M.   *schreitet auf Walther zu und faßt ihn bedeutungsvoll bei der Hand:*

Verachtet mir die Meister nicht,
und ehrt mir ihre Kunst!

Preislied (Liebesthema), Meistersinger-M.   Was ihnen hoch zum Lobe spricht,
fiel reichlich euch zur Gunst.
Nicht euren Ahnen, noch so wert,
nicht eurem Wappen, Speer noch Schwert, –
daß ihr ein Dichter seid,
ein Meister euch gefreit,
dem dankt ihr heut eu'r höchstes Glück.

Kunst-M.   Drum, denkt mit Dank ihr dran zurück,
wie kann die Kunst wohl unwert sein,
die solche Preise schließet ein?

König-David-M.   Das unsre Meister sie gepflegt
grad' recht nach ihrer Art,
nach ihrem Sinne treu gehegt,

Act 3, Scene 5 – Saint Crispin! Saint Crispin!

VS 556 ▶ 1
CD 4/8 6:38
Once more your wit indeed the day has gained

MASTERSINGERS

(solemnly turning to Pogner)

Up, Master Pogner! 'Tis your right, } *king David motif*
now as a Master to name the knight!

POGNER

with a golden chain, on which are three large medals, to Walther:

King David's likeness take from me, } *courtship motif*
of the Masters' Guild thus I make you free!

WALTHER

(refusing the chain impetuously)

Not Master! – No! – } *chalk stroke motif*

He looks tenderly at Eva.

One better way to Heav'n I know! } *baptismal verse (Eva)*

All look at Sachs in great perplexity.

SACHS

VS 559 ▶ 2
CD 4/9 0:01
comes to Walther and takes him impressively by the hand: } *mastersinger motif*

Disdain our Masters not, my friend,
and honour well their art!
What, to their glory, art has gained, } *prize song (love theme), mastersinger motif*
right well has ta'en your part.
For not your ancestors or birth,
nor crest and banner, sword of worth; –
your poet's song alone
the Master's crown hath won,
that brings today your highest bliss.
Then think with thankfulness on this. } *art motif*
How can that art be held as naught,
that prize so rare as this has brought?
Right well our Masters' Guild did tend } *king David motif*
our art, and never swerved
from truth and right to gain their end;

König-David-M.	das hat sie echt bewahrt:	KA 648 ▶ 2798
Kunst-M.	blieb sie nicht adlig, wie zur Zeit,	CD 4/9 1:35
	wo Höf' und Fürsten sie geweiht;	
Naturregel-M.	im Drang der schlimmen Jahr'	
	blieb sie doch deutsch und wahr:	
	und wär' sie anders nicht geglückt,	
	als wie wo alles drängt und drückt,	
	ihr seht, wie hoch sie blieb in Ehr':	
	was wollt ihr von den Meistern mehr?	
Kreidestrich-M.	Habt acht! Uns dräuen üble Streich':	
	zerfällt erst deutsches Volk und Reich,	
	in falscher welscher Majestät	
	kein Fürst bald mehr sein Volk versteht,	
	und welschen Dunst mit welschem Tand	
	sie pflanzen uns in deutsches Land;	
	was deutsch und echt, wüßt' keiner mehr,	
Nürnberg-M.	lebt's nicht in deutscher Meister Ehr'.	
	Drum sag' ich euch:	
Meistersinger-M. ④	ehrt eure deutschen Meister!	
Meistersinger-M.,	Dann bannt ihr gute Geister;	
Preislied (Liebes-	und gebt ihr ihrem Wirken Gunst,	
thema)	zerging' in Dunst	
	das heil'ge röm'sche Reich,	
Kunst-M.	uns bliebe gleich	
	die heil'ge deutsche Kunst!	

Während des folgenden Schlußgesanges nimmt Eva den Kranz von Walthers Stirn und drückt ihn Sachs auf; dieser nimmt die Kette aus Pogners Hand und hängt sie Walther um. Nachdem Sachs das Paar umarmt, bleiben Walther und Eva zu beiden Seiten an Sach-

König-David-M.   *sens Schultern gestützt; Pogner läßt sich, wie huldigend, auf ein Knie vor Sachs nieder. Die Meistersinger deuten mit erhobenen Händen auf Sachs, als auf ihr Haupt. Alle Anwesenden schließen sich dem Gesange des Volkes an.*

Volk

Ehrt eure deutschen Meister,
dann bannt ihr gute Geister;
und gebt ihr ihrem Wirken Gunst,

Act 3, Scene 5 – Saint Crispin! Saint Crispin!

<small>KA 561 ▸ 3
CD 4/9 1:35</small> thus was our art preserved: *king David motif*
and thou not honored as of old, *art motif*
when courts and kings her glories told;
when strife and turmoil grew, *nature rule motif*
German she stood and true:
and though she veiled her worthiness,
amid the mighty storm and stress,
you see, her fame is high and sure:
what would you from the Masters more?
Beware! Ill times now threaten all; *chalk stroke motif*
if we Germans ever fall
in thrall to any foreign land,
no prince his folk will understand,
and foreign mists will blind our eyes,
and o'er our German land will rise:
the art we own were lost for aye,
living in German song today. *Nuremberg motif*
Then hear me now:
        honour your German masters, *mastersinger motif ④*
if you would shun disasters; *mastersinger motif,*
let each hold them deep in his heart; *prize song (love*
then may depart *theme)*
the pomp of holy Rome,
no change will come *art motif*
to holy German art!

> *During the following finale Eva takes the wreath from Walther's head and places it on Sachs, who takes the chain from Pogner's hand, and hangs it round Walther's neck. After Sachs embraced the pair, Walther and Eva remain one on each side of him leaning on his shoulders. Pogner kneels as if in homage before Sachs. The Mastersingers point to Sachs with upraised hands as to their chief. All present join in the song of the people.*

king David motif

People

Honour your German Masters,
if ye would shun disasters;
let each one hold them in his heart,

The Mastersingers of Nuremberg

Kunst-M.,
Meistersinger-M.,
Erregtheitstriller

zerging' in Dunst
das heil'ge röm'sche Reich,
uns bliebe gleich
die heil'ge deutsche Kunst!

> *Das Volk schwenkt begeistert Hüte und Tücher; die Lehrbuben tanzen und schlagen jauchzend in die Hände.*

Heil! Sachs! Nürnbergs teurem Sachs!

Der Vorhang fällt.

Act 3, Scene 5 – Saint Crispin! Saint Crispin!

then may depart
the pomp of holy Rome,
no change will come
to holy German art!

art motif,
mastersinger motif,
excitement trill

> *The people wave hats and kerchiefs in excitement, the prentices dance and joyously clap their hands.*

Hail! Sachs! Nürnberg's poet Sachs!

The curtain falls.

Appendix
Note Samples

The numbers in front of the note samples correspond with those on the enclosed audio CD and on www.musicosa.com/ML17.

🔊 1: anger motif

🔊 2: art motif

🔊 3 awake choral

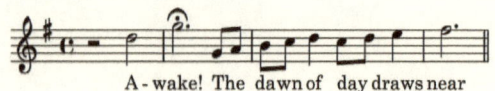

Appendix, Note Samples

🔊 4:   baptismal verse

baptismal verse motif (Sachs)

baptismal verse motif (Eva)

Bright - ly, as the sun up-on my

🔊 5:   beating motif (cf. Beckmesser's courtship motif)

🔊 6:   Beckmesser motif

🔊 7:   Beckmesser's courtship motif (cf. courtship motif)

try - - - ing to win a young maid's hand.

🔊 8:   Beckmesser's passion motif (cf. passion motif)

🔊 9:   Beckmesser's song

I see now dawning day-light, that gives me de-light true.

341

The Mastersingers of Nuremberg

🔊 10: chalk stroke motif

Three squeaky chalk marks on a slate board

🔊 11: chaplet motif

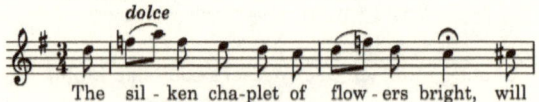

🔊 12: choral of baptism

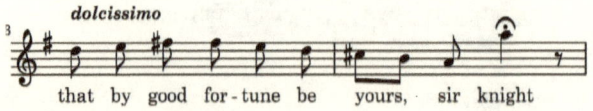

🔊 13: cobbler's labor motif

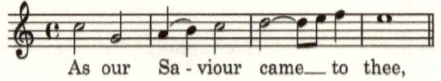

🔊 14: cobbler's song

Appendix, Note Samples

🔊 15: competition motif

🔊 16 courtship motif

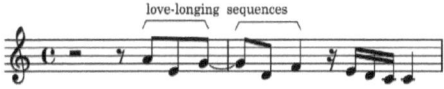

🔊 17: David motif

🔊 18: delight motif

🔊 19 delusion motif

🔊 20: disapproval motif

🔊 21: dream motif

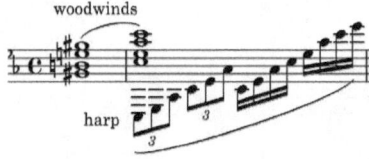

🔊 22: elder motif

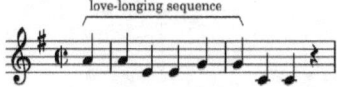

🔊 23: envy motif (cf. Stolzing and Beckmesser motifs)

🔊 24: Eva motif

🔊 25: excitement trill (audio sample with four motifs)

🔊 26: friendship motif

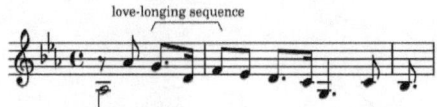

🔊 27: grace motif

Appendix, Note Samples

🔊 28: guild law motif, guild council motif, and guild ideal motif

🔊 29: hope motif

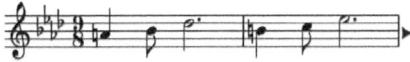

🔊 30: king David motif

🔊 31: liveliness motif

🔊 32: lute motif

The Mastersingers of Nuremberg

🔊 33: mastersinger motif

🔊 34: Midsummer day motif

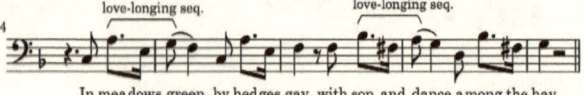

🔊 35: mockery motif

Appendix, Note Samples

🔊 36: nature rule motif (cf art motif, mastersinger motif ②)

🔊 37: Nuremberg motif

🔊 38: passion motif (cf. springtime's behest motif)

🔊 39: prentices motif

🔊 40: prize song (stanza)

The Mastersingers of Nuremberg

🔊 41: prize song (love theme)

🔊 42: rage motif

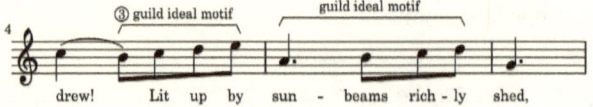

🔊 43: rejection motif

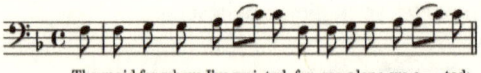

🔊 44: resentment motif

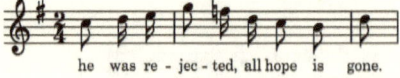

🔊 45: resignation motif (cf. summer night's magic motif)

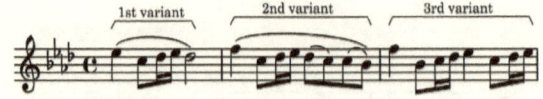

🔊 46: scorn motif

Appendix, Note Samples

🔊 47: singing art motif

The Mas - ters'_tones and_meas - sures are ma-ny in name and kind;

🔊 48: springtime's behest motif (cf. passion motif)

Spring-time's be-hest, with - in his breast

🔊 49: Stolzing motif

🔊 50: summer night's magic motif

🔊 51: Vogelweid motif

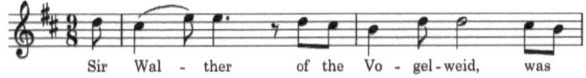

Sir Wal - ther of the Vo - gel - weid, was

🔊 52: work lust motif

🔊 53: youth motif

My friend, when youth's desires compel, and 'twards the goal of loving

349

Index of Motifs

A

anger motif 195, 197, 203, 261, 263, 321, 340
art motif 9, 11, 67, 73, 75, 293, 295, 301, 309, 311, 313, 315, 317, 335, 337, 339, 340, 347
awake choral 229, 311, 340

B

baptismal verse 229, 295, 297, 299, 335, 341
beating motif 189, 205, 207, 209, 211, 213, 215, 217, 219, 221, 223, 225, 227, 231, 235, 241, 261, 263, 265, 267, 279, 341
Beckmesser motif 47, 49, 85, 89, 91, 141, 263, 267, 271, 273, 279, 341
Beckmesser's courtship motif 193, 195, 197, 201, 203, 237, 241, 261, 263, 265, 273, 275, 277, 279, 319, 321, 323, 341
Beckmesser's passion motif 147, 149, 151, 155, 157, 171, 341
Beckmesser's song 181, 191, 193, 195, 197, 199, 201, 203, 213, 217, 219, 221, 223, 225, 227, 235, 241, 247, 261, 263, 319, 321, 323, 341

C

chalk stroke motif 9, 37, 49, 75, 77, 79, 87, 89, 91, 93, 95, 97, 99, 101, 109, 111, 113, 115, 117, 141, 143, 145, 147, 155, 171, 181, 183, 185, 187, 189, 191, 193, 195, 197, 199, 201, 229, 231, 235, 241, 255, 261, 263, 265, 267, 273, 275, 293, 313, 315, 321, 335, 337, 342
chaplet motif 49, 75, 105, 107, 109, 111, 181, 277, 279, 342
choral of baptism 13, 15, 235, 293, 295, 342
cobbler's labor motif 37, 117, 169, 171, 175, 177, 229, 289, 342
cobbler's song 169, 171, 173, 175, 177, 183, 199, 229, 289, 342
competition motif 9, 29, 343

Appendix, Index of Motifs

courtship motif 9, 13, 15, 17, 19, 31, 39, 45, 97, 121, 137, 139, 141, 155, 195, 243, 245, 247, 249, 251, 253, 255, 279, 281, 287, 313, 321, 335, 341, 343

D

David motif 25, 27, 29, 45, 47, 113, 115, 123, 229, 231, 233, 235, 237, 239, 343
delight motif 9, 11, 19, 31, 45, 65, 81, 121, 131, 135, 137, 147, 155, 237, 241, 249, 253, 255, 257, 273, 279, 287, 295, 327, 331, 343
delusion motif 175, 177, 229, 231, 239, 241, 255, 257, 261, 263, 289, 291, 313, 321, 333, 343
disapproval motif 95, 143, 145, 147, 149, 153, 343
dream motif 243, 251, 255, 257, 259, 295, 327, 344

E

elder motif 91, 103, 344
envy motif 85, 89, 93, 261, 263, 265, 267, 269, 273, 275, 315, 317, 319, 321, 325, 344
Eva motif 9, 13, 15, 17, 29, 31, 71, 79, 81, 83, 89, 90, 91, 135, 137, 139, 141, 147, 157, 163, 189, 245, 249, 255, 257, 287, 289, 291, 327, 331, 344
excitement trill 9, 11, 21, 25, 29, 35, 37, 39, 41, 43, 45, 47, 49, 81, 83, 85, 87, 99, 109, 111, 113, 117, 119, 121, 129, 139, 147, 155, 175, 179, 181, 183, 185, 187, 189, 195, 197, 225, 229, 231, 233, 235, 259, 263, 265, 271, 273, 277, 279, 289, 293, 295, 301, 303, 305, 309, 311, 313, 317, 319, 321, 323, 325, 329, 333, 339, 344

F

friendship motif 97, 99, 243, 245, 247, 249, 251, 257, 263, 269, 271, 273, 275, 313, 325, 344

G

grace motif 135, 137, 139, 141, 281, 344
guild council motif 51, 53, 55, 57, 59, 61, 63, 65, 69, 75, 313, 315, 345
guild ideal motif 51, 53, 55, 57, 59, 61, 63, 65, 71, 73, 75, 77, 129, 183, 259, 313, 345
guild law motif 39, 43, 49, 51, 53, 55, 57, 59, 61, 63, 65, 85, 87, 181, 313, 315, 325, 345

H

hope motif 125, 135, 137, 139, 141, 143, 145, 149, 153, 155, 233, 253, 259, 345

K

king David motif 9, 11, 25, 27, 29, 43, 45, 237, 309, 311, 319, 335, 337, 345

L

liveliness motif 33, 43, 49, 155, 157, 345
lute motif 165, 167, 177, 179, 181, 183, 187, 191, 193, 195, 197, 231, 261, 263, 265, 319, 321, 323, 346

M

mastersinger motif 4, 9, 11, 21, 23, 27, 55, 69, 71, 73, 85, 87, 97, 109, 113, 123, 155, 183, 187, 247, 269, 289, 293, 301, 303, 309, 317, 319, 321, 335, 337, 339, 346, 347
Midsummer day motif 65, 67, 69, 75, 97, 99, 113, 115, 117, 241, 279, 301, 305, 313, 315, 346
mockery motif 11, 317, 319, 347

N

nature rule motif 71, 73, 97, 181, 187, 195, 337, 347
Nuremberg motif 55, 121, 181, 241, 257, 259, 263, 279, 299, 301, 313, 337, 347

P

passion motif 9, 11, 13, 15, 89, 91, 95, 103, 105, 107, 131, 141, 147, 149, 151, 155, 157, 171, 239, 247, 249, 251, 257, 341, 347, 349
prentices motif 49, 73, 75, 105, 107, 109, 347
prize song (love theme) 9, 11, 15, 31, 157, 159, 161, 255, 257, 287, 289, 331, 333, 335, 337, 348
prize song (stanza) 241, 243, 251, 253, 255, 257, 263, 275, 285, 287, 295, 297, 299, 327, 329, 331, 348

R

rage motif 265, 267, 323, 348
rejection motif 113, 115, 119, 125, 348

Appendix, Index of Motifs

resentment motif 25, 43, 99, 101, 113, 115, 117, 119, 123, 127, 129, 131, 143, 147, 151, 159, 161, 163, 167, 169, 171, 173, 175, 179, 181, 183, 185, 187, 189, 197, 199, 231, 239, 261, 263, 265, 267, 271, 279, 283, 285, 291, 303, 349
resignation motif 281, 283, 285, 289, 291, 293, 301, 349

S

scorn motif 93, 95, 97, 99, 141, 143, 145, 147, 181, 183, 185, 189, 255, 291, 323, 349
singing art motif 39, 45, 55, 57, 63, 65, 67, 79, 87, 233, 235, 247, 251, 253, 255, 263, 313, 317, 349
springtime's behest motif 89, 91, 103, 105, 109, 131, 155, 239, 249, 347, 349
Stolzing motif 77, 79, 85, 87, 93, 99, 143, 153, 257, 259, 261, 263, 325, 327, 349
summer night's magic motif 157, 159, 161, 163, 185, 189, 191, 225, 227, 241, 281, 285, 349

V

Vogelweid motif 79, 81, 83, 105, 133, 155

W

work lust motif 131, 167, 169, 171, 173, 175, 183, 199, 265, 289, 303, 305

Y

youth motif 247, 249, 251

www.ingramcontent.com/pod-product-compliance
Lightning Source LLC
Chambersburg PA
CBHW022000160426
43197CB00007B/203